Political Institutions and Econo T0167679 **a**

Edited by **Stephen Haber**

Political Institutions and Economic Growth in Latin America

Essays in Policy, History, and Political Economy

Hoover Institution Press Stanford University Stanford, California www.hoover.org

Hoover Institution Press Publication No. 458

First printing, 2000
14 13 12 11 10 09 08 07   9 8 7 6 5 4 3 2

Manufactured in the United States of America

The paper used in this publication meets the minimum requirements
of American National Standard for Information Sciences—Permanence
of Paper for Printed Library Materials, ANSI Z39.48-1984. ⊗

Library of Congress Cataloging-in-Publication Data

Political institutions and economic growth in Latin America : essays in
policy, history, and political economy / edited by Stephen Haber
      p.   cm. — (Hoover Institution Press publication ; no. 458)
    Includes bibliographical references and index.
    ISBN-10: 0-8179-9662-1
    ISBN-13: 978-0-8179-9662-8

    1. Latin America—Economic conditions.   2. Latin America—Politics and
government.   I. Haber, Stephen H., 1957–   II. Series.
HC125.P645   2000
338.98—dc21   99-050375
                                                                      CIP

Contents

Acknowledgments

This volume is the product of a symposium held at the Hoover Institution. The symposium brought together economists, historians, and political scientists in order to understand how political institutions—the rules and regulations that emerge out of political processes—have fundamentally shaped the growth trajectories of the major economies of Latin America. The chapters found herein are not the papers presented at the conference but represent the results of two days of discussion and debate.

I and the other contributors to this volume are indebted to all the symposium participants for their insights and suggestions. The symposium participants included Norma Alvarez, David Brady, Maite Careaga, Gustavo del Angel, Alan Dye, Stephen Krasner, Anne O. Krueger, Moramay López Alonso, Douglass North, Robert Packenham, Kenneth Sokoloff, William Summerhill, Alan Taylor, and Barry Weingast.

Major financial support for the symposium and for this volume was provided by the Hoover Institution and by Peter and Helen Bing, who support my appointment at Hoover. We are much in debt to John Raisian, director of the Hoover Institution, and Richard Sousa, associate director, for their generous support. We are also in debt to them, and the broader community of Hoover scholars, for creating a venue in which scholars could engage in a discussion about the political origins of Latin American underdevelopment from across a broad range of disciplinary perspectives. This is part of the institutional project to study peace and prosperity in Latin America.

We are also indebted to the editorial staff at the Hoover Institution Press, particularly Patricia Baker and Ann Wood, for their editorial guidance, efficiency, and good-natured professionalism. Research assistance for the production of this volume was provided by Aldo Musacchio, Moramay López Alonso, Douglas Grob, and Belinda Yeomans. Finally, we would like to acknowledge the tireless efforts of Scott Wilson, who kept this project on track, even when we were not.

Contributors

ALAN DYE is an assistant professor of economics at Barnard College of Columbia University.

STEPHEN HABER is a professor of history and political science at Stanford University and the Peter and Helen Bing Senior Fellow at the Hoover Institution. He is also the director of Stanford's Social Science History Institute.

ELISA MARISCAL is a doctoral candidate in economics at the University of California, Los Angeles.

DOUGLASS C. NORTH is the Spencer T. Olin Professor in Arts and Sciences at Washington University and a senior fellow at the Hoover Institution. North is the 1993 Nobel laureate in economic science.

KENNETH L. SOKOLOFF is a professor of economics at the University of California, Los Angeles, and a research associate of the National Bureau of Economic Research.

WILLIAM R. SUMMERHILL is an associate professor of history at the University of California, Los Angeles, and (during 1999–2000) a national fellow of the Hoover Institution.

ALAN M. TAYLOR is an associate professor of economics at the University of California, Davis, and a faculty research fellow at the National Bureau of Economic Research. During 1997–98 he was a national fellow at the Hoover Institution and wrote his contribution for this volume during his fellowship year at Hoover.

BARRY R. WEINGAST is the Krebs Family Professor and chair of the Department of Political Science at Stanford University and a senior fellow at the Hoover Institution.

Introduction:
Institutional Change, Economic Growth,
and Economic History

There has been a revolution in the social sciences in recent years emanating from the study of institutions in the process of economic growth. Institutions in this context are understood as the laws, rules, and informal agreements within societies that both permit and bound economic or other types of social behavior. They are not the organizations that societies are composed of (the banks, churches, factories, governments) but are the sets of rules that govern how those organizations work.[1]

The New Institutionalism or New Institutional Economics, as the approach is alternately called, argues that economic growth is the outcome of productivity increases that are brought about by the efficient allocation of factors of production through smoothly functioning firms and markets. All things being equal, societies that create institutions that clearly specify and enforce private property rights, ease the formulation and enforcement of contracts, limit the

---

1. Institutions can be both formal and informal. Formal institutions are often politically determined. Examples include labor laws, environmental laws, regulations governing the operation of banks and securities markets, laws governing the formation and dissolution of families, and other legally codified restrictions on the activities of individuals and corporate bodies. Informal institutions are not legally codified; they include the norms and values that are often culturally embedded in societies. Examples include norms and values related to honesty, civic-mindedness, group identity, and the like.

ability of governments to intervene in the economy for their own short-term advantage, and generally support the operation of free markets will generate more rapid rates of economic growth than those that do not.

The New Institutionalism builds on a long tradition in economic theory and has an impressive theoretical edifice that is widely influential among both scholars and policymakers. Indeed, the New Institutionalism has been particularly influential among those who are designing policies for the transitional economies of Eastern Europe and Latin America. Nowhere is this perhaps more true than at the World Bank, whose recent *World Development Reports* stress the importance of designing institutions that will promote economic growth.

There are essentially three variants in the literature on institutions and growth. One variant focuses on the institutions that govern the operation of markets. This strand of the literature focuses on how changes in institutions make credible commitments possible, property rights more secure, and contracts enforceable, thereby lowering transactions costs and increasing the range of exchanges that are mediated through the market. This, in turn, increases allocative efficiency and encourages entrepreneurs to adopt longer time horizons, thereby increasing investments in physical and human capital.[2] A second, and related, variant of the New Institutionalist literature focuses on the institutions that limit governments. This body of literature argues that economic growth will be enhanced if governments are constrained in their ability to reduce the property rights or increase the tax burdens faced by economic agents. This strand of the literature therefore focuses on the mechanisms that constrain governments from using their authority to engage in opportunistic behavior in order to satisfy their short-term financial

---

2. Douglass C. North, *Institutions, Institutional Change and Economic Performance* (Cambridge: Cambridge University Press, 1990).

needs at the expense of long-term economic growth.[3] A third variant of the literature focuses on the institutions that affect contracts within firms. Changes in the rules and norms that bound or limit the types and nature of intrafirm contracts, it is argued, have an impact on the ability of firms to engage in organizational or technological innovations that increase productivity.[4]

Despite its recent popularity, the New Institutionalism has seldom been subjected to systematic and direct tests of consistency with evidence. The New Institutionalism is advanced by theorists not as a set of necessary truths but as a set of hypotheses to be tested.[5] Yet, of the three types of confirmatory logics employed to sustain truth claims in the social sciences (formal theory, the historical record, and econometric or statistical hypothesis testing), the

3. Douglass C. North and Barry R. Weingast, "Constitutions and Commitment: The Evolution of Institutions Governing Public Choice in Seventeenth Century England," *Journal of Economic History* 44 (December 1989): 803–32; Gregory Clark, "The Political Foundations of Modern Economic Growth: England, 1540–1800," *Journal of Interdisciplinary History* 26 (spring 1996): 563–88; Barry R. Weingast, "The Political Foundations of Limited Government: Parliament and Sovereign Debt in 17th- and 18th-Century England," in John N. Drobak and John V.C. Nye, eds., *The Frontiers of the New Institutional Economics* (San Diego: Academic Press, 1997), pp. 213–46.

4. Oliver E. Williamson, *The Economic Institutions of Capitalism: Firms, Markets, Relational Contracting* (New York: Free Press, 1985).

5. See North, *Institutions, Institutional Change, and Economic Performance*, chap. 1; Douglass C. North, "Toward a Theory of Institutional Change," in William A. Barnett, Melvin J. Hinich, and Norman J. Schofield, eds., *Political Economy: Institutions, Competition, and Representation* (Cambridge: Cambridge University Press, 1983); Leonid Hurwicz, "Toward a Framework for Analyzing Institutions and Institutional Change," in Samuel Bowles, Herbert Gintis, and Bo Gustafsson, eds., *Markets and Democracy: Participation, Accountability, and Efficiency* (Cambridge: Cambridge University Press, 1993); Avner Greif, "Microtheory and Recent Developments in the Study of Economic Institutions through Economic History," in David M. Kreps and Kenneth F. Wallis, eds., *Advances in Economic Theory*. Vol. 2 (Cambridge: Cambridge University Press, 1997), pp. 79–113; Masahiko Aoki, "Towards a Comparative Institutional Analysis: Motivations and Some Tentative Theorizing," *Japanese Economic Review* 47, no. 1 (March 1996): 1–19.

New Institutionalism rests primarily on only one, theory.[6] The success of the approach, as well as the relevance of its policy implications, will ultimately depend, however, on its ability to explain actual economic outcomes, not just theoretical ones.

Social scientists are therefore confronted by a peculiar problem: there is widespread agreement that institutions matter—and matter a great deal—in the process of economic growth. Yet they are simultaneously unsure to what degree institutions affect growth and which particular institutional arrangements are crucial (and which are merely incidental) to economic performance. They therefore have difficulty, as a practical and policy matter, separating the independent impact of particular institutional changes from the effects of other economic transformations.

Unfortunately, operationalizing the testable hypotheses of New Institutional Theory using either the historical record or economet-

---

6. Truth claims in the social sciences are generally supported by one of three types of confirmatory logic: formal models, goodness of fit with the historical record, and hypothesis testing through the econometric analysis of quantitative data. The first confirmatory standard (formal models) assesses truth claims based on the logical consistency of hierarchically organized if-then statements. Such models may take a mathematical form. Although logical models are axiomatically derived, they are often given verisimilitude through the application of *stylized facts* (facts that may or may not be true but are assumed to be true for the purpose of the construction of the model). The second confirmatory standard (goodness of fit with the historical record) stresses the fit between a theory and what actually happened in the past. The third confirmatory standard (econometric hypothesis testing) stresses the explicit specification of hypotheses that operationalize the testable implications of a theory. These hypotheses are then subjected to falsification through the systematic retrieval and analysis of relevant quantitative data. Such tests are set up in such a way as to bias the tests against the hypotheses under consideration in order to ensure that the results are not driven by the choice sampling techniques, functional form, or model specification. In this way, econometric testing seeks to constrain the priors or beliefs of researchers from influencing substantive results. The strongest truth claims in the social sciences are supported by all three types of confirmatory logics. To the degree that there is a consensus about which of the three standards of confirmation takes primacy in theory testing, most social scientists would generally award primacy to econometric standards of proof.

ric analysis has proven elusive. Four factors have hampered research linking theory and the historical record. First, most empirical studies in the New Institutionalism do not, in fact, attempt to test or refine the theory against the past record of economic performance. Rather, they attempt to apply the theory as a metaphorical means to better understand the historical record of economic growth.[7] One potential outcome of this type of research strategy can be the misapplication of theory, or the fitting of history to the theory, rather than the other way around.[8]

The second factor limiting the attempt to assess the fit between theory and the historical record is that the historical case studies selected for analysis are weak and partial tests. Scholars have typically chosen cases for analysis in which putatively more-efficient institutions produced faster economic growth.[9] Yet if positive insti-

7. See, for example, Lee J. Alston, Thráinn Eggertsson, and Douglass C. North, eds., *Empirical Studies in Institutional Change* (Cambridge: Cambridge University Press, 1996); Avner Greif, "Political Organizations, Social Structure, and Institutional Success: Reflections from Genoa and Venice during the Commercial Revolution," *Journal of Institutional and Theoretical Economics* 151, no. 4 (December 1995): 734–40; Avner Greif, "Contract Enforceability and Economic Institutions in Early Trade: The Maghribi Trader's Coalition," *American Economic Review* 83, no. 3 (June 1993): 525–48.

8. Two prominent examples of the misapplication of theory and the fitting of the historical record to suit the theory, rather than the other way around, include dependency theory and trade and development theories current in the 1960s and 1970s. For a discussion of these examples, see Anne O. Krueger, "Trade Policy and Economic Development: How We Learn," *American Economic Review* 87, no. 1 (March 1997): 1–22; Robert A. Packenham, *The Dependency Movement: Scholarship and Politics in Development Studies* (Cambridge: Harvard University Press, 1992); Stephen Haber, "Economic Growth and Latin American Economic Historiography," in Haber, ed., *How Latin America Fell Behind: Essays on the Economic Histories of Brazil and Mexico, 1800–1914* (Stanford: Stanford University Press, 1997), p. 1–33.

9. See, for example, Jean Laurent Rosenthal, *The Fruits of Revolution: Property Rights, Litigation, and French Agriculture, 1700–1860* (Cambridge: Cambridge University Press, 1992); North and Weingast, "Constitutions and Commitment": 803–32. For a critique of North and Weingast, see Clark, "The Political Foundations."

tutional innovations (more-secure property rights, credible commitments by governments to not expropriate private assets, and the like) exert a positive influence on economic growth, then it should also follow that negative institutional changes (such as revolutions that make property rights less secure, the rise of predatory states, or government regulations that distort markets) should produce slow or negative rates of economic growth. The literature to date, however, has not tended to address these types of cases in a systematic fashion.[10]

Third, most of the literature has looked at economies in which institutional change proceeded gradually. The incremental nature of institutional change in these economies, coupled with the fact that there are often multiple institutions undergoing such incremental changes at any one time, means that it is difficult, if not impossible, to pinpoint particular institutional reforms that have been crucial for economic growth. This problem is accentuated by a fourth factor: most of the work done to date has focused on economies that have had long histories of well-developed markets. In these economies, the market has anticipated institutional changes, meaning that it is extremely difficult to demonstrate the effects of any particular institutional reform.[11] Indeed, in economies in which there are well-developed markets, an endogeneity may exist between the market and institutional development; markets as they become more efficient may affect the process of institutional development, which, in turn, feeds back into markets, and so on.

These problems are amplified when scholars attempt to move

10. For an exception, see Stephen Haber and Armando Razo, "Political Instability and Economic Performance: Evidence from Revolutionary Mexico," *World Politics* 51 (October 1998): 99–143.

11. Economic agents realize that there is about to be a reform of institutions and so bid asset prices up or down accordingly before the reform actually takes place. See Clark, "Political Foundations."

beyond stylized historical correlations by developing formalized econometric or statistical tests of the relationship between institutional change and economic growth. Not only do all of the problems of endogeneity and selection bias again emerge, but scholars are confronted by the numerous technical difficulties associated with tying any particular change in institutions to an acceleration in productivity and income growth.

Some scholars, most notably Robert Barro and Alberto Alesina, have attempted to demonstrate the connections between the political or institutional features of societies and the growth of their economies through cross-country growth regressions. The results of these exercises, however, have been inconclusive. First, this body of literature offers no theoretical model of how institutions and growth interact; it is a purely inductive exercise in growth accounting. Second, econometric considerations make these estimates dubious. The statistical results of growth accounting regressions tend to be highly sensitive to the number of observations, the choice of cases, and the specification of the regressions.[12] Third, there are serious problems of measurement error and misspecification of instrumental variables. The instruments we have to measure the institutional or political features of societies are poorly developed. Barro, for example, employs the number of revolutions and coups per year and the number of political assassinations per million population as measures of political instability and then goes on to "interpret [these] variables as adverse influences on property rights."[13]

---

12. Ross Levine and David Renelt, "A Sensitivity Analysis of Cross-Country Growth Regressions," *American Economic Review* 82, no.4 (September 1992): 943.

13. See Robert J. Barro, "Economic Growth in a Cross Section of Countries," *Quarterly Journal of Economics* (May 1991): 432. Other investigators have tried to refine these measures. See Alberto Alesina, Sule Özler, Nouriel Roubini, and Phillip Swagel, "Political Stability and Economic Growth," *Journal of Economic Growth* 1 (June 1996): 189–211.

Finally, there are fundamental concerns about the stability of the statistical relationship between economic and political variables and about the ability of capturing the complex interaction of political and economic institutions through any single linear equation. In situations in which institutions are rapidly changing, the specification itself may no longer hold. This can be a serious problem because, in the pooling of countries with different relationships between politics and economics, it may only require a subset of unstable countries within a larger data set to cause a misspecification in the estimated cross-country equations.[14] In short, on both theoretical and econometric grounds, growth accounting exercises are unlikely ever to produce the level of certainty that most social scientists would find compelling.

In recent years, economists and political scientists interested in the systematic analysis of institutional change and historians of Latin America who have embraced the quantitative and systematic methods of the social sciences have begun a series of collaborative research programs designed specifically to create the kind of basic research that ultimately will be necessary to test and refine New Institutional Theory. They have proceeded from the notion that the most unambiguous results in institutional analysis are to be found in those cases where there have been dramatic changes in institutions, where institutions have at times changed in such a way as to reduce property rights, where markets could not anticipate institutional changes, and where there is sufficient quantitative data to

---

14. Notably, Alesina, Özler, Roubini, and Swagel, "Political Stability," employ a simultaneous equation system to capture the potential feedbacks between economics and politics. Recognizing the inability to properly define instability, they use latent variable methods to model the probabilistic causes of instability. Two questions remain about their analysis, however. One is whether or not the process driving instability, and its linkages to economic growth, is the correct one. Second, even if their specification was the correct one, our critique that under conditions of instability that relationship may break down still holds.

measure the productivity consequences of institutional change. In short, they are attempting to employ the history of Latin American economies as a laboratory for empirical research in the New Institutionalism.

This volume reports on the research of one such collaborative research program that took place at the Hoover Institution in February 1998. It offers a contribution to the literature on institutions and growth through the analysis of historical cases of institutional change and economic growth in Latin America in the nineteenth and twentieth centuries.

To provide the kinds of evidence that most social scientists and policymakers would find compelling, the authors employ three sets of analytic tools: first, the historical approach because the impact of institutional change on economic performance can only be detected over long time periods; second, the methods and approaches of economics because demonstrating that particular institutional reforms had particular effects on market development or firm efficiency requires the careful use of econometric techniques; and third, the methods and tools of modern political science because most formal economic institutions are politically determined. In short, this volume presents not only a set of substantive conclusions about the interaction of particular institutional changes and the economic performance of real world economies but also a methodological framework for the development of similar kinds of research programs.[15]

---

15. One reason single case studies often contribute little to theory development is that they are usually authored by historians who, because of the particular predilections of their discipline, attempt to study all those aspects of the case that they judge interesting or unusual, rather than systematically study particular issues that are relevant to testing or building social science theories. Social scientists are therefore forced to conduct their own case studies, but they do so without the detailed knowledge of past societies, which limits the usefulness of their research. Alexander L. George, "Case Studies and Theory Development: The Method of Structured,

Our theoretical point of departure is the notion that economic institutions cannot be studied in isolation from the institutions that regulate politics. Economic institutions, and their enforcement and refinement, do not emerge from thin air. They are also not simply the result of demands of interest groups. Rather, they are the result of both interest group demands and the specific features of decision making in the polity, which are themselves governed by institutions. On the one hand, these political institutions include the rules about who has the authority to legislate and enforce the regulations that govern economic activity and what are the legitimate extensions of that authority. On the other hand, these political institutions also specify the way in which a polity might change the rules about who has the authority to regulate and the legitimate extent of regulation. Thus, the study of the origins and consequences of economic institutions also requires that we study the institutions that structure political decision making.

The enactment of regulations and general policies, as output of the political system, affects the scope and action of economic agents. That is, the political system generates sets of laws, regulations, and enforcement mechanisms that serve to both permit and bound economic activity. These laws range from those that affect nearly all economic agents (laws regarding the specification of private property, for example) to those that are specific to particular industries, firms, or classes of workers. Examples would include tariffs on specific products, laws that regulate entry into particular lines of economic activity (the regulations that govern the chartering of banks, for example), or laws that regulate wages and hours for particular occupations. These laws, in turn, have a direct impact on the structure and efficiency of firms and markets.

Focused Comparison," in Paul Gordon Lauren, ed., *Diplomacy: New Approaches in History, Theory, and Policy* (New York: Free Press, 1979), pp. 43–68.

There is therefore a complex interaction between the institutions that mediate the polity and the economy, and these need to be studied jointly. Working backward, we can specify the relationship in the following way. There are institutions (laws and regulations governing economic activity) that limit the activities of firms and markets. These economic institutions, by virtue of the fact that they are legally codified, are politically created. Indeed, they are often formulated in order to accomplish political ends, such as the distribution of rewards or benefits to a legislator's constituents. Political decision making is, in turn, governed by its own set of institutions that determine the governance structure of a society (rules about who has the authority to enact and enforce economic legislation) and the specific features of decision making within each branch of the government. On the one hand, these institutions serve to delineate a division of labor to perform government tasks. On the other hand, these institutions structure the process by which the constituent branches of the government go about drafting, debating, and enacting particular pieces of legislation. These institutions are themselves bounded by yet another set of institutions that structure the way that the political system can decide to change the rules about decision making. This type of political institution (rules about the rules, so to speak) includes constitutions and constitutional amendments, as well as the judicial review of proposed policies and laws.

The focus on the interaction of political and economic institutions is clearly articulated by William Summerhill in chapter 2 in this volume, "Institutional Determinants of Railroad Subsidy and Regulation in Imperial Brazil." The economy of imperial Brazil (the period 1822–1889, when Brazil was governed by a monarchy) was characterized by low levels of per capita income, slow rates of economic growth, and widespread market failure. Brazilian policymakers were familiar with the institutional innovations that had accounted for the success of the North Atlantic economies: investments in education and human capital; modern property rights in land; patent laws that made it easy for inventors to earn returns from the fruits of their research; commercial legislation that eased the formation of limited liability companies; and laws that facilitated the development of banks and other financial intermediaries. Surprisingly, they were slow to undertake any of these institutional innovations, and when they did so, the nature of decision making in the Brazilian polity gave rise to policies that strongly departed from the ideal.

Summerhill focuses on one particular set of policies, and the decision-making structure that gave rise to them: the policies related to the subsidization and regulation of railroads. He argues that the nature of Brazilian political organization meant that there were strong incentives for the government to provide railroads as a form of pork. Summerhill generates and tests two hypotheses, one regarding rate regulation and one regarding subsidy levels. He demonstrates that rates were set largely based on the national origin of the owners of the railroad and that subsidies were based largely on whether a railroad was located in a province with high levels of voting power in parliament.

Summerhill's argument can be summarized as follows. Because of Brazil's mountainous topography and lack of navigable rivers, railroads were crucial for economic growth. The cost of creating a railroad system was enormously high, however, and the returns to potential investors were difficult to calculate. Thus, railroads required government subsidization. If railroads were going to be subsidized by the government, this meant that they were also going to be regulated by the government. Inevitably, in the creation of subsidy schemes and rate regulation, distributive politics came into play. In a detailed analysis of the formal rules that governed railroad policy making, Summerhill shows how the nature of decision making gave rise to subsidies for large numbers of railroads whose benefits did not justify their cost. In the end, although railroad technology created large gains for the Brazilian economy, the allocation of resources that resulted from market intervention by the government strongly departed from what would have been economically optimal. The costs of regulation and subsidization, as Summerhill concludes, "proved particularly acute in the context of low levels of overall productivity and income."

One testable implication of Summerhill's chapter, and of New Institutional Theory in general, is that, if the institutions that govern the polity are changed, then the suboptimal economic institutions they give rise to should change as well. Unless political institutions change in a dramatic, discontinuous fashion, however, it is extremely difficult to operationalize this hypothesis as a practical matter.

Stephen Haber, in his contribution to this volume, employs a case of dramatic and discontinuous political change in order to measure the independent impact of changes in political institutions on economic efficiency. He focuses on the overthrow of Brazil's parliamentary monarchy in 1889 and the founding of a federal republic in 1890.

Haber focuses on the laws and regulations that governed the banks and financial markets under each regime, noting that these are notoriously sensitive to the specific features of government regulation. His argument may be summarized as follows. Under the monarchy, the Brazilian central government reserved for itself the right to regulate banks and corporations (as opposed to devolving those responsibilities to provincial governments, as was done in the United States). The rules and regulations created by the central government, however, served to repress the development of the banking system through policies designed to create a succession of semiofficial superbanks that could serve as financial agents of the state. The government also restrained the development of securities markets through a series of laws that made it difficult to obtain a corporate charter and that did not allow for limited liability. The result was that the financial intermediaries necessary to mobilize capital for industrial development were virtually nonexistent. As a result, Brazilian industry's capital was constrained throughout the nineteenth century.

The rules and regulations that constrained the development of financial intermediaries were eliminated in 1890, when the newly founded federal republic completely rewrote the existing legislation. The result was that Brazilian manufacturing firms began to draw on the banking system and the securities markets for finance. In a detailed econometric analysis of firm- and industry-level data on the manufacture of cotton textiles, Haber demonstrates that the easing of capital constraints on firms not only allowed Brazilian industry to grow much faster than it had previously but also allowed capital to be allocated to those firms and entrepreneurs who could use it more efficiently. The end result was that Brazilian industry underwent both extensive growth (an increase in size) and intensive growth (an increase in total factor productivity).

Alan Taylor extends this analysis of domestic institutions and markets to the institutions that governed international capital mobility. His contribution to this volume, "Latin America and Foreign Capital in the Twentieth Century: Economics, Politics, and Institutional Change," argues that one major determinant of Latin America's laggard growth compared to the economies of East Asia has been the presence of barriers to the international movement of capital. These barriers include capital controls, restrictions on the repatriation of profits, multiple exchange-rate systems, and the other policy devices designed to reduce the mobility of capital. In the absence of an increase in domestic rates of saving and investment, these barriers dampened new investment and thus decreased the region's rate of economic growth.

Taylor further argues that the development of capital controls came about in response to changes in political institutions—indeed, that capital controls were politically determined. Borrowing from insights about the political economy of exchange-rate regimes in developed countries, Taylor argues that policymakers faced a tri-lemma—pressures from different constituencies to achieve three mutually inconsistent goals—exchange-rate stability, free capital mobility, and macroeconomic stability (for example, "full employment"). Under a fixed exchange-rate system (such as the gold standard), and in an open economy with free capital mobility, policymakers have no power to use monetary policy as an instrument for the manipulation of the domestic economy. Any attempt to move the interest rate is futile. If, for example, policymakers reduced interest rates to fight unemployment, the result would be a loss in currency reserves, which would soon force rates of interest back to their previous, market-determined, level. Consequently, during economic crises, unemployment rates might be extremely high.

Beginning in the Great Depression of the 1930s, Latin American policymakers decided that they could no longer bear the political costs of maintaining fixed exchange rates and free capital mobility. In order to fight unemployment during the depression, and to maintain high levels of employment thereafter, they needed to be able to chart an independent monetary policy. They therefore had to either abandon fixed exchange rates or the free movement of capital. Inevitably, they chose the latter. Once that decision was made, it proved difficult for governments to return to pre-1930s orthodoxy. The result was that Latin America attracted far less international capital than it should have during the post–World War II period. ·

One implication of Taylor's chapter, and of New Institutional Theory in general, is that suboptimal political and economic institutions work to reinforce one another. Political institutions generate, as output of the political system, specific laws and regulations that benefit particular constituencies. These constituencies, in turn, can oppose any reform of the relevant economic or political institution. The mutually reinforcing character of institutions therefore makes it extremely difficult to carry out reforms, even when the growth-enhancing benefits of such reforms are common knowledge.

Elisa Mariscal and Kenneth Sokoloff, in their contribution to this volume, "Schooling, Suffrage, and the Persistence of Inequality in the Americas, 1800–1945," analyze a canonical case of such institutional deadlock. They note that the positive benefits of widespread literacy and education for economic development are (and were) well known. Yet many societies failed to undertake public policies that would finance education and thus provide high levels of literacy. To understand how and why this happened, Mariscal and Sokoloff examine educational policies and outcomes in a cross section of New World economies during the nineteenth and early twentieth centuries.

Their argument can be summarized as follows. From the outset of the colonial period, there were economic inequalities between Latin and North America that gave rise to political inequalities at the time of independence. The political and economic institutions that fostered inequality in Latin America and relative equality in North America then became mutually reinforcing. In the particular case of education and literacy, North American societies adopted policies that served to support public education. Over time, increasing levels of political equality gave rise to increased support for "common schools." In fact, Mariscal and Sokoloff argue that there was a relationship between the extension of suffrage and increased support for basic education. They also note that most of the impetus for funding schools came at the state and local level. The fact that the costs and benefits were spread more or less evenly across society meant that it was easy to build coalitions (particularly at the local level) that would support taxation for public education. In short, representative democracy and the common school movement went hand in hand.

In most Latin American societies, however, the virtuous cycle described by Mariscal and Sokoloff for the United States and Canada did not come to pass. Most Latin American societies had much greater levels of income and wealth inequality, and marked differences in the distribution of human capital, than did the United States. The result was that at independence these societies did not undertake experiments in representative democracy. With extreme inequality in the distribution of income and political power, Latin American local governments typically did not organize tax-supported schools that were open to all members of the population. Collective action problems frustrated attempts to fund public education at the local level because the costs and benefits of education would not be spread equally across all members of the society. The only way to break the logjam was for federal governments to intervene and support public education at the national level. Such efforts, however, did not begin until the close of the nineteenth century and then proceeded at a modest pace. In sum, political inequality, low investment in public education, limited social mobility, and slow rates of economic growth all mutually reinforced one another.

Summerhill, Haber, and Mariscal and Sokoloff all describe situations in which economic institutions were politically determined. Alan Dye, in his contribution to this volume, "Privately and Publicly Induced Institutional Change: Observations from Cuban Cane Contracting, 1880–1936," reminds us that institutions may also be privately created—that is, be the outcome of the accumulation over time of private decisions. Institutions created by the state may, in fact, be less efficient than those created out of the process of private negotiation. In the first place, centralized decisions about institutional change may suffer from inadequate information (because it is costly, the state is forced to economize on the collection of information). In the second place, echoing points made by Summerhill, the state may not seek to optimize institutional design for the public good. Governments do not generally seek to create institutions that will foment growth; they are interested in providing benefits to their constituencies, at the lowest possible cost to that constituency. The probability of failure of an institution enacted by fiat is therefore relatively high.

Testing hypotheses about the relative efficiency of privately versus publicly induced institutional change is difficult. It requires that researchers be able to identify a particular economic sector in which there were experiments with both forms of institutional creation. It also requires that we have the necessary quantitative data to measure the efficiency outcomes of each type of institutional change.

Dye provides us with exactly this type of case: the Cuban sugar industry. From the 1880s to the 1920s, the institutions that governed sugar production were the product of the endogenous incorporation of information from thousands of privately created contracts. The accumulation of multiple, private contracting decisions led to a convergence on a standard contractual form that minimized transactions costs and enhanced productivity. In the late 1920s, however, the process of the endogenous creation of institutions was reversed. To stabilize the price of sugar, the Cuban government instituted a state-controlled crop restriction program and quota system that allowed inefficient mills to survive because they were guaranteed a share of the market. It also meant increased production costs because contractual relations between growers and mills were less flexible and less easily enforced. Ultimately, it meant an overall reduction in Cuba's share of the world market for sugar.

These essays do not, of course, exhaust all of the testable hypotheses of New Institutional Theory. Neither is it the case that they exhaust all of the cases for analysis provided by Latin America's economic history. Our view, however, is that these cases both present substantive tests of New Institutional Theory and, perhaps more important, provide a model on which further research can be developed.

References

Alesina, Alberto, Sule Özler, Nouriel Roubini, and Phillip Swagel. "Political Stability and Economic Growth." *Journal of Economic Growth* 1 (June 1996): 189–211.

Alston, Lee J., Thráinn Eggertsson, and Douglass C. North, eds. *Empirical Studies in Institutional Change*. Cambridge: Cambridge University Press, 1996.

Aoki, Masahiko. "Towards a Comparative Institutional Analysis: Motivations and Some Tentative Theorizing." *Japanese Economic Review* 47, no. 1 (March 1996): 1–19.

Barro, Robert J. "Economic Growth in a Cross Section of Countries." *Quarterly Journal of Economics*, May 1991.

Clark, Gregory. "The Political Foundations of Modern Economic Growth: England, 1540–1800." *Journal of Interdisciplinary History* 26 (spring 1996): 432–76.

George, Alexander L. "Case Studies and Theory Development: The Method of Structured, Focused Comparison." In Paul Gordon Lauren, ed., *Diplomacy: New Approaches in History, Theory, and Policy*. New York: Free Press, 1979.

Greif, Avner. "Contract Enforceability and Economic Institutions in Early Trade: The Maghribi Trader's Coalition." *American Economic Review* 83, no. 3 (June 1993): 525–48.

———. "Microtheory and Recent Developments in the Study of Economic Institutions Through Economic History." In David M. Kreps and Kenneth F. Wallis, eds., *Advances in Economic Theory*. Vol. 2. Cambridge: Cambridge University Press, 1997.

———. "Political Organizations, Social Structure, and Institutional Success: Reflections from Genoa and Venice during the Commercial Revolution." *Journal of Institutional and Theoretical Economics* 151, no. 4 (December 1995): 734–40.

Haber, Stephen. "Economic Growth and Latin American Economic Historiography." In Haber, ed., *How Latin America Fell Behind: Essays on the Economic Histories of Brazil and Mexico, 1800–1914*. Stanford: Stanford University Press, 1997.

Haber, Stephen, and Armando Razo. "Political Instability and Economic Performance: Evidence from Revolutionary Mexico." *World Politics* 51 (October 1998): 99–143.

Hurwicz, Leonid. "Toward a Framework for Analyzing Institutions and Institutional Change." In Samuel Bowles, Herbert Gintis, and Bo Gustafsson, eds., *Markets and Democracy: Participation, Accountability, and Efficiency.* Cambridge: Cambridge University Press, 1993.

Krueger, Anne O. "Trade Policy and Economic Development: How We Learn." *American Economic Review* 87, no. 1 (March 1997): 1–22.

Levine, Ross, and David Renelt. "A Sensitivity Analysis of Cross-Country Growth Regressions." *American Economic Review* 82, no. 4 (September 1992): 942–63.

North, Douglass C. *Institutions, Institutional Change and Economic Performance.* Cambridge: Cambridge University Press, 1990.

———. "Toward a Theory of Institutional Change." In William A. Barnett, Melvin J. Hinich, and Norman J. Schofield, eds., *Political Economy: Institutions, Competition, and Representation.* Cambridge: Cambridge University Press, 1983.

North, Douglass C., and Barry R. Weingast. "Constitutions and Commitment: The Evolution of Institutions Governing Public Choice in Seventeenth Century England." *Journal of Economic History* 44 (December 1989): 803–32.

Packenham, Robert A. *The Dependency Movement: Scholarship and Politics in Development Studies.* Cambridge: Harvard University Press, 1992.

Rosenthal, Jean Laurent. *The Fruits of Revolution: Property Rights, Litigation, and French Agriculture, 1700–1860.* Cambridge: Cambridge University Press, 1992.

Weingast, Barry R. "The Political Foundations of Limited Government: Parliament and Sovereign Debt in 17th- and 18th-Century England." In John N. Drobak and John V.C. Nye, eds., *The Frontiers of the New Institutional Economics.* San Diego: Academic Press, 1997.

Williamson, Oliver E. *The Economic Institutions of Capitalism: Firms, Markets, Relational Contracting.* New York: Free Press, 1985.

World Bank. *World Development Reports.* Oxford: Oxford University Press, 1996, 1997, 1998.

Institutional Determinants
of Railroad Subsidy and Regulation
in Imperial Brazil

Most work on the role of institutions in Latin American development has focused on economic institutions, namely, the rules, laws, and practices that shape incentives to investment and production. Economic institutions themselves, however, are often outcomes of specific policies and government actions. Institutional arrangements within the polity shape the character of laws, rules, policies, the definition and enforcement of property rights, and just about any form of repeated market intervention that can be considered an economic institution. The division of power and levels of governmental authority responsible for regulating various branches of economic activity, multicameralism, electoral systems, party organizations, and rules relating to the consideration and voting on policy proposals all shape the character of market intervention and affect the efficiency of economic organization. Economic institu-

I am indebted to Douglass North and Barry Weingast for their comments on this essay, to Stephen Haber for organizing the Hoover Conference on Institutions in Latin American Development, as well as to participants in the conference, along with colleagues at the University of California, Los Angeles, and participants in workshops at Northwestern University and the University of Illinois for their suggestions. Support for the research from which this chapter is drawn was generously provided by the Fulbright-Hays program, and the Joint Committee on Latin American Studies of the American Council of Learned Societies and Social Science Research Council. All errors are mine.

tions that directly govern investment, production, and exchange, such as commercial codes, financial regulation and banking laws, tariffs and taxation, and property rights, thus arise in the context of the institutional arrangements of the polity. To the extent that political institutions shape economic institutions that increase or decrease the economic surplus, the polity becomes directly relevant for the study of economic performance. Formal economic institutions are merely the tip of the institutional iceberg, the base of which is political organization and policy making.

Nineteenth-century Brazil's centralized polity is a case where political institutions heavily shaped the character of market intervention by government. A relatively backward economy, Brazil was late to adopt an array of features that account for the success of the advanced industrializing economies of the North Atlantic; investment in human and social overhead capital, modern rights in property, commercial legislation supporting the formation of limited liability companies, and a system of relatively unhindered financial intermediaries are but some leading examples. Unsurprisingly, market failure pervaded the economy. Yet the extent of market failure was but one determinant of the intensity of relative backwardness. The degree to which political organization aided (or hindered) in remedying market failures reveals the contribution (or reduction) that the state made to the level of economic activity in Brazil. Ideally, policies to remedy market failures in an otherwise institution-free setting would maximize the social surplus.[1] By fulfilling the "Gerschenkronian" potential of the state, the most efficient of all possible worlds would obtain, raising income and output appreciably. Defining the gulf between that ideal and the results of the policies Brazil actually pursued helps uncover the role of political institutions in

---

1. This efficiency criterion provides the benchmark against which the chapter contrasts the outcomes obtained by Brazilian political institutions. In the penultimate section, alternative institutional arrangements are considered.

shaping economic outcomes. Of special interest is the way that legislative institutions shaped the aggregation of political preferences and transformed them into policy. Because politicians did not necessarily share the economy's efficiency criteria, policies selected by politicians could depart dramatically from the most efficient outcome, depending on the extent of the market failure addressed by the policy.[2] In choosing policies, politicians do not set out to foster growth, increase gross domestic product, or enhance welfare. Instead, they set out to confer benefits on constituents, while reducing the external and fiscal costs of the policy that their constituents bear. This makes the distributive consequences of market interventions of paramount importance to politicians because policy determines the resulting distribution of benefits and costs. Moreover, the manner in which policymakers "solve" market failures (if solved at all) may prove dissipating and even exacerbate inefficiency. Indeed, only if a market failure was sufficiently widespread and severe was intervention likely to lead to an improvement over the status quo. Even where market failure was widespread, as in nineteenth-century Brazil, efficiency-enhancing intervention by the state may fall well short of realizing the full potential gains of remedying the failure.

The potential gains from transport improvements in nineteenth-century Brazil, and the working of Imperial railroad policy, illustrate this point. Historians and social scientists have long been interested in the impact of measures designed to remedy market failures and the consequences of those policies for growth. This essay poses and answers three questions: By what institutions and mechanisms did the Imperial state promote and regulate railroad

---

2. See Kenneth Shepsle and Barry R. Weingast, "Political Solutions to Market Problems," *American Political Science Review* 78 (1982): 417–43; and Barry R. Weingast, Kenneth A. Shepsle, and Christopher Johnson, "The Political Economy of Benefits and Costs: A Neoclassical Approach to Distributive Politics," *Journal of Political Economy* 89 (1981): 642–64.

investments? How did Brazil's political organization determine the ways in which government selected these policies? What were the consequences of railroad policy for the economy as a whole? The answers to these questions illuminate a broad concern shared by many scholars studying Latin America, namely, the origins and impact of government policy in a relatively backward economy.

In considering Brazilian railroad development, many historians would find much to agree with in the claim that "the plantation- and mine-to-port pattern of Latin American railroad construction did little to provide political integration, to serve local, regional, or national markets, and to encourage industrialization" and that railroads merely "linked Brazil to world markets and thereby deepened dependency."[3] The general impression of railroads in nineteenth-

3. E. Bradford Burns, *The Poverty of Progress: Latin America in the Nineteenth Century* (Berkeley: University of California Press, 1980), p. 136; Bradford Burns, *A History of Brazil* (New York: Columbia University Press, 1993), p. 161. Lest the reader believe this to be a straw man in the making, similarly negative assessments of the consequences of railroad development in Brazil that indict, in varying degrees, foreign investment, government policy, or a short-sighted elite, can be found in a variety of studies, including those by Peter Evans, *Dependent Development: The Alliance of Multinational, State, and Local Capital in Brazil* (Princeton, N.J.: Princeton University Press, 1979), who claims that railroad "concessions and interest guarantees were services to foreign capital" (p. 85) and that "the predilections of British capital" locked Brazil into the classic pattern of dependence (p. 61); Andre Gunder Frank, *Capitalism and Underdevelopment in Latin America: Historical Studies of Chile and Brazil* (New York: Monthly Review Press, 1967), in which he demonstrates how railroads were part and parcel of the overall process of underdevelopment and the export of surplus value (pp. 145–74, passim); Richard Graham, "Sepoys and Imperialists: Techniques of British Power in Nineteenth-Century Brazil," *Inter-American Economic Affairs* 23 (1969): 35–36, discusses how British railroads manifested imperialistic control; John H. Coatsworth, *Growth against Development* (DeKalb: Northern Illinois University Press, 1981), discusses how foreign-owned railroads undercut efficiency and service in Brazil (pp. 145, 176); Eugene Ridings, *Business Interest Groups in Nineteenth-Century Brazil* (Cambridge, Eng.: Cambridge University Press, 1994), p. 262, discusses how railroad policies failed to integrate the national market; and Peter L. Blasenheim, "Railroads in Nineteenth-Century Minas Gerais," *Journal of Latin American Studies* 26 (1994): 347–74, which argues that the planter class's blind ambition in promoting railroad investments in Minas Gerais was short-

century Brazil is that they were extraordinarily efficient at squandering and draining resources, enriching a small planter class while impoverishing the country. Enjoying similarly wide currency is the view that foreign financing of development projects such as railroads necessarily meant that "even the largest, the most stable, and the potentially wealthy countries saw their control over their own economies dissipate."[4] Despite the testable implications embedded in such formulations, for Brazil in particular there are surprisingly few evaluations of the economic consequences of foreign-owned railroads, railroad subsidies, or regulatory policy.[5]

Rather than settling for purely deductive explanations, or stylized impressions, the process of railroad development in Imperial Brazil, and the role of institutional arrangements therein, warrants assessment in terms of its observable consequences. This chapter resituates the inquiry by focusing on the institutional determinants of railroad subsidy and regulation. The chapter proceeds in five

---

sighted and costly. The precedent for these critiques originates in contemporary sentiments that stemmed from natural suspicions about opportunistic behavior on the part of foreign investors, whether real or imagined. What is striking about these assertions on the part of modern scholars is the utter dearth of empirical work that assesses in any systematic or rigorous fashion the benefits and costs of railroad development in Brazil.

4. Burns, *Poverty of Progress*, 138, mainly parrots the line of argument found in Frank, *Capitalism and Underdevelopment*; Fernando Henrique Cardoso and Enzo Faletto, *Dependency and Underdevelopment in Latin America* (Berkeley: University of California Press, 1979); Theotonio dos Santos, "Structure of Dependence," *American Economic Review* 60 (1970).

5. For a detailed study of policy bearing on railroads in one province, see Colin Lewis, *Public Policy and Private Initiative: Railway Building in São Paulo, 1860–1889* (London: University of London, Institute of Latin American Studies, 1991). In terms of empirical assessment, the sole exception is Roberto Fendt Jr., "Investimentos Ingleses no Brasil, 1870–1913: uma Avaliação da Política Brasileira," *Revista Brasileira de Economia* 31, no. 2 (1977): 521–39. Fendt takes the government as a unitary actor and focuses solely on the fiscal costs arising from the use of guaranteed dividends versus outright government ownership of railroads, ignoring all other linkages from railroads, as well as the institutional context within which policy was formulated.

sections. The first briefly discusses the failure of markets to supply railroad transport services, the operation of Brazil's railroad subsidy arrangements, and the growth of the railroad sector from the 1850s until 1887. The second section focuses on the political institutions of Brazil's Chamber of Deputies, examining the legislative choice of the level and distribution of railroad subsidy and its implication for the economic efficiency of Brazilian railroads. The third section examines the political and institutional determinants of the pattern of railroad freight regulation prevailing in Brazil in the 1880s. The fourth section considers some counterfactual alternatives to Brazil's unitary and centralized government to infer the consequences of alternative institutional arrangements. The final section concludes.

The main findings of the study are two. First, during the Imperial era the Brazilian government subsidized and regulated railroad projects in ways that made for strong gains while still registering hefty costs. Railroad technology embodied the potential for large reductions in transport cost. However, key features of domestic policies promoting railroad projects, rather than foreign capitalists or even export agriculture, reduced Brazil's gains below what could have been achieved by railroad technology. Such costs stemmed neither from foreign investment in railroads nor from "export-led growth" and dependency. Instead, costs arose directly from the manner in which Imperial political institutions shaped the distribution of subsidies. Second, government involvement in railroads cut two ways. On the one hand, railroads provide significant savings on transport costs, and the regulation of fares and rates limited the profits that both foreign- and domestically owned railroad companies could earn. Rate controls stanched any excessive leakage from the benefits stream before it could even begin. As a result, the bulk of the social surplus that railroads created remained in Brazil. On the other hand, distributive politics—a central feature of Brazil's parliament and the manner in which it resolved pressures for market interventions—promoted railroad projects in regions with poor agronomic endowments or regions that were otherwise ill-suited to exploit the supply of cheap transport that railroads made possible. As a result the return to Brazil from the capital invested in railroads was a good deal less than what could have been achieved with state-of-the-art transport technology.

These conclusions modify prevailing characterizations in several ways. The history of railroads in nineteenth-century Brazil lies at the intersection of two major currents of interpretation. In the first of these, the quality or character of foreign investment is critical to development. Foreign investment is often viewed by historians as inimical because it was exploitative, misallocated resources, and skewed growth, impoverishing the country and reducing Brazil to a neocolony.[6] Foreign penetration of Brazil, facilitated by policies geared toward attracting foreign capital, led directly to the "development of underdevelopment." The second strand focuses less on the character of foreign investment than on its implications for control of the surplus those investments created.[7] International markets were the background against which the state formulated policy; internalizing the external economic environment in turn shaped domestic class coalitions, resulting in an array of policies that compromised sovereignty and control and fostered business activities that benefited foreign investors disproportionately at the expense of the national economy.[8]

In the case of Brazilian railroads, neither view squares well with the evidence and both gloss over considerable complexity in the relationship between the institutions of government, investors (be they foreign or national), and economic outcomes. Because it had long suffered from high transport costs, the gains Brazil secured

6. Frank, *Capitalism and Underdevelopment*, pp. 147, 171–73, 290–96.
7. A version of this view is Graham, "Sepoys and Imperialists."
8. Cardoso and Faletto, *Dependency and Underdevelopment in Latin America*, p. xvi; dos Santos, "Structure of Dependence," pp. 231–36.

from railroads easily outweighed the costs. The distribution of those gains within Brazil was no doubt tilted to favor the enfranchised, the wealthy, and the powerful. This was a result of the prevailing features of Brazil that long predated the arrival of railroads and thus was in no way an inherent feature of either railroad technology or foreign finance. Foreigners neither captured the bulk of the surplus that railroads created nor controlled policies related to subsidy or pricing. There was no net drain of capital or resources from Brazil. Instead, there were considerable opportunity costs from the way political institutions shaped policies subsidizing and promoting railroad projects. These costs did not stem from foreign control or influence, from the structural imperatives of global capital markets, or from the narrow class interest of the planters. Rather, costs resulted from the way Brazilian political organization shaped the formation of subsidy policies. Policymakers responded not to Brazil's position in the world economy but rather to the imperatives of domestic political interests and institutions.

From Market Failure to Railroad Development

It is now clear railroads in Brazil had a strong direct impact, despite their relatively late start. The first stage of railroad development did not begin until after the middle of the nineteenth century. During Brazil's Second Reign (1840–1889), railroads accounted for the bulk of foreign financing that flowed into the country and constituted the largest "modern" sector of the economy. Private markets, however, failed to supply railroad transport services, despite the fact that the potential return to the economy's producers and consumers from reducing transport costs was large. Railroad development did not begin in earnest until the 1850s, when the government created a guaranteed minimum dividend for investors.[9] Earlier

9. Lei n. 641, June 26, 1852, reprinted in Cyro Diocleciano Ribeiro Pessoa Jr.,

attempts to foster railroads in Brazil foundered on the complexity, cost, and uncertainty inherent to large, capital-intensive investment projects that generated externalities. Five interrelated factors delayed the onset of Brazil's railway age. First, the start-up capital requirements of railroads were hefty. Compared with other investment projects in nineteenth-century Brazil, railroads were easily the most expensive. If mobilizing capital for industrialization was challenging, then doing so for railroads proved difficult in the extreme. Second, much uncertainty attached to the prospects of any individual railroad enterprise. Investors were naturally skittish about projects with uncertain returns, and it was difficult for them to know just how much revenue a railroad stood to earn. As long as the expected private return to the owners of railroad capital could not be pulled more closely in line with the returns to the beneficiaries of cheap transport, the private sector proved unwilling to undertake railroads, no matter how great the benefits they might confer. Third, risk of expropriation figured in the early obstacles to raising railroad capital. The capital intensity of the railroad and its high fixed costs put railroad owners at risk of expropriation through regulation. Po-

---

Estudo Descriptivo das Estradas de Ferro do Brazil (Rio de Janeiro, 1886), p. 3. Unless otherwise noted, the discussion of the overall evolution of Brazil's railroad sector derives from this source and Manoel da Cunha Galvão, *Notícia Sobre as Estradas de Ferro do Brasil* (Rio de Janeiro, 1869); Francisco Picanço, *Viação Ferrea do Brazil* (Rio de Janeiro, 1884); Max Lyon, *Note sur les Chemins de Fer du Bresil* (Paris, 1885); John C. Branner, *The Railways of Brazil, A Statistical Article* (Chicago, 1887); Fernandes Pinheiro, "Chemins de Fer," in F.J. de Santa-Anna Nery, ed., *Le Brésil en 1889* (Paris, 1889), pp. 383–439; Juan José Castro, *Treatise on the South American Railways* (Montevideo, 1893), pp. 344–52; [João] Chrockatt de Sá [Pereira de Castro], *Brazilian Railways, Their History, Legislation, and Development* (Rio de Janeiro, 1893); V.A. de Paula Pessoa, *Guia da Estrada de Ferro Central do Brasil*, vol. 1 (Rio de Janeiro, 1904); Clodomiro Pereira da Silva, *Política e Legislação de Estradas de Ferro* (São Paulo, 1904); Ernesto Antonio Lassance Cunha, *Estudo Descriptivo da Viação Ferrea do Brazil* (Rio de Janeiro, 1909); L. Winer, "The Railways of Brazil," in C.S. Vesey Brown, ed., *The South American Year Book, 1913* (n.p, n.d.), pp. 53–117; and Julian Smith Duncan, *Public and Private Operation of Railways in Brazil* (New York, 1932).

tential investors, either at home or abroad, were naturally wary of a government that could regulate in a way that potentially pushed rates below costs. Brazil's early railroad concessions set the maximum rates that could be charged for freight and passenger services yet did nothing to secure returns to shareholders.[10] Fourth, Brazil's underdeveloped capital market hindered fund-raising, even when the other problems could be solved. The thin capital market meant it was difficult to find enough investors with the right preferences toward risk, and with sufficient funds, to undertake a railroad. Finally, political unrest in Brazil delayed early railroad investment. Instability under the Regency and the early years of the Second Reign (1840–1889) further discouraged investors from taking risks in Brazil. The resources required to quell the revolts of the 1830s and early 1840s rendered government subsidies for internal improvements unfeasible.

Only with the first provision of guaranteed dividends by the Imperial government in 1852 was investment forthcoming.[11] Thereafter, both central and provincial governments in Brazil worked to satisfy landowners' demands for cheap transport by offering guaranteed minimum dividends to railroad projects. Early guarantees were project specific, but follow-up legislation in the 1870s and 1880s expanded central government railroad commitments, making them accessible to all Brazil's provinces.[12] Guaranteed dividends to railroad investors overcame negative perceptions of the country's prospects. The subsidies implicit in the guarantee policy reduced

10. Lei no. 101, October 31, 1835; Decreto, November 4, 1840. The appropriate annual volumes of *Coleção das Leis do Império do Brazil* published railroad legislation and administrative decrees bearing on railroad policy.

11. The railroad law of 1852 retained for the government the power to set maximum passenger fares and freight charges; the major difference between it and the earlier concession was the guarantee of a minimum dividend; Cyro Diocleciano Ribeiro Pessoa Junior, *Estudo Descriptivo das Estradas de Ferro*, pp. 3–4.

12. *Coleção das Leis do Império do Brazil*, Decreto 2450, September 24, 1873; Decreto 6995, August 10, 1878; Decreto 7959, August 29, 1880.

risk and permitted railroads either to obtain capital that they would not have received or to obtain it more cheaply than would be otherwise possible.[13] Government subsidies to transport were common in the nineteenth century, and guaranteed dividends were not unique to Brazil. After midcentury the nature of Brazil's guaranteed dividend policy had much in common with local aid to railroads in the United States and similar policies in India, Russia, Tuscany, France, and Sweden.[14] Brazil's guarantee arrangement with each railroad set a minimum dividend rate on an agreed-upon value of the firm's capital. When the railroad's net earnings failed to attain the prescribed level, the government aided the company by paying it the difference between its profits and the legislated rate of return. When the company achieved net earnings in excess of the prescribed dividend level by a sufficient margin, the additional profits were divided with the government in order to reimburse any prior guarantee payments. Even higher dividends occasioned the lowering of freight and passenger fares. Although the specific arrangements varied from line to line, the gist of the dividend guarantees was that they provided subsidized, need-based loans to railroads.

This led to two outcomes. For railroads that proved viable, only the nominal value of the guaranteed dividend payments received by the railroad was repaid to the government, and the value of the subsidy was the interest that the railroad escaped. For railroads that never turned a sufficient profit, the value of the subsidy that the firm enjoyed equaled the entire stream of guarantees that the government paid out. In either case, the quid pro quo of the guarantee was rate regulation by government authorities. With controls on

13. Mercer, *Railroads and Land Grant Policy*, pp. 19–26.
14. Albert Fishlow, *American Railroads and the Transformation of the Ante-Bellum Economy* (Cambridge, Eng.: Cambridge University Press, 1965), pp. 191–92; Manoel da Cunha Galvão, *Notícia Sobre as Estradas de Ferro do Brasil* (Rio de Janeiro, 1869), p. 21.

TABLE 1

Track and Output on Brazilian Railroads, 1855–1887

Year	Total Track (in route kilometers)	Railroad Output (in 1887 milreis)*
1855	15	200,155
1860	223	2,078,514
1865	498	3,611,287
1870	744	6,571,833
1875	1,801	14,306,998
1880	3,398	26,744,889
1885	6,930	34,966,580
1887	8,400	37,368,187

SOURCE: Drawn from Summerhill, "Benefits and Costs."
*Deflated by the extended wholesale price index for Rio de Janeiro.

freight and passenger fares, the minimum dividend policy created a rate-of-return band for guaranteed railroads.

Brazil's first railroad opened in 1854, yet the growth of the railroad sector proceeded slowly until after the war with Paraguay (1864–1870). Railroad development accelerated thereafter, with both track and output expanding at a steady pace through the end of the Empire. By 1887 Brazil had some 8,400 kilometers of track open for service. Table 1 sketches the growth of the railroad sector in Brazil through 1887 by reference to two basic indicators. The first is track route kilometers, a crude index of sectoral capacity and capital formation.[15] The second is total railroad operating revenues, the bulk of which came from railroad freight and passenger services.

15. The growth of route kilometers is a lagging indicator of investment since a fair amount of the capital formation occurs in the year or two prior to placing the track in operation. Track as an index of capital formation implies that the cost of constructing a kilometer of track was the same throughout Brazil from year to year and that outlays on rolling stock, structures, and the like were a constant share of total outlays. None of these are likely to hold, but route distance nonetheless provides a useful measure of capacity.

These are deflated to 1887 prices using the extended wholesale price index for Rio de Janeiro[16] and thus provide a rough measure of railroad output. Both indicators show sustained growth in railroad activity. Transport capacity and traffic grew especially rapidly after 1875. Increases in route mileage resulted first from the increase in Brazilian government subsidies to new railroad projects and then later from the dramatic fall in the price of rails and rolling stock occasioned by the diffusion of the Bessemer process. Between 1855 and 1887 the average increase in railroad output was almost 15 percent a year.

By the end of the Empire in 1889, the railroad sector had developed to the point that the material gains to Brazil were appreciable. Railroads created an economic surplus because they improved on other modes of overland shipment prevalent in Brazil, namely, animal-drawn carts, mule trains, and in some cases human porters. By combining capital, labor, and raw materials to produce a unit of transport services at lower cost than did the old modes of shipment, railroads permitted the integration and extension of markets. Gains to shippers appeared as a significant reduction in the charges of securing transport services.

The social savings created when the railroad supplanted more

16. The series of nominal revenues was rather painstakingly constructed from the annual revenues of individual railroads, found in Pessoa, *Estudo Descriptivo das Estradas de Ferro*; Picanço, *Viação Ferrea do Brazil*; Brazil, *Relatório do Ministério da Agricultura*, for 1886 and 1887; Liberato de Castro Carreira, *História Financeira e Orçamentária do Império no Brasil*, pp. 777–830. By 1887 there were forty-seven separate railroads in operation that reported to the government, making Brazil's railroad sector the least concentrated, and the most intractable for researchers, in all of Latin America. The output series excludes urban tramways and some smaller railroads that reported only to provincial authorities. The nominal revenues are deflated by the wholesale price index in Luis A.V. Catão, "A New Wholesale Price Index for Brazil during the Period 1870–1913," *Revista Brasileira de Economia* 46, no. 4 (1992): 519–33. The index is extended backward from 1870 by regressing it on a related index, that for Rio de Janeiro consumer prices, presented in Eulália Maria Lahmeyer Lobo, *História do Rio de Janeiro* (Rio de Janeiro, 1978), pp. 804–05.

costly forms of transport were large. The details of the railroad's aggregate impact are presented elsewhere, but a brief summary suggests the importance of the new transport technology.[17] In 1887 Brazil's railroads produced 221.1 million ton kilometers of freight service, charging on average 0.123 milreis per ton kilometer.[18] This was well less than the best-practice prerail charge of about 0.417 milreis (adjusted to 1887 prices). Estimated social savings on freight shipment were 64.9 million milreis in 1887, fully 9.5 percent of Brazil's gross domestic product.[19] This magnitude may be further expressed in terms of the economy's advance in the last decades of the Second Reign. From 1861 to 1887 Brazil's gross domestic product almost doubled, rising from 336.2 million milreis to 657.7 million in 1887 prices. Controlling for the increase in population, the implied productivity gain was some 130.4 million milreis. The upper-bound measure of the social savings comes to a full 50 percent of this increase; alternative lower-bound measures exceed 25 percent of the total productivity advance. Brazilian railroads were no doubt the single most important force at work in raising output per capita between 1861 and 1887.

17. William Summerhill, "Railroads in Imperial Brazil," in John H. Coatsworth and Alan M. Taylor, eds., *Latin America and the World Economy Since 1800* (Cambridge, Mass.: Harvard University Press, 1998), pp. 383–406.

18. The output, revenues, and capital in the railroad sector in 1887 come from the company reports of the major railroads, the report of the Ministry of Agriculture for 1887, and the report of the president of the province of Rio de Janeiro. Detail on the sources may be found in the appendix to the lengthier paper from which this chapter is drawn; Summerhill, "Benefits and Costs: The Political Economy of Railroads in the Empire of Brazil," ms. 1997.

19. The gross domestic product estimate for 1887 is from Cláudio R. Contador and Cláudio L. Haddad, "Produto Real, Moeda e Preços: A Experiência Brasileira no Período 1861–1970," *Revista Brasileira de Estatística* 36 (1974): 407–40.

Institutional Origins of Railroad Subsidy

Previous studies of Brazilian railroads stressed the role of external constraints, agrarian classes, and local interests in shaping their development. Curiously, none of those studies examined the determinants of the pattern of subsidy. Moreover, those analyses eschewed the role of political institutions. Adding only a modest amount of political institutional detail reveals the forces underpinning the pattern of actual subsidy. By providing dividend guarantees to railroads, the Imperial parliament solved a problem that the market alone had failed to solve. Where guarantees were insufficient to bring sufficient investment within the interval desired by public authorities, the government constructed and operated railroads. Central to this market intervention was the influence of the "pork barrel" in the legislative politics of the era. Given that the onset and course of railroad development depended on the character and extent of market intervention by government, this section turns to the institutional origins of railroad subsidy. The following section focuses on the nature of freight rate regulation.

While no full description of Brazilian political organization is possible here, in general public goods and scarce projects were distributed by means of voting within parliament. Two chambers considered legislation; projects that passed both chambers then went to the emperor for sanction or veto. Senators with lifetime tenure constituted the upper house, and deputies elected for a fixed term of four years made up the lower chamber. Considerable turnover and innovation characterized the membership of the lower house.[20] Provincial assemblies also passed legislation, but these acts were subject to the review of the national parliament. Provincial subsidies

20. Eul-Soo Pang, *In Pursuit of Honor and Power: Noblemen of the Southern Cross in Nineteenth-Century Brazil* (Tuscaloosa: University of Alabama Press, 1988), p. 200.

to railroads, for example, had to withstand the scrutiny of central government authorities. In several cases, provinces were unable to cover the costs of those subsidies and the national government stepped in to pay them. Unlike a federal arrangement, such as that of the nineteenth-century United States, which pitted subnational administrative units against one another in competition for mobile factors of production, Brazilian centralism pitted provincial delegations against one another in the competition for pork and patronage within parliament.

The economic impact of market intervention on the part of parliament was influenced by three main institutional factors: (1) the perception of the incidence of the benefits and costs of such intervention by legislators; (2) the use of a majority voting rule, which selected the median legislator's preferred level of subsidy as the one prevailing for the entire country; and (3) the incentives for legislators from the same electoral district or province to cooperate in supporting a subsidy policy. The result was that institution-bound incentives systematically promoted subsidy policies that departed from those that were economically efficient.

To understand the role of Brazilian political institutions in subsidy policies, consider first the problem of an optimal subsidy to a railroad. An efficient subsidy policy, x, that maximizes the social surplus ($x = \arg\max E(x) = B(x) - C(x)$) would be one that subsidizes a railroad up to the point where the marginal social benefit of the subsidy equals the marginal social cost of the policy, $B'(x) = C'(x)$ (where benefits and costs are present-value adjusted). By contrast, a legislator considers how the political costs and benefits bear on his political support in choosing x, the subsidy policy:

$$N_i(x) = B_{i1}(x) + C_{i1}(x) - C_{i2}(x) - t_i T(x),$$

where $N_i(x)$ is the political support that legislator i expects from policy x, $B_{i1}(x)$ are the benefits created by the policy within his electoral district, $C_{i1}(x)$ are the direct outlays from the policy received within the district, $C_{i2}(x)$ are the indirect costs borne by the district, and $t_i T(x)$ is the district's share of the total tax burden arising from the policy.[21] To garner the most political support possible, the legislator seeks a policy (that is, a magnitude of x) that maximizes the benefits enjoyed by his constituents, and minimizes their costs. The costs of interest to the legislator thus differ from the true resource costs of the policy. Part of the costs, namely, outlays within the district, are enjoyed by constituents as benefits; only those external costs that weigh on constituents within the district figure into the legislator's choice.

Two factors create a gap between the efficient policy and that adopted by the legislature. First is the geographic partition of the polity, whereby legislators represent particular electoral-administrative districts. Legislators ignore an economically relevant component of cost because it does not bear on their political support. Summing across all political support functions (and all districts) gives what would be a "politically efficient" level and distribution of railroad subsidy:

$$x = \arg\max \sum_i N_i(x) = B(x) + C_1(x) - C_2(x) - T(x).$$

Since the outlays on the subsidy equal the tax costs of the policy, the two terms cancel,

$$N(x) = B(x) - C_2(x),$$

21. The basic model of the legislator's choice in a setting of distributive politics is adapted from Weingast et al., "The Political Economy of Benefits and Costs," pp. 642–64. For simplicity, the analysis here treats the subsidy as one that generates benefits only within the legislator's district or province. Allowing benefits to arise outside the district simply distorts the economic consequences of the political calculus even further since the legislator considers only those benefits that accrue to his constituents.

leaving

$$x = \arg\max N(x) = B(x) - C_2(x)$$

which differs from the efficient subsidy:

$$x^E = \arg\max E(x) = B(x) - C_1(x) - C_2(x),$$

where the two cost components are direct outlays and negative externalities. The political mechanism causes legislators to consider only the costs that fall within their districts and treats part of the cost as a benefit. Because of the way legislators perceive the relevant benefits and costs within their district (and thereby treat one of the components of economic cost as a political benefit), they collectively choose a level of subsidy that is larger than the efficient one. The politically efficient subsidy thus exceeds that warranted by economic efficiency.

The second factor that makes even the politically "efficient" level of subsidy unlikely is majority rule. Institutional arrangements in Brazil's legislature guaranteed the existence of an equilibrium policy by separating the space of policy alternatives into single policy dimensions, considered by the legislature one at a time.[22] Thus,

22. The significance of the separability of issues cannot be understated since it guarantees a stable policy equilibrium, avoids cycles in the collective choice, and enables legislators to consider and vote on proposals one issue at a time; see Joseph B. Kadane, "On Division of the Question," *Public Choice* 13 (1972): 47–54; Gerald H. Kramer, "Sophisticated Voting over Multidimensional Choice Spaces," *Journal of Mathematical Sociology* 2 (1972): 165–80; Kenneth A. Shepsle, "Institutional Arrangments and Equilibrium in Multidimensional Voting Models," *American Journal of Political Science* 23 (1979): 27–59; Douglas Dion, "The Robustness of Structure-Induced Equilibrium," *American Journal of Political Science* 36 (1992): 462–82. In Brazil's Chamber of Deputies, the internal rules required separation of issues into distinct sections of a bill, and each section was voted on separately; see Brazil, Camara dos Deputados, *Regimento Interno da Camara dos Deputados* (Rio de Janeiro, 1875), pp. 148–50, for the sections that establish separability and germaneness of amendments.

on the subsidy dimension the winning policy is that preferred by the median legislator. To be politically efficient in the sense elaborated above, the level of subsidy must correspond to the mean of the levels preferred by all legislators. Instead, majority rule guarantees that the median preference prevails. The relationship between the median preference and the mean level is indeterminate. That they would equate is a knife-edge condition that could prevail but is unlikely to do so.

Those two factors—geographic partition and majority rule—provide the first hypothesis on Brazilian railroad subsidies: because they were approved by a parliament composed of legislators seeking political support, subsidies tended to be excessive. At the same time, because the market failure implied by having no railroads was widespread throughout Brazil, market intervention under those political arrangements was likely to improve on the status quo solution in which Brazil had no railroads at all. Because subsidy proposals would be selected under majority rule, however, the degree to which the subsidy policy departs from the efficient one varied, depending on the distribution of legislator preferences.

A third factor modifies the first two: Brazilian politicians not only chose a level of railroad subsidies but also chose a particular distribution of subsidies across provinces. There are three distinct analytic approaches to the problem of distributing projects in a majority rule legislature. The first of these treats the distributive problem as a zero-sum game: every pound sterling of subsidy enjoyed by one district was viewed as lost to another. In that case, the predicted outcome is the emergence of a minimum-sized winning coalition that distributes subsidies only to its members.[23] Adding ad-

23. William Riker and Peter Ordeshooke, *An Introduction to Positive Political Theory* (Englewood Cliffs, N.J.: Prentice Hall, 1973), pp. 176–91; James M. Buchanan and Gordon Tullock, *The Calculus of Consent* (Ann Arbor: University of Michigan Press, 1962).

ditional members to the coalition distributes the benefits more thinly; removing members from the coalition causes it to lose. Hence, minimum winning coalitions dominate all others. Legislators that are members of the winning coalition garner subsidies for their districts, net of their districts' share of taxes, while the other legislative districts receive a negative payoff in the form of tax costs. Although the approach cannot indicate which minimum winning coalition will prevail (and there are many potential candidates), it does strongly predict that only a minimum winning coalition will emerge. Opposed to this view of a legislature is one that does not involve the zero-sum assumption, allowing subsidies to create benefits enjoyed by constituents that are not lost to others, while also making legislators uncertain over whether they will be a member of the minimum winning coalition. In that case, a universal coalition emerges that distributes the subsidies across all districts. If individual legislators' perceptions of the uncertainty over whether they will be in a less-than-universalistic coalition weaken, however, universalism breaks down at the level of the legislature as a whole (even though it may still operate at lower levels of aggregation).

Exploiting the possibility that legislators are less than fully uncertain about whether they stand to be in a winning coalition provides a third avenue for considering how distributive coalitions might arise. Consider a proposed railroad project, the benefits of which may be enjoyed across much of a Brazilian province and especially so by the enfranchised elite that own land and raise commercial crops. Those near the railroad see an increase in the value of their land; those farther removed look to the possibility of future railroad extensions and in the interim enjoy increasing competition among nonrailroad modes of shipment due to the decline in the demand for their services in areas served by the railroad. Deputies from the province seek to obtain a railroad subsidy for their constituents, sharing in the political credit for doing so. In parliament provincial blocs of legislators could coordinate their actions to attain outcomes preferred to those they might be able to secure individually. Projects apportioned by parliament to generate geographically specific benefits created incentives for representatives from a single electoral district to vote together, irrespective of ideology, party, and the like.[24] Since a distributive project concentrates direct outlays and spillovers in the province by banding together, legislators from that province increase the chances that at least some of them can secure a position in the winning coalition and that their constituents would be the recipients of the largesse of that coalition. Clearly, provinces with large numbers of deputies stood a greater chance of having at least one deputy—and hence their province's proposed railroad subsidy—in the winning coalition. This provides an intuitive hypothesis on subsidies: provinces with large delegations in the Chamber of Deputies secured more railroad subsidies.

Assessing the mechanism by which the government distributed subsidies requires a measure of what is being distributed. The two components of railroad subsidy were (1) guaranteed dividends and (2) direct outlays on the part of the government for railroads that it either took over or undertook itself. In the latter case subsidies include both capital expenditures and operating losses covered by tax revenues. Although the largest government-owned line (the Dom Pedro II) usually covered its operating expenses before 1887 and yielded a surplus that would have been a competitive rate of return, most other government-owned railroads operated at a loss. The experiences of the guaranteed lines reveal a similar diversity in performance. Some, such as the San Paulo Railway or the Companhia

---

24. For much of this period, Brazil operated with multimember electoral districts often as large as the province itself. These are notorious for the incentives they create for cultivating a personal vote and the corollary, weak party organizations. Deputies thus had ample reason to try and obtain expenditures targeted to their districts, if they were concerned with maintaining their electoral support. That the province is the proper unit of analysis is suggested by the province-specific character of most railroad projects under the Empire.

Paulista, needed guaranteed dividends only in the early years of operation. Many of the other privately owned railroads with guaranteed dividends, such as the Bahia and San Francisco and the Great Western of Brazil, needed those payments almost every year that they operated.[25]

A first approximation to the level of the government's subsidy commitments is derived as follows. On government-owned lines, the value of the subsidy equals the sum of capital costs and any operating losses. On guaranteed lines the value of the government commitment to those projects is taken as the agreed-upon minimum dividend rate for each railroad. Operating losses on those lines were absorbed by shareholders, which covered them out of the dividend guarantees and reserves. The measure elaborated here is for 1888, the last full year of the monarchy.[26] The value of the central government's commitment to underwrite railroads in any province i is

$$G_i = OC_i + rK_{1i} + \delta K_{2i} ,$$

where OC_i is the sum of operating losses on government-owned lines in province i, rK_{1i} is the value of the direct capital "subsidy" on all government-owned lines in province i, and δK_{2i} is the value of the dividend guarantee on guaranteed lines in province i. The capital subsidy is taken to be 6 percent of the construction cost of the government-owned lines in operation in 1888 (operating losses on government-owned lines are taken from the same year). The value of the commitment embodied in the dividend guarantee equals the product of the agreed-upon value of the railroad and the dividend

25. Detail of the experiences of the main railroads through 1913 may be found in Summerhill, "Market Intervention in a Backward Economy," *Economic History Review*, August 1998.

26. The components of those commitments are taken from the report of the Brazilian minister of agriculture in 1888.

rate (both codified in the concession or later legislation), which varied from 6 to 7 percent depending on the railroad. In only one case—the government-owned Estrada de Ferro Dom Pedro II, which traversed Rio de Janeiro province and ran into Minas Gerais—were any of the major railroads "shared" by more than one province. There the value of the government's commitment was partitioned in accordance with the share of total track in each province.[27] Summing across provinces gives the maximum outlay the Brazilian government would confront in a worst-case year (see table 2 for the resulting valuation of the imperial state's commitment to railroad projects in 1888, by province). As can be seen, the distribution of these commitments was uneven. Eight of Brazil's twenty provinces had received none of these commitments on the eve of the Republic. Among the twelve provinces that did receive them, the level of total subsidy varied widely.

The allocation of railroad dividend guarantees and government railroad outlays by the Brazilian Imperial Parliament is modeled using cooperative game theory to measure provincial voting power in the Chamber of Deputies. Such a measure of voting power, based solely on the structure of representation, predicts how rent-generating projects such as railroad subsidies will be distributed among Brazil's provinces.

The measure of voting power for each province derives from the possibilities of coalition formation in a cooperative setting. It expresses the likelihood that a deputy from a particular province could turn a losing coalition into a winner, on the basis of all possible permutations of deputies. The resulting Shapley-Shubik index of voting power expresses how often, on average, a particular province

---

27. The Minas share of track in 1888 is taken from Rodolpho Jacob, *Minas Gerais no XXo Seculo* (Bello Horizonte, 1910), p. 447. The Rio share is calculated residually based on total track reported in E.F.D. Pedro II, *Relatorio, 1888* (Rio de Janeiro, 1889).

TABLE 2
Government Railroad Subsidies and Voting Power, by Province

Province	Subsidy Commitment, 1888 (in milreis)	Shapley-Shubik Index until 1881	Shapley-Shubik Index from 1884
Rio de Janeiro	4,472,898	0.0993	0.0970
Minas Gerais	4,159,397	0.1808	0.1761
Bahia	3,723,732	0.1181	0.1153
Pernambuco	3,667,260	0.1086	0.1060
São Paulo	2,815,439	0.0726	0.0709
Rio Grande do Sul	1,501,365	0.0472	0.0462
Ceará	930,393	0.0640	0.0626
Alagôas	826,686	0.0390	0.0381
Paraná	804,443	0.0153	0.0149
Santa Catarina	392,651	0.0153	0.0149
Rio Grande do Norte	384,514	0.0153	0.0149
Paraíba	302,188	0.0390	0.0381
Maranhão	0	0.0472	0.0462
Sergipe	0	0.0310	0.0303
Pará	0	0.0231	0.0462
Piauí	0	0.0231	0.0226
Amazonas	0	0.0153	0.0149
Espírito Santo	0	0.0153	0.0149
Goiás	0	0.0153	0.0149
Mato Grosso	0	0.0153	0.0149

SOURCES: Guaranteed capital and rates from "Estradas de ferro em trafego, em construção e em projecto até 31 de dezembro de 1888," *Relatório do Ministério da Agricultura* (Rio de Janeiro, 1889). Indexes of voting power computed as described in text, based on information in Barão de Javari, *Organizações e Programas Ministeriais desde 1822 a 1889* (Rio de Janeiro, 1889).

NOTE: Subsidy commitment is the value of all central government railroad commitments in 1888, by próvince. In the case where a railroad traversed more than one province, the guaranteed capital for each province is proportional to the extension of that railroad within the respective provincial borders. The value of the commitments equals the product of the guaranteed stock of capital and the guaranteed rate per annum. The first type of commitment is based on the recognized value of the railroad capital formed by foreign and domestic investors that enjoyed dividend guarantees, typically established at 7 percent a year. The second is those lines owned by government, where a slightly lower rate of 6 percent is imputed (this is higher than the 4.5 percent used in the benefit-cost assessments in order to allow for depreciation). The Shapley-Shubik index is a measure of the voting power of a province's delegation in the Chamber of Deputies.

can expect one of its deputies to be pivotal in a winning coalition.[28] The index captures the intuition that participants in a coalition receive a share of the spoils on the basis of their relative contribution to that coalition but modifies that share on the basis of the majority voting rule. (See table 2 for indexes of the voting power of the provinces in Brazil's Chamber of Deputies.)[29] The distribution of seats in the chamber changed slightly in the early 1880s, giving rise to the two different series presented in the table.[30] An inspection of the sum of railroad dividend guarantees and government outlays on railroads by province reveals a close relationship between them and the amount of voting power held by a province in the chamber. The correlation coefficient between the two is 0.89, indicating that variation in voting power is associated with 89 percent of the variation in the amount of railroad subsidies received by the provinces. The larger the share of seats controlled by the province, the larger its share of railroad commitments.

There are departures in the table from predicted outcomes and these will be understood only after a much closer examination of

28. Other indexes also serve as measures on voting power, most prominently the Banzhaf index. Nonetheless, "the two [the Banzhaf and Shapley-Shubik indexes] can be regarded as equivalent for many practical purposes if we grant that law and politics are far from being exact sciences." Pradeep Dubey and Lloyd S. Shapley, "Mathematical Properties of the Banzhaf Power Index," *Mathematics of Operations Research* 4, no. 2 (1979): 100.

29. The computation of the index of the upper house is left aside here. The proportions of seats by province in both chambers were virtually identical under the constitution of 1824. As such, Imperial Brazil differed from the United States. Unequal voting power in the lower house of the U.S. Congress would be tempered heavily by the equal seat allocations in the Senate, and voting power in the lower house would be a poor predictor of the division of the spoils from distributive projects as a result.

30. It is not the case that the share of seats held by a province reflected its share of population. Unlike the United States, Brazil had no regular reapportionment mechanism. For most of the Empire the basic distribution of seats reflected the impressions of Brazil's provincial population in the 1820s.

the process of policymaking.[31] Rio Grande do Sul, for example, received a disproportionately large share of railroad subsidies mainly because of concerns about moving troops quickly to the far south in case of the renewal of conflict in the Rio de la Plata. Also, nothing in the analysis explains why some "weak" provinces received guarantees while other provinces that were no weaker received none at all. Some of those in the north received subsidies as part of drought relief programs provided by the central government. More generally, exploring why such departures from the predicted level of subsidy occurred requires reference to additional features of distributive policies in Brazil's parliament.[32] It is clear, however, that voting power was a major determinant of a province's pulling down railroad subsidies. Bigger provinces (in the sense of having a larger share of total seats) captured more subsidies. The politicization of the benefits from those subsidies—the way in which politicians created support by providing subsidies to projects that benefited their constituents—meant that projects that should not have been un-

31. For example, representatives of contiguous provinces might join together to secure projects whose benefits spilled into both districts. For example, a railroad from Minas to the coast could run through Bahia, Espirito Santo, Rio de Janeiro, or São Paulo. Moreover, a railroad skirting Minas Gerais and running through the Paraiba valley would cross São Paulo and Rio de Janeiro, as well as have effects in southern Minas. In particular, given the administrative boundaries of the provinces, and the large number of votes commanded by the contiguous provinces of Brazil's center-south, their provincial delegations could vote together to secure subsidies for projects benefiting the larger region. It comes as little surprise, then, that a large share of Brazil's railroads concentrated in that region of the country. Similarly, bargaining for support of a particular policy between a "powerful" province and the Cabinet might lead to a log roll in which the Cabinet authorizes subsidies to that province under standing legislation. These various actions are difficult to observe in practice, and the index of voting power proves especially useful because it captures the underlying ability to turn a losing coalition into a winner on a vote.

32. There are several of these, one of them being the role of Cabinet government and the Emperor's "moderating power." For an analysis of how the executive could shift the induced preference of the median legislator, see Summerhill, "Moderating Power and Confidence Vote Procedure: Executive Agenda Setting in Brazil's Imperial Parliament," ms. 1998.

dertaken came to enjoy extensive government support in Imperial Brazil.

Although the distribution of railroad subsidies was clearly related to the distribution of voting power, it remains to be shown the extent to which the pattern of subsidy was inefficient. As a starting point, an aggregate measure of the social return on all Brazilian railroads provides a benchmark to gauge performance of individual railroad projects. The first hypothesis—that railroad subsidies were inefficient by virtue of having been distributed not in terms of economic criteria but rather in pursuit of political objectives—suggests that the social return on railroad projects should be low.

There are two conceptual distinct measures of the social rate of return. The first examines whether the return on investments in railroads justified the resources devoted to them. The answer to that is given by the average social return.[33] As long as the return to society on railroad capital was no less than the return on alternative investments, then railroads were a good use of capital in Brazil. The second measure addresses whether Brazil invested too much or too little in its railroads. That is answered by estimating the marginal social return,[34] which although derived from the average social return, reveals just how much an additional milreis of capital invested in the railroad sector generated for the economy as a whole. This second measure serves as the efficiency benchmark. Ideally, the Brazilian government should have promoted investment in projects with good prospects and then subsidized them right up to the point where the return on an additional milreis invested equaled the returns from other activities in the economy. If the railroad returned less than that, then the government oversubsidized. At least some

33. Fishlow, *American Railroads*, pp. 52–54; Marc Nerlove, "Railroads and American Economic Growth," *Journal of Economic History* 26 (1966): 111–15.

34. On the challenges involved in estimating the marginal social return, see Peter McClelland, "Social Rates of Return on American Railroads in the Nineteenth Century," *Economic History Review* 25 (1972): 471–88.

of the subsidized investment would have been better applied elsewhere. If the railroad returned more than that, then the level of
subsidy was too low and the state should have promoted investment until it drove the additional return down to the point where it
equaled the relatively riskless private return.

For an aggregate estimate of the social profitability of Brazil's
railroad sector in 1887, see table 3,[35] which derives the average social
return on railroad capital. To do so, it computes the social benefits
across all railroads by reference to the transport cost savings on
freight shipment they provided over a system of improved wagon
roads.[36]

The table adds to these social benefits the net revenues of the
railroads (minus subsidy payments to investors). The ratio of that
sum to the total reproducible physical capital in railroads in 1887 is
the average social rate of return. In 1887 Brazilian railroads enjoyed
an unsubsidized private rate of return of a little less than 3 percent.
This was higher in the eyes of investors in guaranteed lines, who
enjoyed both net revenues and subsidies. Outlays on guaranteed
dividends that year came to 9.9 million milreis. Combined with the
net operating revenues, the return actually received by owners of
railroad capital came to 4.75 percent. A relatively low-risk return at
that time was that on government debt instruments, which ran a
little more than 4 percent in 1887. Summing the lower-bound social
savings to the unsubsidized capital earnings of the railroads yields
a social rate of return of 9.4 percent. The average social return is
converted to the marginal return by multiplying it by the share of
capital earnings in total subsidized revenues. This approximates the
capital elasticity of output on the railroad sector, which is imputed

35. Details of the derivation are found in Summerhill, "Benefits and Costs."
36. Railroads of course carried passengers as well, and these should figure into
the benefits measure. However, cost savings on railroad passenger services were
actually low, and ignoring them here leaves out little.

in this way for Brazil at 0.52. The resulting estimate of the social rate of return at the margin comes to 4.9 percent in 1887 (see table 3). In aggregate, Brazil had not overinvested in railroads and may have slightly underinvested in them at the end of the Empire.

The aggregate measure serves as a benchmark, but it obscures the fact that individual railroad projects may have been systematically over- or undersubsidized. Disaggregating the sector into its constituent lines reveals the extent to which individual railroads returned greater or less than the market rate of return. (See table 3 for the marginal social rates of return, net of subsidy, on individual railroads in Brazil in 1887.)[37] It is clear that although a number of Brazil's railroads presented strong positive returns, fully three-fourths of them did not. Their combined private and social returns at the margin reveal that they generated well less than the 4.5 percent return that could have been earned on public debt. The minority of lines that exceeded the 4.5 percent cutoff had a social return at the margin of 7.5 percent, revealing that additional subsidy was warranted. The group that performed poorly also had dismal social returns. After deducting subsidy payments (including implicit capital subsidies on government-owned lines), these poor performers as a group earned for Brazil around −2.2 percent at the margin. These lines constituted just over half the total capital of the railroad sector in 1887.

From the perspective of a social benefit-cost analysis, the poor-performing railroads were not good investments for Brazil. The aggregate result, obtained above for the railroad sector as a whole, is in fact driven by relatively few large railroads that exhibited high marginal returns. Since all railroads in Brazil used the same tech-

37. The social return from a railroad in a single year is admittedly not the best measure. This problem is unavoidable here because the assessment rests on a rich cross section of data that cannot be readily reproduced for earlier years. For an assessment of the social returns from Brazil's major railroads over a lengthy interval of time, see Summerhill, "Market Intervention in a Backward Economy."

TABLE 3
Social Rate of Return at the Margin, by Railroad, 1887

Railroad	Marginal Social Rate of Return
Santos a Jundiaí	0.18
Macahe e Campos e Santo Antonio de Padua	0.10
Paulista	0.11
S.Carlos do Pinhal	0.08
Recife a Limoeiro	0.03
Mogiana	0.07
Recife a Palmares	0.05
Dom Pedro II	0.06
Leopoldina	0.05
Sorocabana-Ituana	0.04
São Paulo e Rio	0.03
Taquary a Cacequi	0.03
Baturite	0.03
Maceio a Imperatriz	−0.04
Bahia a Alagoinhas	−0.04
Central da Bahia	−0.03
Rio Grande a Bage	−0.03
Rio do Ouro	0.02
Oeste de Minas	0.03
Principe do Grao Para	0.03
Barao de Araruama	0.03
Conde d'Eu	−0.04
Campos a Carangola	−0.01
Paranagua a Corytiba	−0.02
Bragantina	−0.03
Recife a Caruaru	0.01
Minas e Rio	−0.04
Itapemirim	−0.04
Porto Alegre a Novo Hamburgo	−0.02
Uniao Valenciana	0.01
Campos a S.Sebastiao	0.01
Rio das Flores	0.01
Camocim a Sobral	0.00
Ramal do Timbo	−0.04
Bahia e Minas	0.01
Palmares a Caranhuns	0.00

TABLE 3
(continued)

Railroad	Marginal Social Rate of Return
Paulo Affonso	−0.01
Alagoinhas a S. Francisco	0.00
Natal a Nova Cruz	−0.04
Quarahim a Itaqui	−0.06
E.F. do Norte	0.00
Ramal de Cantagallo	0.00
Sant'Anna	0.00
Santa Isabel do Rio Preto	−0.03
D. Thereza Christina	−0.06
Rezende a Areas	−0.02
All Railroads	0.03

SOURCE: Summerhill, "Benefits and Costs," provides a detailed discussion of the derivation of these social rates of return.

NOTE: Marginal return is the product of lower-bound freight social savings and share of capital in total costs.

nology—steam locomotion to pull carriages on fixed tracks made of iron and steel rails—there was little difference among them. There were, however, substantial differences among the regions where those railroads operated. Brazil was not homogeneous; different regions had different agronomic endowments and different production possibilities. As a result, some areas could easily support the capacity of the railroad services, responding in a flexible fashion to exploit the opportunities of cheap transport, whereas other areas could not. By the end of the Empire, a good chunk of Brazil's railroad capacity was in the wrong place. As many as 75 percent of the individual lines, and half the total railroad capital, could not generate transport demand sufficient to use their capacity with a minimal degree of social efficiency.

Just how costly this misallocation was in Brazil is best illustrated through a simple hypothetical (see table 4). If the capital invested in

TABLE 4

Hypothetical Increase in Social Savings from Reallocating Railroad Capital from Low-Return to High-Return Lines, 1887

Lower-bound social return at the margin for high-return lines	0.075
Lower-bound social return at the margin for low-return lines	−0.022
Difference	0.097
Physical reproducible capital of low-return lines	239.3 million milreis
Hypothetical increase in social savings from reallocation of capital	23.2 million milreis
Upper-bound direct social savings	64.9 million milreis
Increase in social savings	36 percent
Increase in gross domestic product	3.4 percent

SOURCE: William Summerhill, "Benefits and Costs: The Political Economy of Railroads in the Empire of Brazil," ms. 1997.

NOTE: High-return railroads are those with marginal social returns exceeding the government bond rate in 1887, a relatively low-risk measure of the private return in Brazil. Those railroads in 1887 were the Dom Pedro II, the Recife and San Francisco Railway (Recife a Palmares), the Great Western of Brazil Railway (Recife ao Limoeiro), the San Paulo Railway (Santos a Jundiaí), the Leopoldina, the Mogyana, the Sorocabana e Ituana, the Macahe-Campos, the Companhia Paulista, and the São Carlos do Pinhal. The low-return railroads encompass the other thirty-five lines for which data is available.

low-return railroads could be redeployed to the high-return areas, the increase in the railroad's social savings would have been appreciable. With a social return on railroad capital equal to 7.5 percent at the margin for high-return lines, and a return on the poor performers of −2.2 percent, reallocating the capital from low-return lines to high-return lines would increase the surplus from railroads by at least 23.2 million milreis. If Brazil had captured no more than this lower-bound, conservative measure of additional gains from the reallocation of capital, it would have increased the estimated upper-bound freight social savings in 1887 by almost 36 percent. This comes to more than 3 percent of gross domestic product, much of which, if realized, could have been captured by Brazil's slave- and land-owning elite. Members of that elite in the regions where railroads generated high returns certainly had an incentive to work in the political arena to garner those benefits.

The fact that so many individual railroads had returns condemning their worth means that the mechanisms that channeled the investments in those particular railroads were costly. There were, however, other reasons that some of these investments were poor. One was simple prediction error—because it was difficult to know how a region would respond to a railroad, it would be easy to build one in the wrong place. Writing off pervasive low returns to a lack of perfect foresight, however, would be naive, ignoring the prevailing mechanisms of railroad subsidies in Imperial Brazil. Foresight of a different sort, namely, political foresight with respect to distributive policies, was an inherent feature of policy formulation. The government promoted railroad investments not in keeping with some abstract development strategy but rather in response to political concerns. Low-return railroads generated geographically specific benefits to shippers, while the costs of those lines were spread across the tax base. The poor efficiency results here were not a political mistake but the result of splendid political acumen, and the government targeted its railroad subsidies accordingly. The result was a pattern of social returns across railroads (see table 3) and opportunity costs (see table 4). The results underscore the importance of political institutions in shaping economic outcomes.

The hypothesis of misallocation of subsidy, and hence railroad capital, is supported by two factors (see table 3): first, institutional incentives caused legislators to ignore overall benefits and costs and focus instead on district- or province-specific incidences; second, in the centralized legislature the uneven distribution of voting power impelled subsidies in provinces and areas where legislative delegations succeeded in capturing a share of those subsidies proportional to the province's voting power, not where railroads had their highest economic payoff.

The Political Economy of Freight Rate Regulation

Since the quid pro quo of guaranteed dividends was regulated rates, it is appropriate to examine how freight rates were set in Brazil. Freight rates were an important feature of government railroad policy, and through a number of mechanisms it was possible to set rates in a reasonably efficient manner. In Brazil the high cost of prerail transport, and the possibility of monopoly pricing by the railroads, was sufficiently pervasive that rate regulation was likely to improve a good deal on the old transport system. As in the previous section, the assumption here is that politicians set rates not in the interest of efficiency but to garner and maintain political support. Deputies considered not the benefits and costs of regulation but the incidence of the various components of costs and benefits in their respective districts.

Just as in the case of subsidies, in setting rates a legislator considers how the political costs and benefits bear on his political support when choosing x, a regulatory policy:

$$N_i(x) = B_{i1}(x) - C_{i2}(x),$$

where $N_i(x)$ is the political support that legislator i expects from policy x, $B_{i1}(x)$ are the benefits created by the project within his electoral district, and $C_{i2}(x)$ are the indirect costs borne by the district. Rate regulation in and of itself did not involve direct outlays. In the case where the railroad was overregulated, reducing its revenues below cost, the government had to pay the guaranteed dividends (or absorb the loss, if it was a government-owned line), thus creating a tax burden. But that burden stemmed from the existence of a subsidy policy, not regulation.[38] As in the case of subsidy, ma-

---

38. While they were clearly related, the political choice of levels of subsidy and regulation were delinked by virtue of the separability of issues in the parliament

jority rule makes it unlikely that the level of regulation is efficient. It is not possible to predict whether the level chosen exceeds the efficient level or falls below it. It is possible, however, to predict how different types of railroads were regulated. The key insight is that the indirect political costs of regulation on electoral districts in Brazil varied with railroad ownership. For a railroad with predominantly Brazilian owners, the costs of rate regulation within the district were positive since regulation reduced shareholder profits (which potentially include rents those investors would like to receive and which they see as a benefit to them of setting rates high). In that case, the legislator would choose a smaller project—that is, less regulation. For a railroad with predominantly British ownership (or complete public ownership), those costs were zero. No countervailing force against tight regulation existed, and tighter control of rates prevailed. In that case, the legislator did not have to balance the political gains of providing shippers with cheap transport against the political costs of reducing shareholder profits. With no railroad owners among the district's voters, the indirect electoral costs arising from shareholders who received lower profits were of no concern to the legislator.

Few constituents of Brazilian deputies received rents in the form of railroad profits on British-owned or government-owned lines. Profits on British railroads went predominantly to shareholders in London, while profits on government lines went to the treasury. In particular, British-owned railroads on average suffered heavier regulation that similar Brazilian railroads. Brazilian shippers naturally preferred the lowest possible freight rates. As constituents seeking the benefits that policy could confer on them, they differed from one another only in a trivial fashion. The same cannot, however, be

---

that guaranteed the existence of equilibrium policy. By way of comparison, in the U.S. rate regulation could also reduce revenues below costs. But in and of itself this did not stipulate compensatory outlays by government.

said for the owners of Brazil's railroads, who for the purposes of Brazilian politicians were quite heterogeneous. The "comparative statics" of this regulatory model predict that railroads owned by foreign shareholders, or by the government, would be saddled with heavier rate regulation than those owned by Brazilian investors. Indeed, it may be reasonably inferred that the political distance separating each company's shareholders from the regulatory apparatus of the Brazilian government accounts in large part for the different rates adopted for Brazil's railroads. That Brazilian shareholders in domestically owned railroads constituted an important political constituency suggests that they enjoyed some success at resisting downward pressure on rates. British shareholders were less effective in this regard because they had less direct representation within the political system, and no politician was concerned with currying favor among shareholders in London. Ownership made a difference in the division of the surplus made possible by railroad investment.

Guided by this simple model of policy choice, the hypothesis is that ownership and operation of railroads by either the state or foreigners is associated with lower freight rates. A rough test of the rate-setting hypothesis is specified in the following form:

$$RATE = \alpha + \beta_1 EXPORT + \beta_2 IMPORT + \beta_3 GOV + \beta_4 BRITISH,$$

where *RATE* is the railroad's charge for one ton-kilometer of freight service, *EXPORT* is a dummy on high unit-value products bound largely for export, *IMPORT* is a dummy for similarly high unit-value products typically imported from abroad, *GOV* is a dummy for government ownership of the railroad, and *BRITISH* is a dummy for predominantly British ownership. The *EXPORT* and *IMPORT* dummies account for rate discrimination imposed (or permitted) across different categories of freight by the government.[39] Discrimination worked to set the highest rates on high-value imports, similarly high rates on export goods, and lower rates on domestically produced and consumed foodstuffs. Such discrimination was broadly consistent with Brazil's fiscal structure, where most revenues derived from import and export tariffs. Moreover, it reduced some of the distortion within Brazil from regulation. To the extent that the higher freight rates on exports fell mainly on landowners, who were also the chief beneficiaries of railroad development, then the beneficiaries of railroads paid a large share of their cost. Similarly, the planter class no doubt directly or indirectly consumed many of Brazil's imports, resulting in a similar pattern of tax incidence.

The results of the regression on this specification for the rates of twenty-two railroads in the 1880s are seen in table 5. This was a period of relatively little change in the level of general prices, and as such the rates do not require deflation to a common year. The results clearly support the hypothesis relating ownership to rates, via the legislative choice of regulation. Privately owned Brazilian lines enjoyed higher freight rates. British companies, whose shareholders were predominantly abroad, had less room for maneuver within Brazil's polity and could not effectively make demands on Brazil's legislature beyond the guaranteed minimum dividends. As a result British-owned railroads had to charge significantly lower freight rates than average. The largest departure from the average freight rates is found on the government-owned lines, not surprisingly, for there were no shareholders to require a minimum rate of return. The targeting of specific regions for government railroad projects, combined with the spreading of the costs of such projects across the tax base, meant that rates on these lines could be pushed well below

39. Because demand for Brazil's leading export was inelastic, a higher freight rate for coffee raised the price to consumers abroad to a greater degree than it lowered the price received by Brazilian producers.

TABLE 5
Determinants of Railroad Freight Rates in Brazil, 1880s
(dependent variable: rate per ton kilometer of freight service)

Independent Variable	Coefficient	T-Statistic
Constant	0.305	11
Export merchandise	0.097	3
Import merchandise	0.211	6.5
Government railroad	−0.24	−7
British-owned railroad	−0.165	−5.5
R-squared	0.62	
Adjusted R²	0.6	
N	66	

SOURCES: *Coleção das Leis do Brasil* (Rio de Janeiro, various years); *Relatório das Obras Públicas do Estado do Rio de Janeiro* (Rio de Janeiro, 1895). A listing of the lines is available in Summerhill, "Benefits and Costs."

NOTE: The freight categories employed are export freight (typically coffee or sugar, depending on the region of the railroad), import freight (typically consumer goods such as dishes or nonagricultural machinery), and domestic freight (typically agricultural foodstuffs, such as corn and beans). These charges are spot observations and are not weighted by the shares of these categories of freight in total shipment. In cases where the government assigned a railroad a differential tariff schedule, the rate used here represents the unit freight charge at a distance equal to that particular railroad's average haul for all freight in 1887. Government-owned railroads include those owned by the Imperial government and the provinces. British-owned railroads are those that obtained the bulk of their financing from the London Stock Exchange. Brazilian-owned joint stock railroads that issued fixed-interest debt in London but whose equity shareholders were largely in Brazil, such as the Companhia Paulista, are not treated as British.

those required to provide a competitive return on capital. Rate regulation proved to be an integral element of distributive politics in Imperial Brazil. But unlike subsidy, where the distributive dimension ran along provincial lines, in this case what mattered was the presence of shareholders among a deputy's constituents.

The pattern of railroad regulation in Brazil is well explained by the politicization of the costs and benefits of setting railroad rates. Unlike the United States, where widespread railroad regulation awaited the creation of the Interstate Commerce Commission, in Brazil the government regulated railroads from the outset. Although in some cases rates were set directly by parliament in the course of granting concessions or subsidies, in most cases rates were set within the Ministry of Agriculture, in accordance with the preferences of the parliament. That the ministry operated under ministerial responsibility, and could not venture far from the preferences of the parliamentary majority without putting the government at risk, made it possible for parliament to avoid legislating all rates yet still obtain the desired outcome for its constituents. This political check and balance served to offset any pressure on the ministry by foreign shareholders to raise their rates.[40] As in the case of subsidy, distributive politics provide valuable insights into the pattern of regulation, especially how government-owned and British-owned railroads were saddled with lower freight rates than Brazilian-owned lines.

Comparative Institutional Statics and Counterfactual Conjectures

The preceding sections assessed the impact of Brazilian political institutions on the economic consequences of railroad development by comparing actual outcomes with a "first-best" standard of efficiency. Although a useful tool in positive and normative analysis, the ability of first-best efficiency criteria to illuminate particular historical circumstances is naturally limited. Historical relevance derives from historically relevant alternative institution arrangements, not just the first-best ideal. Different institutional arrangements might well fall short of full efficiency yet could still improve on the highly centralized pork barrel politics of Imperial Brazil's unitary government. By way of illustration, consider two counterfactual scenarios. The first suggests how things might have been different if

40. See Summerhill, "Benefits and Costs," for estimates of the profits earned by British railroad investors in the 1880s.

the Brazilian state had been organized on the basis of federalism as opposed to centralism. Because the monarchy was followed by a federal republic, a comparison with Brazil after 1889 would appear especially relevant. But Brazilian "federalism" was peculiar, lacking many of the elements of a market-preserving set of federal arrangements. Instead, Brazil's centralized Imperial polity, which took distributive politics to an extreme, may be contrasted with a set of federal arrangements such as that enjoyed by the United States. The latter certainly involved distributive politics and pork that emanated from the national government but differed in two key respects from Brazil. First, the central government protected a common market. Second, lower levels of government (states) intervened in markets to provide subsidies and formulate other policies bearing on local economic activity. It is in this second regard that railroad subsidy policy could have been quite different. Since Brazil's railroads under the Empire were by and large province- or region-specific, they were largely local in their benefits. Under a federal system provincial railroads would be subsidized and regulated in accordance with provincial policy, not national policy. In a federal polity, provincial-level governments are more likely to subsidize local projects at levels closer to that of economic efficiency.[41] Market-preserving federalism reinforces that tendency; in providing subsidies each province would compete with others for mobile factors of production.[42] Oversubsidizing local railroads would create a tax burden that would limit the province's attractiveness to capital and labor; undersubsidizing relative to other provinces would do the same by limiting the opportunities for new economic activities. Although

41. Robert P. Inman and Daniel L. Rubinfeld, "The Political Economy of Federalism," in Dennis C. Mueller, ed., *Perspectives on Public Choice* (Cambridge, Eng.: Cambridge University Press, 1997), p. 99.

42. Barry R. Weingast, "The Economic Role of Political Institutions: Market Preserving Federalism and Economic Development," *Journal of Law, Economics, and Organization* 11 (1995): 1–31.

contrasting Brazil's centralized political economy with market-preserving federalism is less tractable than comparing Brazil with its railroads and without, the implication of the different institutional arrangements is clear. A Brazilian federalism that promoted more efficient railroad subsidy would have allowed it to capture a portion of the losses from the centralized distributive politics established in table 4.

The second comparison is with institutional arrangements more rooted in Brazil's own history, namely, what would have happened if Brazil possessed an absolute monarch, as it did through the colonial era and in the period 1808–1822, when it was raised to the status of a kingdom. In this case, the allocative distortions imposed by the institutions of representative parliamentary government vanish because the political calculus is very different. The sovereign, rather than delegating authority over public policy to the elected representatives of the enfranchised citizenry, would instead bargain with producers over tax rates and policy. Trading control over policy in exchange for revenues has a clear-cut implication; capital, as opposed to landowners or labor, gains disproportionate control over policy by virtue of its greater mobility.[43] In a setting where the sovereign sought to promote railroad development, capitalists (including foreigners), not landowners represented in a parliament, would command the terms of subsidy and regulation. The outcome would be remarkably similar to that often asserted in dependency analyses.

In short, the political organization of the Brazilian monarchy

43. Robert H. Bates and Da-Hsiang Donald Lien, "A Note on Taxation, Development, and Representative Government," *Politics and Society* 14, no. 1 (1985): 53–70. The authors employ their results to reveal, among other things, the logic underpinning *dependentista* assessments of foreign capital in Latin America. In the results derived from their model, capital, by virtue of its mobility (and hence higher elasticity of supply), leverages control over policy from a tax-seeking sovereign. Importantly, no political institutions figure into the model, other than the sovereign.

avoided this particular dependency-type outcome because representative institutions tailored policies responsive to Brazilian landowners and railroad investors, not foreign capitalists. It fell well short of full efficiency because centralization exacerbated and compounded the pressures inherent to distributive politics. Because neither market-preserving federalism nor an absolutist monarchy obtained while Brazil was in its first stage of railroad development, no rigorous test of the impact of alternative institutions is possible in terms acceptable to historians. As such, both the counterfactual propositions necessarily remain conjectural. Even if these alternatives had created the predicted consequences on the level and distribution of railroad subsidies, they would have led neither to unparalleled success nor outright disaster. Under an absolutist-dependency scenario, Brazil would have still obtained some gains from railroads. Even with strong federalism, it is unlikely that Brazil would have secured the economic success of the United States irrespective of its success at crafting policies closer to the efficiency benchmark. Too many other factors contributed to the process of underdevelopment. That Brazilian railroads created the benefits they did is testimony not to the advantages of the iron horse as a transport technology but to the way in which institutions of representative government responded flexibly to the demands of domestic interests and constituents. The manner in which legislative-electoral systems systemically drove a wedge between political and economic benefit-cost relationships shows how and why Brazil did not enjoy the full promise that advanced transport technology offered.

Conclusion

This chapter has presented results that alter our understanding of how investment in railroads, and policies bearing on those investments, operated in Imperial Brazil. By the end of the Empire, railroad technology had created large gains for the economy. Those gains were a good deal lower than they could have been, however, since many individual railroads produced mediocre outcomes. This was not the result of foreign investment, exploitation, dependency, the export of surplus value, or foreigners conspiring to undercut efficient service. Instead, it stemmed directly from the way in which Brazil's political organization channeled investment subsidies. The polity was neither endogenous to the structure of the international market nor bending to the demands of foreign investors. Indeed, many of its features were common to stable, successful, representative polities at that time. One key difference was the highly centralized character of the political institutions that were empowered to undertake market intervention.

Since the market's failure to provide railroads in Brazil was pervasive and widespread, market intervention improved considerably on the status quo. Even then, however, the results fell short of maximizing the potential gains from railroad projects. In intervening, the state did not pursue a development strategy in a single-minded fashion, nor did it act as a simple agent of the collective elite. Instead, institutional arrangements that made up the state structured distributive politics in such a way as to make railroad subsidy and regulation politically attractive. Political expediency was the reason the state pursued the strategy it did.

The importance of the polity in allocating subsidies derives from the opportunities for intervention created by market failures. But unlike the economy, where market prices convey scarcity, in the polity there are no political markets and no relative political prices that allocate resources. Instead, political institutions and procedural details transform preferences into outcomes.[44] Because policies,

---

44. Peter Ordeshook, "The Emerging Discipline of Political Economy," in James E. Alt and Kenneth A. Shepsle, eds., *Perspectives on Political Economy* (Cambridge, Eng.: Cambridge University Press, 1990), p. 20.

laws, regulations, and administrative decrees involve the efficiency of economic organization, formal political institutions bear directly on economic performance. Although representative government, majority rule, and distributive incentives all contributed to the gap between Brazil's policy equilibrium and economic efficiency, political centralization exacerbated the costs of that gap. For a relatively backward economy those costs proved particularly acute in the context of low levels of overall productivity and income.

References

Bates, Robert H., and Da-Hsiang Donald Lien. "A Note on Taxation, Development, and Representative Government." *Politics and Society* 14, no. 1 (1985).

Blasenheim, Peter L. "Railroads in Nineteenth-Century Minas Gerais." *Journal of Latin American Studies* 26 (1994).

Branner, John C. *The Railways of Brazil, A Statistical Article.* Chicago, 1887.

Brazil. Camara dos Deputados. *Regimento Interno da Camara dos Deputados.* Rio de Janeiro, 1875.

———. *Coleção das Leis do Brazil.* Rio de Janeiro, various years.

———. *Coleção das Leis do Império do Brazil,* various years.

———. Ministerio da Agricultura. "Estradas de ferro em trafego, em construção e em projecto até 31 de dezembro de 1888." *Relatório do Ministério da Agricultura.* Rio de Janeiro, 1889.

———. *Relatório das Obras Públicas do Estado do Rio de Janeiro.* Rio de Janeiro, 1895.

———. *Relatório do Ministério da Agricultura,* 1886 and 1887.

Buchanan, James M., and Gordon Tullock. *The Calculus of Consent.* Ann Arbor: University of Michigan Press, 1962.

Burns, E. Bradford. *A History of Brazil.* New York: Columbia University Press, 1993.

———. *The Poverty of Progress: Latin America in the Nineteenth Century.* Berkeley: University of California Press, 1980.

Cardoso, Fernando Henrique, and Enzo Faletto. *Dependency and Underdevelopment in Latin America.* Berkeley: University of California Press, 1979.

Castro, Juan José. *Treatise on the South American Railways.* Montevideo: La Nación Steam Printing Office, 1893.

Castro Carreira, Liberato de. *História Financeira e Orçamentária do Império no Brasil.* Imprensa Nacional Reprint, Brasília: Fundação Casa de Rui Barbosa, 1980.

Catão, Luis A.V. "A New Wholesale Price Index for Brazil during the Period 1870–1913." *Revista Brasileira de Economia* 46, no. 4 (1992).

Coatsworth, John H. *Growth against Development.* DeKalb: Northern Illinois University Press, 1981.

Contador, Cláudio R., and Cláudio L. Haddad. "Produto Real, Moeda e Preços: A Experiência Brasileira no Período 1861–1970." *Revista Brasileira de Estatística* 36 (1974): 407–40.

Cunha Galvão, Manoel da. *Notícia Sobre as Estradas de Ferro do Brasil.* Rio de Janeiro, 1869.

de Javari, Barão. *Organizações e Programas Ministeriais desde 1822 a 1889.* Rio de Janeiro, 1889.

Dion, Douglas. "The Robustness of Structure-Induced Equilibrium." *American Journal of Political Science* 36 (1992).

dos Santos, Theotonio. "Structure of Dependence." *American Economic Review* 60 (1970).

Dubey, Pradeep, and Lloyd S. Shapley. "Mathematical Properties of the Banzhaf Power Index." *Mathematics of Operations Research* 4, no. 2 (1979).

E.F.D. Pedro II. *Relatorio, 1888.* Rio de Janeiro, 1889.

Evans, Peter. *Dependent Development: The Alliance of Multinational, State, and Local Capital in Brazil.* Princeton, N.J.: Princeton University Press, 1979.

Fendt, Roberto, Jr. "Investimentos Ingleses no Brazil, 1870–1913: uma Avaliação da Política Brasileira." *Revista Brasileira de Economia* 31, no. 2 (1977).

Fishlow, Albert. *American Railroads and the Transformation of the Ante-Bellum Economy.* Cambridge, Eng.: Cambridge University Press, 1965.

Frank, Andre Gunder. *Capitalism and Underdevelopment in Latin America: Historical Studies of Chile and Brazil.* New York: Monthly Review Press, 1967.

Graham, Richard. "Sepoys and Imperialists: Techniques of British Power in Nineteenth-Century Brazil." *Inter-american Economic Affairs* 23 (1969).

Inman, Robert P., and Daniel L. Rubinfeld. "The Political Economy of Federalism." In Dennis C. Mueller, ed., *Perspectives on Public Choice*. Cambridge, Eng.: Cambridge University Press, 1997.

Jacob, Rodolpho. *Minas Gerais no XXo Seculo*. Belo Horizonte: Impressores Gomes, Imão & C., 1910.

Kadane, Joseph B. "On Division of the Question." *Public Choice* 13 (1972).

Kramer, Gerald H. "Sophisticated Voting over Multidimensional Choice Spaces." *Journal of Mathematical Sociology* 2 (1972).

Lahmeyer Lobo, Eulália Maria. *História do Rio de Janeiro*. Rio de Janeiro: IBMEC, 1978.

Lassance Cunha, Ernesto Antonio. *Estudo Descriptivo da Viação Ferrea do Brazil*. Rio de Janeiro: Imprensa Nacional, 1909.

Lewis, Colin. *Public Policy and Private Initiative: Railway Building in São Paulo, 1860–1889*. London: University of London, Institute of Latin American Studies, 1991.

Lyon, Max. *Note sur les Chemins de Fer du Bresil*. Paris, 1885.

McClelland, Peter. "Social Rates of Return on American Railroads in the Nineteenth Century." *Economic History Review* 25 (1972).

Nerlove, Marc. "Railroads and American Economic Growth." *Journal of Economic History* 26 (1966).

Ordeshook, Peter. "The Emerging Discipline of Political Economy." In James E. Alt and Kenneth A. Shepsle, eds., *Perspectives on Political Economy*. Cambridge, Eng.: Cambridge University Press, 1990.

Pang, Eul-Soo. *In Pursuit of Honor and Power: Noblemen of the Southern Cross in Nineteenth-Century Brazil*. Tuscaloosa: University of Alabama Press, 1988.

Pereira da Silva, Clodomiro. *Política e Legislação de Estradas de Ferro*. São Paulo, 1904.

[Pereira de Castro], [João] Chrockatt de Sá. *Brazilian Railways, Their History, Legislation, and Development*. Rio de Janeiro: Typographia de C. Leuzinger & Filhos, 1893.

Pessoa, V.A. de Paula. *Guia da Estrada de Ferro Central do Brasil*. Vol. 1. Rio de Janeiro: Impensa Nacional, 1904.

Picanço, Francisco. *Viação Ferrea do Brazil*. Rio de Janeiro: Typographia do Machado & C., 1884.

Pinheiro, Fernandes. "Chemins de Fer." In F.J. de Santa-Anna Nery, ed., *Le Brésil en 1889*. Paris: C. Delagrave, 1889.

Ribeiro Pessoa, Cyro Diocleciano, Jr. *Estudo Descriptivo das Estradas de Ferro do Brazil*. Rio de Janeiro: Imprensa Nacional, 1886.

Ridings, Eugene. *Business Interest Groups in Nineteenth-Century Brazil.* Cambridge, Eng.: Cambridge University Press, 1994.

Riker, William, and Peter Ordeshooke. *An Introduction to Positive Political Theory.* Englewood Cliffs, N.J.: Prentice Hall, 1973.

Shepsle, Kenneth A. "Institutional Arrangements and Equilibrium in Multidimensional Voting Models." *American Journal of Political Science* 23 (1979).

Shepsle, Kenneth, and Barry R. Weingast. "Political Solutions to Market Problems." *American Political Science Review* 78 (1982).

Smith Duncan, Julian. *Public and Private Operation of Railways in Brazil.* New York: Columbia University Press, 1932.

Summerhill, William. "Benefits and Costs: The Political Economy of Railroads in the Empire of Brazil." Manuscript, 1997.

———. "Market Intervention in a Backward Economy." *Economic History Review*, August 1998.

———. "Moderating Power and Confidence Vote Procedure: Executive Agenda Setting in Brazil's Imperial Parliament." Manuscript, 1998.

———. "Railroads in Imperial Brazil." In John H. Coatsworth and Alan M. Taylor, eds., *Latin America and the World Economy since 1800.* Cambridge, Mass.: Harvard University Press, 1998.

Weingast, Barry R. "The Economic Role of Political Institutions: Market Preserving Federalism and Economic Development." *Journal of Law, Economics, and Organization* 11 (1995).

Weingast, Barry R., Kenneth A. Shepsle, and Christopher Johnson. "The Political Economy of Benefits and Costs: A Neoclassical Approach to Distributive Politics." *Journal of Political Economy* 89 (1981).

Winer, L. "The Railways of Brazil." In C. S. Vesey Brown, ed., *The South American Year Book, 1913.* N.p, n.d.

The Political Economy of Financial Market Regulation and Industrial Productivity Growth in Brazil, 1866–1934

In recent years economists and economic historians have become increasingly interested in the role of institutional change in the process of economic growth. One major variant of the recent research on institutions, most commonly associated with Douglass North, holds that economic growth is the outcome of productivity increases that are brought about by the efficient allocation of the factors of production through smoothly functioning markets. At the core of increases in the efficiency of markets is the reform of institutions—the rules and regulations enforced by the state that both permit and bound the operation of markets.[1]

---

1. The literature on institutions and growth suggests various avenues through which institutional reform can enhance productivity growth. For example, institutions also include rules governing contracts within firms. Changes in labor laws, to cite one example, can produce significant changes in work rules, which may allow for organizational innovation by firms, thereby increasing productivity. This chapter considers only one variant of the institutional literature and therefore concentrates on how changes in the institutions governing markets enhance productivity growth. For the most succinct statement of this view see Douglass C. North, *Institutions, Institutional Change, and Economic Performance* (New York: Cambridge University Press, 1990). For a survey and analysis of the different institutionalist approaches see Avner Greif, "Micro Theory and Recent Developments in the Study of Economic Institutions through Economic History," in David M. Kreps and Kenneth F. Wallis, eds., *Advances in Economic Theory*, vol. 2 (Cambridge, Eng.: Cambridge University Press, 1997).

Institutional theory alone, however, cannot answer the question of which institutions are crucial and which are merely incidental for the process of economic development. To answer these questions it is necessary to integrate institutional theory with economic history.

This chapter examines the history of capital market regulation and industrial productivity growth in Brazil during the period 1866 to 1934. I focus on capital market regulation because capital markets are especially crucial for economic growth and are also notoriously subject to government regulation. Indeed, it is widely accepted that the details of such regulation have profound effects on the structure of banking and securities markets. What is less clear is whether these differences have any discernible impact on the performance of the rest of the economy.[2]

2. The term *capital markets* is used here to mean the organized process by which banks, brokers, and exchanges raise, securitize, distribute, trade, and continually value investment funds. Although the exact mechanisms are rarely examined empirically, one can infer from the literature that there are four channels through which the development of capital markets increases the efficiency of the rest of the economy. First, by eliminating the need for savers and investors to have direct knowledge of one another, capital markets increase allocative efficiency; funds flow to those entrepreneurs who can provide savers with the highest risk-adjusted rate of return. Second, by lowering the cost of capital to firms (and potential firms), capital markets allow entrepreneurs greater flexibility in their choice of the capital-labor ratio. Third, by allowing firms to grow far more rapidly than they would be able to otherwise, capital markets permit firms to rapidly reach the size at which they can take advantage of potential scale economies in production. Fourth, by lowering the cost of capital to entrepreneurs and potential entrepreneurs, new firms come into existence that would not have existed otherwise. The result is an increase in the rate of technical change (because new firms are putting physical plants of more recent vintage into service) and increased competition, which intensifies entrepreneurial efforts to raise productivity through new technological and organizational innovations. For a comparison of the U.S. and German cases, arguing that Germany had a more efficient financial system because of differences in the regulation of banking, see Charles W. Calomiris, "The Costs of Rejecting Universal Banking: American Finance in the German Mirror, 1870–1914," in Naomi Lamoreaux and Daniel Raff, eds., *The Coordination of Economic Activity within and between Firms* (Chicago: University of Chicago Press, 1994).

I focus on the case of Brazil during the period 1866–1934 for two reasons. First, Brazil provides a counterfactual test of the proposition that the specific features of government regulation profoundly affect the development of securities markets because the overthrow of the Brazilian monarchy in 1889 and the founding of a federal republic brought about a dramatic revision of the preexisting laws. Second, Brazil is unusual in that abundant data at the firm level permit the estimation of productivity growth by firm type and size. It is therefore possible in the Brazilian case to estimate the efficiency gains afforded to manufacturers by calculating the differences in the levels of total factor productivity between those firms that mobilized capital by selling debt and equity to the investing public and those that used more traditional, personalized channels.

I carry out this analysis using panel data techniques, which involve linking together eighteen censuses covering the period 1866–1934 with production, financial, and dummy variable information for 558 textile firms. I estimate time series, cross-sectional regressions for the census years 1905–1927, following the institutional reforms of the 1890s, which permit the measurement of the impact of the ability of firms to take the joint stock corporate form, sell equity on the public markets, and issue bonded debt on their level of total factor productivity.

I argue that changes in government regulations had a profound effect on the growth and performance of industry. The first reform was the establishment of limited liability, which overcame a fundamental asymmetry in incentives: Before 1890 the law created disincentives for entrepreneurs to issue debt and for investors to purchase equity because an investor was held to be fully liable for a firm's debts in the case of insolvency, even if the investor had traded away the stock. From the point of view of founding groups of investors, the new limited-liability law meant that they could go out to the debt markets and not be personally liable for those debts if the company failed. From the point of view of potential investors from outside the founding groups, limited liability meant that they could purchase equity shares in firms and not have to be concerned that they would be held personally liable for the firm's debts if it went bankrupt.

The second crucial reform in securities markets was related to mandatory disclosure. The 1890 regulatory law required firms to produce financial statements, reprint at least the balance sheets in public documents, such as a newspaper or state gazette, and include a statement in the report about the identities of each stockholder and the number of shares they owned. In the market's early stages investors likely made decisions about which firms to invest in on the basis of the reputations of the founding group of entrepreneurs. Over time, however, potential investors had far more information to go on; they knew who held controlling interest in the firm, and they had a great deal of financial information available, including the firm's history of dividend payments, its level of indebtedness, the size of its reserves, and the liquidity of their investment.

These regulatory reforms reduced transaction and monitoring costs, thereby lowering the cost of capital to firms that adopted the joint stock, limited liability form. First, mandatory disclosure made it easier for investors to monitor managers. Second, limited liability eliminates the need for investors to monitor one another. In a situation in which liability is not limited, investors must create costly covenants that restrict the transferability of ownership rights to individuals with sufficient wealth to cover their share of any liability resulting from insolvency. Alternatively, investors must engage in costly monitoring to verify the liquidity of their partners.[3]

Before the reforms few firms utilized the market to mobilize capital, and Brazilian industry was small in size—even by Latin

---

3. See Jack L. Carr and G. Frank Mathewson. "Unlimited Liability as a Barrier to Entry," *Journal of Political Economy* 96, no. 4 (1988): 766–84.

American standards. After the reforms, large numbers of firms were financed through the sale of stocks and bonds to the investing public. The result of lower capital costs was that already existing firms were able to grow faster than they could have otherwise and that new firms could enter the market because their cost of capital was lower than their expected risk-adjusted rate of return. Not only did industry grow by leaps and bounds (capacity, as measured by spindlage, grew nearly thirtyfold from 1881 to 1925), but limited-liability joint-stock companies became the dominant form of corporate organization. In the case under study here—the cotton textile industry—70 percent of the industry's installed capacity in 1925 was located in joint-stock firms.

The use of the securities markets had similarly unambiguous effects on the performance of industry. There was a sizable difference in levels of productivity between firms that used the markets to obtain finance and those that continued to mobilize capital through traditional, informal avenues. These differences in total factor productivity (TFP) hold regardless of firm size. The primary impact of the securities markets on productivity was not, therefore, that joint-stock firms could take advantage of economies of scale in production but that limited-liability joint-stock companies were able to move into the market for fine-weave, high-quality output, which earned a price premium. Because the production of high-quality output requires machines to be run more slowly, it necessitates more machines per worker than the production of low-quality cloth. Under these conditions, firms with access to low-cost capital had a distinct advantage. The result was increased allocative efficiency; those entrepreneurs who could best combine the factors of production and choose the optimal output mix were able to mobilize capital that otherwise would not have been available to them. The implication is that, had it been difficult for small entrepreneurs to use the securities markets to obtain investment capital, the growth of TFP in Brazilian cotton textile manufacturing would have been significantly lower.

One might argue that causality ran the other way, that firms did not have high TFP because they were publicly owned but were publicly owned because they had high TFP or because they were founded by entrepreneurs with a proven track record of business success in other areas. There are two problems with this line of reasoning. The first is that most limited-liability joint-stock companies did not start out as privately owned firms that at some point in their life cycle decided to change corporate form. In the vast majority of cases, publicly owned firms were entirely new enterprises without track records in the textile industry; their initial finance came from the sale of equity to the investing public. The second problem is that from the point of view of economic growth it does not matter whether entrepreneurs were screened in some way by brokers or other intermediaries based on their previous record. Had the securities markets not existed, or had access to them been limited in some way, these more able entrepreneurs would have been capital constrained. They therefore would have directed smaller enterprises or perhaps not founded firms at all.

This is not to argue that the only constraint faced by Brazilian industry was access to capital or that the only relevant policy change in Brazil related to the regulation of financial markets. Coterminous with the reform of financial market regulations were increases in tariff protection and the expansion of the railroad network, which had begun to develop in the 1880s but which now grew rapidly under the combined influence of federal subsidies and the availability of foreign capital.[4] It is to argue, however, that one crucial

---

4. On the impact of Brazil's inefficient railroad system, see William R. Summerhill, "Transport Improvements and Economic Growth in Brazil and Mexico," in Stephen Haber, ed., *How Latin America Fell Behind: Essays on the Economic Histories of Brazil and Mexico, 1800–1914* (Stanford: Stanford University Press, 1997). On the myriad problems constraining growth in nineteenth-century Brazil, see Nathaniel

piece of the puzzle explaining the lack of industrial development before 1890 and rapid industrial growth after 1890 was access to capital. Changes in the rules and regulations governing the operation of banks and capital markets were a necessary, but not a sufficient, condition for the expansion of Brazilian industry.

This chapter is organized into four sections. In the first section I explain the choice of the textile industry as a test case and discuss the data sources and their limitations. In the second section I discuss the institutional history of financial market regulation in Brazil. In the third section I examine the effects of these reforms, paying particular attention to the impact of greater use of the financial markets on industrial productivity. The fourth section contains my conclusions.

Cotton Textiles as a Test Case

This chapter focuses on cotton textile manufacture, but I would expect that the relationships between access to capital, firm size, and TFP growth would extend to a broad range of industries in early twentieth-century Brazil. In fact, Brazil's securities markets were used to mobilize capital for urban tramways and municipal railroads, utility companies, navigation companies, banks, insurance companies, and sugar refineries, as well as a diverse range of manufacturing enterprises.

I focus on the cotton textile industry for both practical and theoretical reasons. First, cotton textiles were the most important manufacturing industry in Brazil during the period under study.[5]

Leff, *Underdevelopment and Development in Brazil* (London: George Allen & Unwin Publishers, 1982), and Nathaniel Leff, "Economic Development in Brazil, 1822–1913," in Haber, *How Latin America Fell Behind*.

5. As Kuznets points out, the first manufacturing industry to develop as economies modernize is that of textiles. Brazil conformed to this general pattern. At the time of Brazil's first full-scale industrial census in 1920, cotton textiles accounted

Second, both the Brazilian government and Brazil's various manu-facturers' associations regularly gathered systematic census-type data on the textile industry, which permits the estimation of TFP. Third, there are compelling theoretical reasons to focus on cotton textiles. Textile manufacturing is characterized by capital divisibili-ties and modest scale economies. Thus, the minimum efficient scale of production is small enough that firms may be financed through traditional sole proprietor and partnership arrangements, as well as through the use of impersonal financial markets. This permits pro-ductivity comparisons across various firm types and sizes that would not be possible in most other mechanized industries, such as ce-ment, beer, chemicals, or steel, where there were few firms that were not financed through the sale of equities.[6]

The Data

The analysis presented here rests on three bodies of evidence. The first is the censuses that cover all of the mechanized cotton textile companies—both privately and publicly owned—operating in Brazil. I have retrieved and put into machine-readable form the cen-suses from 1866, 1875, 1881, 1883, 1895, 1898, 1901, 1905, 1907–08,

---

for 24.4 percent of manufacturing value added, a higher percent than any other manufacturing activity. See Simon Kuznets, *Economic Growth of Nations: Total Output and Production Structure* (Cambridge, Mass.: Belnap Press of Harvard University Press, 1971), pp. 111–13; see also Stephen Haber, "Business Enterprise and the Great Depression in Brazil: A Study of Profits and Losses in Textile Manufacturing," *Business History Review* 66, no. 2 (1992): 335–63.

6. This does not mean that there were no scale economies in cotton textile production. Indeed, had the minimum efficient scale of production been extremely small—such as that found in industries like beeswax candle making, differences in access to low-cost capital could not have played a role in raising productivity. It does mean, however, that economies of scale were exhausted in textiles at relatively small firms compared to industries such as steel, cement, and chemicals. Indeed, the estimates of firm level TFP later in this chapter indicate a minimum efficient scale equivalent to a market share of less than one-half of 1 percent.

1914–15, 1923–27, and 1934. The second is the semiannual financial statements of fifteen publicly traded cotton textile manufacturing firms covering the years 1895 to 1940. These fifteen firms are not a random sample but were chosen because it was possible to retrieve complete sets of their financial statements.[7] These fifteen firms controlled 42 percent of the industry's installed capacity in 1905 and 24 percent even as late as 1934. Their financial statements permit a more detailed study of the structure of debt and equity than do the censuses. The third is data on the secondary markets for textile firm securities that I retrieved from the major Rio de Janeiro and São Paulo newspapers.

7. The fifteen firms are: Companhia de Fiaçao e Tecidos Alliança, Companhia America Fabril, Companhia Brasil Industrial, Companhia de Fiaçao e Tecelagem Carioca, Companhia de Fiaçao e Tecidos Industrial Campista, Companhia de Fiaçao e Tecidos Cometa, Companhia de Fiaçao e Tecidos Confiança Industrial, Companhia de Fiaçao e Tecidos Corcovado, Companhia de Fiaçao e Tecidos Industrial Mineira, Companhia de Fiaçao e Tecidos Mageénse, Companhia Manufactora Fluminense, Companhia Petropolitana, Companhia Progresso Industrial do Brasil, Companhia de Fiaçao e Tecidos Santo Aleixo, and Companhia Fabrica de Tecidos Sao Pedro de Alcantara.

Some of these reports were located in the Bibliotheca Nacional in Rio de Janeiro, filed erroneously in the periodicals section. Most were retrieved from the *Journal do Commercio* (Rio de Janeiro's major financial daily) and the *Diario Official* (Brazil's equivalent of the Federal Register). In theory, it would be possible to retrieve the reports of all publicly traded companies from these and similar sources—such as the *Diario Official* for each state and the major financial dailies of all the major cities because under Brazilian law firms had to reprint abbreviated versions of their financial statements in public venues. In practice, however, this is a costly procedure because none of the relevant publications are indexed and each runs to roughly 20,000 pages a year. I therefore concentrated on the months of January, February, March, April, July, and August (when most firms produced their financial statements) for the *Jornal do Commercio* and the *Diario Official*. Research in progress is retrieving reports published in *O Estado de São Paulo* (São Paulo's major newspaper) and the *Diario Official do Estado de São Paulo*. Even restricting analysis to these four publications and concentrating solely on the months listed above still requires the researcher to look at roughly 1 million frames of microfilm to cover the sixty years from 1880 to 1940.

Textile Finance before 1890

Throughout most of the nineteenth century, institutions designed to mobilize impersonal sources of capital were largely absent in Brazil. An organized stock exchange had functioned in Rio de Janeiro since early in the century, but it was small and seldom used to finance industrial companies. Brazil's mill owners could also not appeal to the banking system to provide them with capital; as late as 1888 Brazil had only twenty-six banks, whose combined capital totaled only 145,000 contos (roughly US$48 million). Only seven of the country's twenty states had any banks at all, and half of all deposits were held by a few banks in Rio de Janeiro.[8]

The slow development of these institutions can be traced in large part to public policies designed to restrict entry into banking and limit abuses of the public by unscrupulous corporate promoters. The imperial government, which held the right to charter banks, was primarily concerned with creating a small number of superbanks that could serve as a source of government finance and that would promote monetary stability. Unfortunately, the government's continual shift in regulatory policies prevented the development of even a tightly controlled, centralized banking system along the lines of many Western European countries.[9]

8. Steven Topik, *Political Economy of the Brazilian State, 1889–1930* (Austin: University of Texas Press, 1987), p. 28.

9. Topik, *Political Economy*, p. 28. Carlos Manuel Peláez and Wilson Suzigan, *História monetária do Brasil: análise da política, comportamento e institucões monetárias* (Rio de Janeiro, Brazil: IPEA/INPES [Instituto de Planejamento Economico e Social, Instituto de Pesquisas], 1976), chaps. 2–5; Flávio Azevedo Marques de Saes, *Crédito e bancos no desenvolvimento da economia paulista, 1850–1930* (São Paulo, Brazil: Instituto de Pesquisas Economicas, 1986), pp. 22, 27–86; Maria Bárbara Levy, *História da bolsa de valores do Rio de Janeiro* (Rio de Janeiro, Brazil: IBMEC [Instituto Brasileiro de Mercados de Capitais], 1977), pp. 109–12; Stanley J. Stein, *The Brazilian Cotton Textile Manufacture: Textile Enterprise in an Underdeveloped Area* (Cambridge, Mass.: Harvard University Press, 1957), pp. 25–27; Richard E. Sylla, *The American Capital Market, 1846–1914* (New York: Arno Press, 1975), pp. 52, 209.

The imperial government also created regulations designed to discourage the corporate form of ownership. Brazil's 1860 incorporation law required the promoters of joint-stock companies to obtain the special permission of the imperial government, prohibited investors from purchasing stocks on margin, and restricted banks from investing in corporate securities. In addition, it did not permit limited liability. In fact, under Brazilian law an investor could be held liable for a firm's debts for a period of five years after he had sold the stock.[10]

Given these constraints on the formation of financial intermediaries, the securities markets were rarely used to mobilize capital for industry. Not coincidentally, the textile industry remained small. In 1866 the entire modern sector of the industry numbered nine firms, none of which were joint-stock companies. The early 1870s witnessed the creation of two joint-stock companies that raised their initial capital through public offerings in Rio de Janeiro.[11] Even with these two joint-stock companies, however, the capacity of the Brazilian cotton textile industry was only 85,000 spindles in 1881 (see table 1).[12] This was not only minuscule by the standards of the United States, which in 1880 had an industry of some 10.6 million

10. Presumably this provision of the law was meant to protect individuals and enterprises doing business with joint-stock companies, as well as to protect outside investors from being fleeced by unscrupulous corporate promoters. The fear evidently was that individuals would found a firm, take on large amounts of debt, sell virtually all of the stock to outsiders, transfer the wealth of the firm to themselves, and then leave their creditors holding unrepayable debts and the outside investors holding watered stock. Levy, *História da bolsa*, p. 117; Peláez and Suzigan, *História monetária*, pp. 78–83, 96–97; Saes, *Crédito e bancos*, pp. 22, 86; Anne Hanley, "Capital Markets in the Coffee Economy," Ph.D. diss., Stanford University, 1995; Ridings, *Business Interest Groups*.

11. Agostino Vioto de Borja Castro, "Relatorio do segundo grupo," in Antonio José de Souza Rego, ed., *Relatorio da segunda Exposição Nacional de 1866* (Rio de Janeiro, 1869), pp. 3–73; Commissão de Inquerito Industrial, *Relatorio ao Ministerio da Fazenda*.

12. Spindlage is used as the index for capacity because it is widely agreed that it provides the best proxy for physical capital.

TABLE 1

Participation of Limited-Liability Joint-Stock Firms in the Brazilian Cotton Textile Industry, 1866–1934

Year	Total firms	Total spindles	NUMBER OF JOINT-STOCK FIRMS				CAPACITY OF JOINT-STOCK FIRMS (MEASURED IN SPINDLES)			
			Rio de Janeiro [a]	São Paulo	All states [b]	Percent of total	Rio de Janeiro [a]	São Paulo	All states [b]	Percent of total
1866	9	14,875	1		1	9%	20,000		20,000	44%
1875	11	45,830	2		2	8	29,660		29,660	35
1881	24	84,956	2		2	8	25,500		25,500	32
1883	24	78,908								
1885 [c]		66,466 [c]								
1895 [c]	22	260,842	9	2	13	—	164,405	8,204	192,275	—
1898 [d]	18	279,666 [d]	14		14	—	255,578		255,578	—
1905	90	778,224	17	3	25	28	316,310	27,606	358,740	46
1907	117	823,343	19	5	30	26	321,783	65,329	402,863	49
1908 [c]	119	761,816 [c]	10	6	16	13	267,011	62,857	329,867	—
1914	205	1,634,449	25	29	66	32	512,387	384,206	983,404	60
1915	170	1,598,568	25	25	63	37	517,757	358,096	972,935	61
1921 [c]	242	1,621,300 [c]								
1923 [c]	243	1,700,000 [c]								
1924	184	2,200,612	23	27	69	38	821,682	521,934	1,475,982	67
1925	183	2,397,380	25	34	80	44	870,226	668,710	1,689,357	70
1926	215	2,558,433	23	44	92	43	890,902	700,261	1,751,761	68
1927	228	2,692,077	25	41	94	41	880,561	719,871	1,788,244	66
1934	203	2,507,126	26	32	83	41	796,696	624,314	1,618,310	65

SOURCES: Agostino Vioto de Borja Castro, "Relatorio do segundo grupo," in Antonio José de Souza Rego, ed., *Relatorio da segunda Exposição Nacional de 1866* (Rio de Janeiro, 1869), pp. 3–73; Commissão [para] Exposição Universal [em] Philadelphia, *The Empire of Brazil at the Universal Exhibition of 1876 in Philadelphia* (Rio de Janeiro: Typographia e Lithographia do Imperial Instituto Artistico, 1876), pp. 285–87 and statistical tables; Biblioteca da Associação Industrial, *Archivo da Exposição da Industria Nacional de 1881* (Rio de Janeiro: Typographia Nacional, 1882), pp. xcvi–xcvii; Commissão de Inquerito Industrial, *Relatorio ao Ministerio da Fazenda* (Rio de Janeiro, 1882), p. 15; John C. Branner, "Cotton Factories in Brazil—1883," *Cotton in the Empire of Brazil*, U.S. Department of Agriculture, Miscellaneous Special Report No. 8 (Washington, D.C.: Government Printing Office, 1885); Consul W. Ricketts, *Report*, C4657, 1xv (1886), pp. 187–88 from British Consular Reports, *Consular Reports: Accounts and Papers* (London, 1870–1900), as cited by Stanley J. Stein, *The Brazilian Cotton Textile Manufacture: Textile Enterprise in an Underdeveloped Area* (Cambridge, Mass.: Harvard University Press, 1957), appendix I; Antonio Olyntho dos Santos Pires, *Relatorio apresentado ao Presidente da Republica dos Estados Unidos do Brasil pelo Ministerio de Estado dos Negocios da Industria, Viação e Obras Publicas* (Rio de Janeiro, 1896), pp. 24–25; José Carlos de Carvalho, "O Algodão: sua historia," and "O Cafe: sua historia," in *Sociedad Nacional de Agricultura, Fasciculo No. 7* (Rio de Janeiro, 1900); Cunha Vasco, "Industria de Algodão," *Boletim do Centro Industrial do Brasil*, Fasciculo 111 (Rio de Janeiro, 1905); Prefeitura do Distrito Federal, *Noticia sobre o desenvolvimento da industria fabril no Distrito Federal e sua situação actual* (Milano: Tipografia Fratelli Trevos, 1908); William Alexander Graham Clark, *Cotton Goods in Latin America, Part I, Cuba, Mexico, and Central America* (Washington, D.C.: Government Printing Office, 1909); Cunha Vasco, *Fabrica de fiação e tecelagem de Algodão* (Rio de Janeiro, 1908); Antonio F. Bandeira Junior, *A Industria no Estado de São Paulo* (São Paulo, 1908); Centro Industria do Brasil, *Relatorio da Directoria para ser Apresentado a Assemblea Geral Ordinaria do anno de 1915* (Rio de Janeiro, 1915); Centro Industria do Brasil, *O Centro Industrial na Conferencia Algodeira* (Rio de Janeiro, 1917); Centro Industrial de Fiação e Tecelagem de Algodão (hereafter, CIFTA), *Relatorio da Directoria 1921–1922* (Rio de Janeiro, 1922); CIFTA, *Exposição de Tecidos de Algodão* (Rio de Janeiro, 1923); CIFTA, *Relatorio da Directoria 1923* (Rio de Janeiro, 1924); CIFTA, *Relatorio de Directoria do Centro Industrial de Fiação e Tecelagem de Algodão do Anno 1925* (Rio de Janeiro, c. 1925); CIFTA, *Relatorio da Directoria* (Rio de Janeiro, c. 1926); CIFTA, *Fabricas filiadas* (Rio de Janeiro, c. 1926); CIFTA, *Relatorio da Directoria* (Rio de Janeiro, c. 1928); CIFTA, *Fiação e Tecelagem: Censo Organizado pelo Centro Industrial de Fiação e Tecelagem de Algodão* (Rio de Janeiro, 1935).

[a] Includes Distrito Federal firms.

[b] This is a national count of limited-liability joint-stock companies, including Rio de Janeiro and São Paulo firms.

[c] Estimate based on partial information.

[d] Includes only Rio de Janeiro and Distrito Federal firms.

spindles, but small even by Latin American standards. Circa 1880, Mexico's cotton textile industry was more than three times the size of Brazil's (249,000 spindles) even though Mexico's national income was only 55 percent that of Brazil's.[13]

Regulatory Reforms and Outcomes

In the last decades of the nineteenth century a dramatic reform of the regulations governing Brazil's capital markets took place. These changes began in 1882, when the government removed the requirement that joint-stock companies obtain special charters from parliament. This reform also lowered, from 25 to 20 percent, the amount of paid-in capital required before the stock could be traded. Investors were still liable in the case of insolvency, however, for the firm's debts, even if those shares had been traded away as long as five years before.[14] As one might imagine, the lack of limited liability meant that these reforms had little effect on the use of the stock and bond markets as sources of industrial investment.

The real impetus to regulatory reform did not get under way until 1888, when the imperial government abolished slavery. The end of slavery produced a series of unexpected and unintended outcomes that set in motion both the overthrow of the monarchy and the complete reform of banking and securities market regulation. Abolition drove a wedge between Brazil's planter class, which historically had been the mainstay of the monarchy, and the imperial government. In an effort to placate the planters by making credit

---

13. Mexican textile data from Stephen Haber, "Financial Markets and Industrial Development: A Comparative Study of Governmental Regulation, Financial Innovation, and Industrial Structure in Brazil and Mexico, 1840–1930," in Haber, *How Latin America Fell Behind*, p. 33. National income data from John Coatsworth, "Obstacles to Economic Growth in Nineteenth-Century Mexico," *American Historical Review* 83, no. 1 (1978): 82. Note that Mexico and Brazil had roughly similar population sizes in the early 1880s, 9.1 million and 9.9 million, respectively.

14. Hanley, "Capital Markets," pp. 24, 27.

more easily available to them, the imperial government awarded concessions to twelve banks of issue and provided seventeen banks with interest-free loans. The easy credit policies of 1888 were not enough, however, to stem the tide of Brazil's republican movement, which saw the monarchy and its policies as inimical to the creation of a modern economy and society. In November 1889, Dom Pedro II, Brazil's emperor, was overthrown and a federal republic was created.

The newly created federal government avidly moved to rewrite the regulations that constrained Brazil's financial markets. First, the government deregulated the banking industry; banks could now engage in whatever kind of financial transactions they wished, including the right to extend long-term loans and to invest in corporate securities. Second, the government dramatically reduced shareholder liability. Shareholders were still liable for the face value of their shares but only until the annual shareholder's meeting, when the financial records were approved. This effectively limited their liability to a twelve-month period.[15] Third, the government instituted a set of mandatory disclosure laws that were highly unusual for the time. Brazil's publicly owned corporations were required to produce financial statements annually (many in fact produced them twice a year) and reprint them in public documents, such as state or federal gazettes or the newspaper. In addition, their annual reports had to list the names of all shareholders and the number of shares they controlled. Finally, the annual report had to list the number of shares that had changed hands during the year, including information on the number of shares traded in each transaction. Investors could thus obtain reasonably good information on the health of

15. Hanley, "Capital Markets," pp. 24–28; Topik, *Political Economy*, pp. 28–32; Peláez and Suzigan, *História monetaria*, pp. 141–43. Stein, *Brazilian Cotton Textile Manufacture*, p. 86.

firms, the potential liquidity of their shares, and the identities of their major shareholders.[16]

The results of these reforms were dramatic. The nominal capital of corporations listed on the Rio de Janeiro and São Paulo exchanges, which had stood at 410,000 contos (roughly $136 million) in May 1888, grew fourfold by December 1891, when it reached 3,778,695 contos.[17]

In the short term, the speculative bubble created by the Encilhamento[18] financed large numbers of banks that provided loans to Brazil's textile industry. In some cases, banks directly organized and ran textile companies. Bank-financed industrial development was not, however, to be long lasting in Brazil. The speculative bubble burst in 1892, bringing down many of the banks. The government therefore decided in 1896 to once again restrict the right to issue currency to a single bank acting as the agent of the treasury. These more restrictive regulations, coupled with the already shaky financial situation of many of the banks, produced a massive contraction of the banking sector. After that contraction, Brazil's banks appear to have lent little money for long-term investment. Banks played an important role, however, in providing short-term, working capital to manufacturers by discounting commercial paper. For the fifteen firms whose balance sheets I have retrieved, during the period 1895–1915 short-term debt accounted for from 29

16. Shareholder lists were not always published in the abbreviated reports reprinted in the newspapers, but they were published in the original reports.

17. The data for 1888 are from Paulo Neuhaus, *História monetária do Brasil, 1900–45* (Rio de Janeiro, Brazil: Instituto Brasileiro de Mercado de Capitais, 1975), p. 19ff. Data for 1889, 1890, and 1891 calculated from *O Estado de São Paulo* and *Jornal do Commercio*, consolidated stock tables (see table 1). A conto was equal to 1,000 milreis, the basic unit of Brazilian currency. There were roughly three milreis to the dollar in 1890.

18. Encilhamento refers to the boom that resulted from the aforementioned series of regulatory and financial reforms implemented by the Brazilian government (beginning in 1889) to loosen the constraints on its financial markets.

to 42 percent (depending on the year) of their total indebtedness (see table 2).

The more important, long-run effect of the Encilhamento was that the regulatory reforms of the securities markets gave rise to the widespread sale of equity and bonded debt to the investing public in order to mobilize long-term capital. Essentially, corporate finance took the following form: A group of entrepreneurs tied through kinship or established business relationships would come together and found a joint-stock company. They would then issue a prospectus, find a broker or bank to act as an intermediary, and sell shares to the public. These offerings would often be advertised in newspapers or state gazettes. As a firm's capital requirements grew it would either issue new shares, which would be advertised in a public offering and handled by a broker, or they would issue bonds, which would also be subscribed by the public through the services of a broker or a bank. In the early stages of the market's development it looked much like the Boston Stock Exchange, with stocks tending to be closely held by the founding groups. Gradually, however, stock ownership became more diversified, particularly for the larger, more successful companies. By the 1920s, larger companies typically had more than a hundred shareholders and the rate of turnover of shares in the secondary markets was roughly 10 percent a year. It was also generally the case that no individual stockholder controlled more than 10 percent of a firm's shares (see table 1).

In 1866 there were no joint-stock companies in the cotton textile industry. By the early 1880s there were two, accounting for 32 percent of the industry's installed capacity. By 1895, thirteen joint-stock firms had been founded with a capacity seven times that of the joint-stock companies in 1883. This mushroomed to sixty-six joint-stock firms (accounting for 60 percent of industry capacity) by 1914 and to eighty joint-stock firms (accounting for 70 percent of capacity) by 1925.

As important as the development of the equities markets in

TABLE 2

Debt-Equity Ratios and Sources of New Capital for Fifteen-Firm Sample, 1895–1940 (Estimated From Balance Sheets, Includes Short-Term Debt)

PANEL I: LIABILITIES (IN MILLIONS OF MILREIS)

Year	Paid capital	Retained earnings	Short-term debt	Bond debt	Total liabilities	Debt-equity ratio
1895	10	1	2	5	19	0.68
1900	53	16	9	19	96	0.39
1905	61	30	7	16	115	0.26
1910	76	28	19	26	149	0.43
1915	81	30	26	38	175	0.57
1920	115	43	21	45	224	0.41
1925	145	118	54	39	357	0.35
1930	137	100	65	78	380	0.60
1935	135	124	66	64	389	0.50
1940	145	143	74	46	409	0.42

PANEL II: SOURCES OF NEW CAPITAL (WEIGHTED BY TOTAL LIABILITIES)

Period	Growth of debt and equity (in percent)	Short-term debt (in percent)	Bond debt (in percent)	Retained earnings (in percent)	Paid capital (in percent)
1895–1900	410.8%	8.1%	17.1%	18.9%	55.9%
1900–1905	19.3	−6.2	−13.0	77.5	41.8
1905–1910	30.3	33.2	28.8	−5.0	43.0
1910–1915	16.9	28.8	45.2	5.9	20.1
1915–1920	28.1	−11.3	14.8	27.5	69.0
1920–1925	59.4	25.1	−4.2	56.3	22.8
1925–1930	6.5	46.1	170.1	−78.8	−37.3
1930–1935	2.5	13.5	−145.2	251.0	−19.3
1935–1940	4.9	41.3	−96.0	100.9	53.8

SOURCES: *Diario Official da Federacão* (Rio de Janeiro, Brazil, 1890–1940); *Diario Official do Estado de São Paulo* (São Paulo, Brazil, 1891–1940); *Jornal do Commercio* (Rio de Janeiro, Brazil, 1880–1940); and *O Estado de São Paulo* (São Paulo, Brazil, 1888–1921).

Brazil was the simultaneous development of markets for long-term debt. As with equities, debt issues came in small denominations; virtually all had a par value of 200 milreis (about $50 at the rate of exchange at the turn of the century), implying that they could be held by medium-sized savers. These debts took the form of general obligation bonds, were callable, carried nominal interest rates of from 5 to 8 percent, and had terms of twenty years or more.

These debt issues raised significant amounts of capital. A comparison of the 1905 and 1915 censuses indicates that firms located in Rio de Janeiro or the Distrito Federal, where the market was well developed, financed 69 percent of their growth in total capitalization through the sale of debt. For the country as a whole, 29 percent of new investment came in the form of long-term debt (see table 3). In 1915 the average (weighted) debt-equity ratio for firms in Rio de Janeiro or the Distrito Federal was .43:1.00, three times its level in 1905. For the country as a whole, the debt-equity ratio in 1915 was .27:1.00, nearly twice its level in 1905 (see table 4).

This analysis, which is based on census data, significantly understates the importance of debt financing because it does not include trade debt from suppliers, short-term liabilities (mostly commercial paper), and the small quantity of mortgage debt owed to banks. For that reason, I have estimated financial ratios for the fifteen-firm sample of publicly owned companies from their balance sheets. In 1915 the average (weighted) debt-equity ratio for these fifteen firms was .57:1.00 (see table 2). The balance sheet data also corroborate the census data in regard to the pattern of bond finance; the use of the bond market was most important during the periods 1905–10, when new bond debt accounted for 29 percent of all new investment, and 1910–15, when new bond debt accounted for 45 percent of all new investment (see panel II of table 2).

TABLE 3

Sources of New Capital for Brazilian Cotton Textile Firms, 1905–1934 (does not include short-term debt)

Period	Location	Firms	Growth of Total Capital (in percent)	New Paid Capital (in percent)	Long-Term Debt (in percent)	New Reserves (in percent)	Capital plus Reserves (in percent)
1905–1915	All Brazil	174	88%	—	29.2%	—	70.8%
	Firms located in Rio de Janeiro or Distrito Federal	30	45	—	68.9	—	31.1
	Firms located in São Paulo	43	272	—	14.4	—	85.6
	Joint-stock firms in Rio de Janeiro	25	55	—	53.6	—	46.4
	Joint-stock firms in São Paulo	25	834	—	13.5	—	86.5
	Joint-stock firms in other states	12	208	—	31.1	—	68.9
	Total joint-stock firms	62	135	—	29.1	—	70.9
	Total private firms	112	35	—	29.8	—	70.2
1915–1925	All Brazil	189	137	37.5%	4.2	58.3%	—
	Firms located in Rio de Janeiro or Distrito Federal	28	118	36.1	3.5	60.4	—
	Firms located in São Paulo	53	244	39.2	6.9	53.9	—
	Joint-stock firms in Rio de Janeiro	25	136	35.9	6.5	57.6	—
	Joint-stock firms in São Paulo	33	270	37.9	7.0	55.1	—
	Joint-stock firms in other states	20	109	33.9	1.1	65.0	—
	Total joint-stock firms	78	181	36.9	6.4	56.7	—
	Total private firms	111	54	41.3	-10.2	68.9	—

1925–1934						
All Brazil	244	19	80.3	64.7	–45.1	—
Firms located in Rio de Janeiro or Distrito Federal	35	7	67.4	89.6	–56.9	—
Firms located in São Paulo	98	13	127.1	147.7	–174.7	—
Joint-stock firms in Rio de Janeiro	25	2	18.2	243.9	–162.1	—
Joint-stock firms in São Paulo	31	1	578.4	2215.3	–2693.7	—
Joint-stock firms in other states	25	102	65.9	26.5	7.6	—
Total joint-stock firms	81	9	84.0	158.7	–142.7	—
Total private firms	163	56	78.3	12.2	9.5	—

SOURCES: Agostino Vioto de Borja Castro, "Relatorio do segundo grupo," in Antonio José de Souza Rego, ed., Relatorio da segunda Exposição Nacional de 1866 (Rio de Janeiro, 1869), pp. 3–73; Commissão de Inquerito Industrial, Relatorio ao Ministro da Fazenda (Rio de Janeiro, 1882); John C. Branner, Cotton in the Empire of Brazil, U.S. Department of Agriculture, Miscellaneous Special Report No. 8 (Washington, D.C.: Government Printing Office, 1885); Ministerio da Industria, Viação e Obras Publicas, Relatorio, 1896 (Rio de Janeiro, 1896); Cunha Vasco, "Industria de Algodão," Boletim do Centro Industrial do Brasil, Fasciculo 111 (Rio de Janeiro, 1905); Centro Industrial do Brasil, O Brasil: suas riquezas naturaes, suas industrias. Industria de Transportes, Industria Fabril, vol. 3 (Rio de Janeiro, 1909); Centro Industria do Brasil, Relatorio da Directoria para ser Apresentado a Assemblea Geral Ordinaria do anno de 1915 (Rio de Janeiro, 1915); Centro Industrial de Fiação e Tecelagem de Algodão (CIFTA), Relatorio da Directoria 1921–1922 (Rio de Janeiro, 1922); CIFTA, Relatorio da Directoria (Rio de Janeiro, 1924); CIFTA, Relatorio da Directoria do Centro Industrial de Fiação e Tecelagem de Algodão do Anno 1925 (Rio de Janeiro, c. 1925); CIFTA, Fabricas filiadas (Rio de Janeiro, c. 1926); CIFTA, Estatisticas da industria, commercio e lavoura de Algodão (Rio de Janeiro, 1935); Stanley J. Stein, The Brazilian Cotton Textile Manufacture: Census Organizado pelo Centro Industrial de Fiação e Tecelagem de Algodão relativos ao anno de 1927 (Rio de Janeiro, 1928); CIFTA, Fiação e Tecelagem: Censo Organizado pelo Centro Industrial de Fiação e Tecelagem de Algodão (Rio de Janeiro, 1935); Stanley J. Stein, The Brazilian Cotton Textile Manufacture: Textile Enterprise in an Underdeveloped Area (Cambridge, Mass.: Harvard University Press, 1957), Appendix I.

TABLE 4

Financial Structure of Brazilian Cotton Textile Firms, 1905–1934 (in millions of current milreis; does not include short-term debt)

Year	Location	Firms	Paid Capital	Long-Term Debt	Reserves	Capital plus Reserves	Total Capital	Debt-Equity Ratio
1905	All Brazil	90	—	28	—	177	205	0.16
	Firms located in Rio de Janeiro or Distrito Federal	19	—	13	—	93	106	0.14
	Firms located in São Paulo	17	—	4	—	24	28	0.16
	Joint-stock firms in Rio de Janeiro	17	—	13	—	77	91	0.17
	Joint-stock firms in São Paulo	3	—	4	—	6	10	0.68
	Joint-stock firms in other states	4	—	—	—	7	8	0.06
	Total joint-stock firms	24	—	18	—	90	108	0.20
	Total private firms	66	—	11	—	87	97	0.12
	Percent of joint-stock firms in Brazil		—	62.8%	—	51.1%	52.7%	
1915	All Brazil	174	264	81	41	305	386	0.27
	Firms located in Rio de Janeiro or Distrito Federal	30	87	46	21	108	154	0.43
	Firms located in São Paulo	43	79	15	8	88	103	0.17
	Joint-stock firms in Rio de Janeiro	25	79	40	21	100	140	0.40
	Joint-stock firms in São Paulo	25	67	15	8	75	90	0.20
	Joint-stock firms in other states	12	17	6	2	19	24	0.30
	Total joint-stock firms	62	163	60	31	194	255	0.31
	Total private firms	112	101	21	9	111	131	0.19
	Percent of joint-stock firms in Brazil		61.6%	74.5%	76.8%	63.7%	65.9%	
1925	All Brazil	189	463	103	350	813	916	0.13
	Firms located in Rio de Janeiro or Distrito Federal	28	152	52	131	284	336	0.18
	Firms located in São Paulo	53	178	32	143	321	353	0.10

Joint-stock firms in Rio de Janeiro	25	148	52	131	279	331	0.19
Joint-stock firms in São Paulo	33	159	32	142	300	332	0.11
Joint-stock firms in other states	20	26	6	19	45	51	0.13
Total joint-stock firms	78	332	90	292	624	714	0.14
Total private firms	111	130	14	58	188	202	0.07
Percent of joint-stock firms in Brazil		71.8%	86.9%	83.4%	76.8%	78.0%	
1934 All Brazil	244	605	218	271	875	1,093	0.25
Firms located in Rio de Janeiro or Distrito Federal	35	168	73	118	286	359	0.25
Firms located in São Paulo	98	235	98	65	300	398	0.33
Joint-stock firms in Rio de Janeiro	25	149	73	118	267	340	0.27
Joint-stock firms in São Paulo	31	176	98	61	237	335	0.42
Joint-stock firms in other states	25	60	20	23	84	103	0.24
Total joint-stock firms	81	385	191	202	587	778	0.32
Total private firms	163	219	27	69	288	315	0.10
Percent of joint-stock firms in Brazil		63.7%	87.4%	74.5%	67.1%	71.1%	

SOURCES: Agostino Vioto de Borja Castro, "Relatorio do segundo grupo," in Antonio José de Souza Rego, ed., *Relatorio da segunda Exposição Nacional de 1866* (Rio de Janeiro, 1869). pp. 3–73; Commissão de Inquerito Industrial, *Relatorio ao Ministro da Fazenda* (Rio de Janeiro, 1882); John C. Branner, *Cotton in the Empire of Brazil*, U.S. Department of Agriculture, Miscellaneous Special Report No. 8 (Washington, D.C.: Government Printing Office, 1885); Ministerio da Industria, Viação e Obras Publicas, *Relatorio, 1896* (Rio de Janeiro, 1896); Cunha Vasco, "Industria de Algodão," *Boletim do Centro Industrial do Brasil*, Fasciculo 111 (Rio de Janeiro, 1905); Centro Industrial do Brasil, *O Brasil: suas riquezas naturaes, suas industrias. Industria de Transportes, Industria Fabril*, vol. 3 (Rio de Janeiro, 1909); Centro Industria do Brasil, *Relatorio da Directoria para ser Apresentado a Assemblea Geral Ordinaria do anno de 1915* (Rio de Janeiro, 1915); Centro Industrial de Fiação e Tecelagem de Algodão (CIFTA), *Relatorio da Directoria 1921–1922* (Rio de Janeiro, 1922); CIFTA, *Relatorio da Directoria* (Rio de Janeiro, 1924); CIFTA, *Relatorio da Directoria do Centro Industrial de Fiação e Tecelagem de Algodão do Anno 1925* (Rio de Janeiro, c. 1925); CIFTA, *Fabricas filiadas* (Rio de Janeiro, c. 1926); CIFTA, *Estatisticas da industria, commercio e lavoura de Algodão relativos ao anno de 1927* (Rio de Janeiro, 1928); CIFTA, *Fiação e Tecelagem: Censo Organizado pelo Centro Industrial de Fiação e Tecelagem de Algodão* (Rio de Janeiro, 1935); Stanley J. Stein, *The Brazilian Cotton Textile Manufacture: Textile Enterprise in an Underdeveloped Area* (Cambridge, Mass.: Harvard University Press, 1957), Appendix I.

Financial Market Reforms and Industrial Productivity

The reform of the regulations governing the operation of the securities market had significant impacts on the growth in size, industrial structure, and productivity of the textile industry. The most obvious change in the industry was its size; a small industry that appears to have been stagnating in the 1880s began to grow rapidly (see table 1). Even according to the partial census of 1895, which seriously undercounted the industry's installed capacity, the industry had tripled in size since 1885. From 1895 to 1905 the industry tripled in size again and then doubled from 1905 to 1915, making it the largest cotton textile industry of any Latin American country. It then grew an additional 70 percent up until 1927, when the depression cut short its growth.

This rapid rate of growth, it should be pointed out, was not confined to the cotton textile industry. According to Nathaniel Leff's estimates, real agricultural output increased from 1900 to 1909 by 3.5 percent a year, industrial output by 5.6 percent a year, and aggregate real output at a rate of 4.2 percent a year. From 1900 to 1947, the annual rate of growth of aggregate real output rose at 4.4 percent a year and per capita real output grew by 2.3 percent a year. This impressive rate of aggregate growth was accompanied by structural transformations in which industry came to be the fastest-growing sector of the economy. Indeed, the period after 1900 marked the rapid expansion of a wide variety of manufacturing industries in Brazil, including steel, cement, glass, beer, food processing, and machine tools.[19]

This is not to argue that the only obstacle to growth before the 1890s was capital immobilities and that the only relevant policy change in Brazil related to the regulation of financial markets. Co-

---

19. Leff, "Economic Development," p. 58; Wilson Suzigan, *Indústria brasileira: origem e desenvolvimento* (São Paulo: Editora Brasiliense, 1986).

terminous with the reform of financial market regulations were increases in tariff protection and the expansion of the railroad network, which had begun to develop in the 1880s but which now grew rapidly under the combined influence of federal subsidies and the availability of foreign capital.[20] It is to argue, however, that one crucial piece of the puzzle explaining the lack of industrial development before 1890 and the rapid industrial growth after 1890 was access to capital. Indeed, had problems in the mobility of capital not been an issue before 1890 it would be hard to explain the vast change in the way that firms used the securities markets to obtain their investment funds; the industry could simply have grown using the traditional sole proprietor and partnership forms of business organization.

There are two ways that we can at least partially control for these other changes in the Brazilian economy, thereby measuring the *marginal effects* of the capital market reforms. One is to look at firm size. Panel I of table 5 looks at sixty-two firms that appear in both the 1905 and 1915 censuses, segmenting them into five categories: private firms (partnerships or sole proprietorships), nontraded joint-stock companies, publicly traded joint-stock companies, private firms that switched to nontraded joint-stock companies, and private firms that switched to publicly traded joint-stock companies. Panel II of the same table repeats the operation, this time looking at 111 firms that appear in both the 1915 and 1925 censuses. The results of both panels are unambiguous. First, joint-stock firms were anywhere from two and a half to four times the size of private firms (the exact ratio depending on the year). Second, the rate of growth of new investment (as measured by spindlage) in joint-stock com-

20. On the impact of Brazil's inefficient railroad system, see Summerhill, "Transport Improvements." On the myriad problems constraining growth in nineteenth-century Brazil, see Leff, *Underdevelopment and Development;* and Leff, "Economic Development."

TABLE 5
Growth in Installed Capacity by Firm Type, 1905–1915 and 1915–1925

PANEL I. FIRMS THAT APPEAR IN BOTH THE 1905 AND 1915 CENSUSES

Firm type	Firms	Total spindles in 1905	Total spindles in 1915	Average spindles per firm in 1905	Average spindles per firm in 1915	Change in average firm size (in percent)
Private	41	291,334	402,824	7,283	9,825	35%
Nontraded joint stock						
Traded joint stock	13	244,812	369,278	18,832	28,406	51
Firms that switched:						
Private to nontraded joint stock	1	31,884	36,000	31,884	36,000	13
Private to traded joint stock	7	69,712	171,292	9,959	24,470	146

PANEL II. FIRMS THAT APPEAR IN BOTH THE 1915 AND 1925 CENSUSES

Firm type	Firms	Total spindles in 1915	Total spindles in 1925	Average spindles per firm in 1915	Average spindles per firm in 1925	Change in average firm size (in percent)
Private	72	549,332	613,155	7,630	8,516	12%
Nontraded joint stock	3	72,180	109,860	24,060	36,620	52

Traded joint stock	32	634,292	1,001,784	19,822	31,306	58
Firms that switched:						
Private to nontraded joint stock	3	28,900	36,108	9,633	12,036	25
Private to traded joint stock	1	7,000	10,000	7,000	10,000	43

SOURCES: Agostino Vioto de Borja Castro, "Relatorio do segundo grupo," in Antonio José de Souza Rego, ed., *Relatorio da segunda Exposição Nacional de 1866* (Rio de Janeiro, 1869). pp. 3–73; Commissão [para] Exposição Universal [em] Philadelphia, *The Empire of Brazil at the Universal Exhibition of 1876 in Philadelphia* (Rio de Janeiro: Tipographia e Lithographia do Imperial Instituto Artistico, 1876), pp. 285–87 and statistical tables; Biblioteca da Associação Industrial, *Archivo da Exposição da Industria Nacional de 1881* (Rio de Janeiro: Tipographia Nacional, 1882), pp. xcvi–xcvii; Commissão de Inquerito Industrial, *Relatorio ao Ministerio da Fazenda* (Rio de Janeiro, 1882), p. 15; John C. Branner, "Cotton Factories in Brazil—1883," *Cotton in the Empire of Brazil*, U.S. Department of Agriculture, Miscellaneous Special Report No. 8 (Washington, D.C.: Government Printing Office, 1885); Consul W. Ricketts, *Report*, C4457, 1xv (1886), pp. 187–88 from British Consular Reports, *Consular Reports: Accounts and Papers* (London, 1870–1900) as cited by Stanley J. Stein, *The Brazilian Cotton Textile Manufacture: Textile Enterprise in an Underdeveloped Area* (Cambridge, Mass.: Harvard University Press, 1957), appendix I; Antonio Olyntho dos Santos Pires, *Relatorio apresentado ao Presidente da Republica dos Estados Unidos do Brasil pelo Ministerio de Estado dos Negocios da Industria, Viacão e Obras Publicas* (Rio de Janeiro, 1896), pp. 24–25; José Carlos de Carvalho, "O Algodão: sua historia," and "O Cafe: sua historia," in *Sociedad Nacional de Agricultura*, Fasciculo No. 7 (Rio de Janeiro, 1900); Cunha Vasco, "Industria de Algodão," *Boletim do Centro Industrial do Brasil*, Fasciculo 111 (Rio de Janeiro, 1905); Centro Industrial do Brasil, *O Brasil: suas riquezas naturaes, suas industrias. Industria de Transportes, Industria Fabril*, vol. 3 (Rio de Janeiro, 1909); Prefeitura do Distrito Federal, *Noticia sobre o desenvolvimento da industria fabril no Distrito Federal e sua situação actual* (Milano: Tipografia Fratelli Trevos, 1908); William Alexander Graham Clark, *Cotton Goods in Latin America, Part I, Cuba, Mexico, and Central America* (Washington, D.C.: Government Printing Office, 1909); Cunha Vasco, *Fabrica de fiação e tecelagem de Algodão* (Rio de Janeiro, 1908); Antonio F. Bandeira Junior, *A Industria no Estado de São Paulo* (São Paulo, 1908); Centro Industria do Brasil, *Relatorio da Directoria para ser Apresentado a Assemblea Geral Ordinaria do anno de 1915* (Rio de Janeiro, 1915); Centro Industria do Brasil, *O Centro Industrial na Conferencia Algodeira* (Rio de Janeiro, 1917); Centro Industrial de Fiação e Tecelagem de Algodão (hereafter, CIFTA), *Relatorio da Directoria 1921–1922* (Rio de Janeiro, 1922); CIFTA, *Exposição de Tecidos de Algodão* (Rio de Janeiro, 1923); CIFTA, *Relatorio da Directoria 1923* (Rio de Janeiro, 1924); CIFTA, *Relatorio da Directoria* (Rio de Janeiro, 1924); CIFTA, *Relatorio da Directoria do Centro Industrial de Fiação e Tecelagem de Algodão do Anno 1925* (Rio de Janeiro, c. 1925); CIFTA, *Fabricas filiadas* (Rio de Janeiro, c. 1926); CIFTA, *Relatorio da Directoria* (Rio de Janeiro, c. 1928); CIFTA, *Fiação e Tecelagem: Censo Organizado pelo Centro Industrial de Fiação e Tecelagem de Algodão* (Rio de Janeiro, 1935).

panies was consistently faster than in private firms. Third, firms that switched from sole proprietorships or partnerships to publicly traded joint-stock companies consistently grew faster than firms that did not switch. In fact, from 1905 to 1915 private firms that became traded joint-stock companies outgrew the other traded firms by three to one and outgrew private firms by four to one. The implication is clear: Privately owned firms were capital constrained; their growth was limited by the rate at which they could plow back retained earnings or the rate at which their owners could divert their wealth from other sources into their textile mill. Limited-liability joint-stock companies, in contrast, were not as constrained. They could mobilize capital from a broad range of individual and institutional investors through a variety of financial instruments, including stocks, bonds, and commercial paper.

Brazilian industry would therefore have been smaller had there not been financial markets to mobilize capital—but how much smaller? One way to get a first-order approximation is to assume that the same number of firms would have existed but that the publicly owned firms would have been as capital constrained as the privately owned firms. They therefore would have been the same size as privately owned firms. The total size of the industry in any year would therefore have been the actual number of censused firms multiplied by the average size of privately owned firms (see table 6). Had all firms been privately owned, in 1905 the industry would have been 28 percent smaller, in 1915, 32 percent smaller, and in 1925, 49 percent smaller.

One might argue that the absence of joint-stock limited-liability companies would have opened up the possibility for investments in the industry by existing and potential private firms and thus that the industry would not in fact have been any smaller. Doubtless this would have happened. The implication, however, is that these potential firms would have been less efficient than the joint-stock firms they would have replaced; otherwise they would have come into existence anyway and outcompeted the joint-stock companies. Either way there would have been a loss for Brazil: a smaller, but equally efficient industry or a less efficient, but equal-sized industry. We will return to this latter possibility in some detail shortly.

The second impact of the institutional reforms that allowed for the creation of limited-liability joint-stock companies in Brazil was an increase in productivity; joint-stock firms were more efficient than those that were privately owned. These results are indicated by estimates of Cobb-Douglas production functions on the panel data set. We measure output two ways, by real value and by physical units (meters of cloth). Each measure of output has its advantages and disadvantages: Real output is sensitive to the price index we construct to measure changes in the price of cloth; physical output eliminates the price index problem but understates output because it cannot capture differences in the quality of the cloth over time (which was significant).

The real value estimates require first the estimation of a price index for cotton textile goods. We assume that Brazilian manufacturers priced their products at the milreis price of foreign imports plus the tariff. It then follows that the rate of change of domestic prices is equal to the sum of the changes in the nominal exchange rate, the tariff, and the value of foreign cotton goods. Since most Brazilian imports were from Great Britain, we employ the British cotton goods' price series.

Following Kane's work on the United States, we employ the number of spindles as a proxy for the capital input of each company.[21] Following Atack and Sokoloff on productivity in the United States, and Bernard and Jones on international productivity com-

---

21. See, for instance, N. F. Kane, *Textiles in Transition: Technology, Wages, and Industry Relocation in the U.S. Textile Industry, 1880–1930* (New York: Greenwood Press, 1988).

TABLE 6

Average Capacity by Firm Type, 1866–1934

Year	NUMBER OF FIRMS				AVERAGE NUMBER OF SPINDLES			INDUSTRY SIZE		
	Total [a]	Private	Joint-stock traded	Joint-stock not traded	Private	Joint-stock traded	Joint-stock not traded	If all firm private	Actual	Difference (in percent)
1866	9	9	0	0	1,653	—	—	14,875	14,875	0%
1875	11	11	0	0	4,166	—	—	45,830	45,830	0
1881	24	22	2	0	2,513	14,830	—	60,323	84,956	29
1883	24	22	2	0	2,428	12,750	—	58,264	78,908	26
1905	90	72	16	2	6,210	11,932	20,270	558,900	778,224	28
1907	117	95	21	1	4,790	15,758	37,340	560,430	823,343	32
1914	204	152	49	3	5,495	16,608	6,346	1,120,980	1,634,449	31
1915	170	120	45	5	6,355	16,701	16,874	1,080,350	1,598,568	32
1924	184	132	42	10	6,610	31,320	17,685	1,216,240	2,200,612	45
1925	183	122	44	17	6,720	30,010	15,120	1,229,760	2,397,380	49
1926	214	141	50	23	6,391	26,578	14,594	1,367,674	2,558,433	47
1927	228	146	48	34	6,702	27,820	11,126	1,528,056	2,692,007	43
1934	203	131	41	31	7,491	26,828	13,739	1,520,673	2,507,126	39

SOURCES: Agostino Vioto de Borja Castro, "Relatorio do segundo grupo," in Antonio José de Souza Rego, ed., *Relatorio da segunda Exposição Nacional de 1866* (Rio de Janeiro, 1869), pp. 3–73; Commissão [para] Exposição Universal [em] Philadelphia, *The Empire of Brazil at the Universal Exhibition of 1876 in Philadelphia* (Rio de Janeiro: Tipographia e Lithographia do Imperial Instituto Artistico, 1876), pp. 285–87 and statistical tables; Biblioteca da Associação Industrial, *Archivo da Exposição da Industria Nacional de 1881* (Rio de Janeiro: Tipographia Nacional, 1982), pp. xcvi–xcvii; Commissão de Inquerito Industrial, *Relatorio ao Ministerio da Fazenda* (Rio de Janeiro, 1882), p. 15; John C. Branner, "Cotton Factories in Brazil—1883," *Cotton in the Empire of Brazil*, U.S. Department of Agriculture, Miscellaneous Special Report No. 8 (Washington, D.C.: Government Printing Office, 1885); Consul W. Ricketts, *Report*, C4657, 1xv (1886), pp. 187–88 from British Consular Reports, *Consular Reports: Accounts and Papers* (London, 1870–1900) as cited by Stanley J. Stein, *The Brazilian Cotton Textile Manufacture: Textile Enterprise in an Underdeveloped Area* (Cambridge, Mass.: Harvard University Press, 1957), appendix I; Antonio Olyntho dos Santos Pires, *Relatorio apresentado ao Presidente da Republica dos Estados Unidos do Brasil pelo Ministerio de Estado dos Negocios da Industria, Viacão e Obras Publicas* (Rio de Janeiro, 1896), pp. 24–25; José Carlos de Carvalho, "O Algodão: sua historia," and "O Cafe: sua historia," in *Sociedad Nacional de Agricultura*, Fasciculo No. 7 (Rio de Janeiro, 1900); Cunha Vasco, "Industria de Algodão," *Boletim do Centro Industrial do Brasil*, Fasciculo 111 (Rio de Janeiro, 1905); Prefeitura do Distrito Federal, *Noticia sobre o desenvolvimento da industria fabril no Distrito Federal e sua situação actual* (Milano: Tipografia Fratelli Trevos, 1908); William Alexander Graham Clark, *Cotton Goods in Latin America, Part I, Cuba, Mexico, and Central America* (Washington, D.C.: Government Printing Office, 1909); Cunha Vasco, *Fabrica de fiação e tecelagem de Algodão* (Rio de Janeiro, 1908); Antonio F. Bandeira Junior, *A Industria no Estado de São Paulo* (São Paulo, 1908); Centro Industrial do Brasil, *Relatorio da Directoria para ser Apresentado a Assemblea Geral Ordinaria do anno de 1915* (Rio de Janeiro, 1915); Centro Industria do Brasil, *O Centro Industrial na Conferencia Algodeira* (Rio de Janeiro, 1917); Centro Industrial de Fiação e Tecelagem de Algodão (hereafter, CIFTA), *Relatorio da Directoria 1921–1922* (Rio de Janeiro, 1922); CIFTA, *Exposição de Tecidos de Algodão* (Rio de Janeiro, 1923); CIFTA, *Relatorio da Directoria 1923* (Rio de Janeiro, 1924); CIFTA, *Relatorio da Directoria do Centro Industrial de Fiação e Tecelagem de Algodão do Anno 1925* (Rio de Janeiro, c. 1925); CIFTA, *Fabricas filiadas* (Rio de Janeiro, c. 1926); CIFTA, *Relatorio da Directoria* (Rio de Janeiro, c. 1928); CIFTA, *Fiação e Tecelagem: Censo Organizado pelo Centro Industrial de Fiação e Tecelagem de Algodão* (Rio de Janeiro, 1935).

ᵃ Includes only those firms with spindle data.

parisons, we employed the number of workers as the measure of the labor input.[22]

The estimates presented here break firms into two categories, joint stock and privately owned, and into two sizes, those smaller than 13,500 spindles and those larger than 13,500 spindles (13,500 spindles was the median firm size observed in the panel data set). Conveniently, it also represents a firm size equivalent to a capacity share of 0.5 percent at the time of the last census under analysis. As we shall see later on, when we use survivor methods to cross-check our TFP regressions, 0.5 percent turns out to be the minimum efficient scale of production. We used an unbalanced panel procedure to estimate basic pooled- and fixed-effects specifications of regressions for the years 1905–27 of the following type:

$$Y_{it} = \alpha + \beta \cdot X_{it} + u_{it},$$

where Y_{it} is the dependent variable of firm i at time t; α is the overall intercept term for all firms; β is a vector of coefficients corresponding to the X_{it} vector of independent variables; and u_{it} is a stochastic term.[23] We assume usual normality and independence conditions to obtain least-squares estimates of β.[24]

---

22. See J. Atack, *Estimation of Economies of Scale in Nineteenth-Century United States Manufacturing* (New York and London: Garland Publications, 1985); K. L. Sokoloff, "Was the Transition from the Artisanal Shop to the Nonmechanized Factory Associated with Gains in Efficiency? Evidence from the U.S. Manufacturing Censuses of 1820 and 1850," *Explorations in Economic History* 21, no. 4 (1984): 351–82; and A. B. Bernard and C. I. Jones, "Productivity across Industries and Countries: Time Series Theory and Evidence," *Review of Economics and Statistics* 78, no. 1 (1996): 135–46.

23. For ordinary least squares estimates, this coefficient would be the same for all firms; for fixed effects, it was not estimated as it was allowed to vary freely among cross sections. Both models, the basic pooled and fixed effects, produced the same qualitative results with minor differences in the magnitude of the estimated coef-

We assume a Cobb-Douglas production function of the form $Y = A \cdot K^\gamma \cdot L^{1-\gamma}$ with constant returns to scale where K and L represent the capital and labor inputs and A is a function that captures improvements in technology over time. In order to use linear estimation procedures, we take natural logarithms of a normalized production function of the form $y = k^\alpha$ where $y = Y \div L$ and $k = K \div L$ and add explanatory variables to arrive at the following model:

$$Ln\ y = \alpha + \beta_1 \cdot Ln\ k + \beta_2 \cdot Ln\ L + \beta_3 \cdot time\ trend + \delta \cdot dummies$$

This specification allows us to both test for economies of scale as well as obtain the rate of total factor productivity growth, the coefficient on the time trend. We use variations of this equation to estimate the impact of other features of firms (location, traded status, vintage, and other relevant variables) for the specifications whose results are reported in table 7.[25]

---

ficients. In some cases, as with the time trend, the estimates were nearly identical. Thus, to avoid repetition, we report only results from the basic pooled model.

24. In the construction of time series for each observation unit, it is evident that plain OLS techniques would result in biased estimates because some of the variables in later periods could be predicted from earlier years (e.g., spindles at time t could very well be equal to spindles at time $t+1$). The panel procedure individually identifies each company over time to correct for potential autocorrelation in its variables.

25. This specification provides a simple test for economies of scale, following the methodology of Atack, *Estimation of Economies of Scale*. The sign of β_2 would indicate whether, if negative, there are decreasing returns to scale or, if positive, increasing returns to scale. The magnitude of β_2 would indicate the level to which production deviates from the standard case of constant returns to scale. A coefficient of small magnitude that is not statistically significant would corroborate the hypothesis of constant returns to scale. The additional variables, *dummies* and *interaction terms*, are vectors of dummy explanatory variables (including limited-liability status, trading in the stock market, and location in the central region), respectively; δ and γ are the corresponding coefficient vectors. We use these to further decompose the rate of growth (β_3) of TFP. We obtain the same results if we use a specification where the variables were not normalized by the labor input, but in that case we would not be able to test for economies of scale. Whether or not we normalize by labor, β_3 remains the rate of total factor productivity growth because, in both cases,

TABLE 7
Alternate Specifications of Cobb-Douglas Production Functions, Brazilian Cotton Textile Industry, 1905–1927

Dependent Variable	LOG(REAL VALUE OF PRODUCTION/WORKER)				
	Specification 1	Specification 2	Specification 3	Specification 4	Specification 5
1. Intercept	6.502 (39.678)	6.389 (38.909)	6.268 (38.652)	6.154 (40.351)	6.256 (37.689)
2. Ln(spindles/worker)—proxy for capital	0.316 (8.765)	0.331 (9.100)	0.348 (9.603)	0.304 (8.607)	0.298 (8.336)
3. Ln(workers)—proxy for firm size	−0.012 (−0.613)	0.002 (0.088)	0.018 (0.985)	0.034 (1.958)	0.019 (0.978)
4. Time	0.061 (21.310)	0.062 (21.545)	0.063 (21.376)	0.061 (21.627)	0.061 (21.435)
5. Vintage—dummy for firms founded on or after 1905	0.076 (2.037)	0.089 (2.344)	0.087 (2.284)	0.065 (1.756)	0.059 (1.583)
6. Joint stock—dummy for limited-liability joint-stock company	0.226 (5.770)				
a. Joint-stock out—dummy for joint-stock firm outside competitive region					0.285 (2.248)
7. Traded—dummy for firms listed in stock exchange markets		0.165 (3.872)			
8. Bonds—dummy for bonded debt			0.093 (1.842)		
9. Region—dummy for firms in Minas Gerais, Rio de Janeiro, Distrito Federal, São Paulo				0.300 (8.281)	

a. Privately owned in Minas Gerais, Rio de Janeiro, Distrito Federal, São Paulo					0.279 (6.394)
b. Joint stock in Minas Gerais, Rio de Janeiro, Distrito Federal, São Paulo					0.354 (8.138)
N	1,017	1,017	1,017	1,017	1,017
Adjusted R^2	0.40	0.39	0.39	0.42	0.43

SOURCES: Agostino Vioto de Borja Castro, "Relatorio do segundo grupo," in Antonio José de Souza Rego, ed. *Relatorio da segunda Exposição Nacional de 1866* (Rio de Janeiro, 1869), pp. 3–73; Commissão [para] Exposição Universal [em] Philadelphia, *The Empire of Brazil at the Universal Exhibition of 1876 in Philadelphia* (Rio de Janeiro: Tipographia e Lithographia do Imperial Instituto Artistico, 1876), pp. 285–87 and statistical tables; Biblioteca da Associação Industrial, *Archivo da Exposição da Industria Nacional de 1881* (Rio de Janeiro: Tipographia Nacional, 1982), pp. xcvi–xcvii; Commissão de Inquerito Industrial, *Relatorio ao Ministerio da Fazenda* (Rio de Janeiro, 1882), p. 15; John C. Branner, "Cotton Factories in Brazil—1883," *Cotton in the Empire of Brazil*, U.S. Department of Agriculture, Miscellaneous Special Report No. 8 (Washington, D.C.: Government Printing Office, 1885); Consul W. Ricketts, *Report*, C4657, 1xv (1886), pp. 187–88 from British Consular Reports, *Consular Reports, Accounts and Papers* (London, 1870–1900) as cited by Stanley J. Stein, *The Brazilian Cotton Textile Manufacture: Textile Enterprise in an Underdeveloped Area* (Cambridge, Mass.: Harvard University Press, 1957), appendix I; Antonio Olyntho dos Santos Pires, *Relatorio apresentado ao Presidente da Republica dos Estados Unidos do Brasil pelo Ministerio de Estado dos Negocios da Industria, Viação e Obras Publicas* (Rio de Janeiro, 1896), pp. 24–25; José Carlos de Carvalho, "O Algodão: sua historia," in *Sociedad Nacional de Agricultura*, Fasciculo No. 7 (Rio de Janeiro, 1900); Cunha Vasco, "Industria de Algodão," *Boletim do Centro Industrial do Brasil*, Fasciculo 111 (Rio de Janeiro, 1905); Prefetura do Distrito Federal, *Noticia sobre o desenvolvimento da industria fabril no Distrito Federal e sua situação actual* (Milano: Tipografia Fratelli Trevos, 1908); William Alexander Graham Clark, *Cotton Goods in Latin America, Part I, Cuba, Mexico, and Central America* (Washington, D.C.: Government Printing Office, 1909); Cunha Vasco, *Fabrica de fiação e tecelagem de Algodão* (Rio de Janeiro, 1908); Antonio F. Bandeira Junior, *A Industria no Estado de São Paulo* (São Paulo, 1908); Centro Industria do Brasil, *Relatorio da Directoria para ser Apresentado a Assemblea Geral Ordinaria do anno de 1915* (Rio de Janeiro, 1915); Centro Industria do Brasil, *O Centro Industrial na Conferencia Algodeira* (Rio de Janeiro, 1917); Centro Industrial de Fiação e Tecelagem de Algodão (hereafter, CIFTA), *Relatorio da Directoria 1921–1922* (Rio de Janeiro, 1922); CIFTA, *Exposição de Tecidos de Algodão* (Rio de Janeiro, 1923); CIFTA, *Relatorio da Directoria 1923* (Rio de Janeiro, 1924); CIFTA, *Relatorio da Directoria* (Rio de Janeiro, 1924); CIFTA, *Relatorio da Directoria do Centro Industrial de Fiação e Tecelagem de Algodão do Anno 1925* (Rio de Janeiro, c. 1925); CIFTA, *Fabricas filiadas* (Rio de Janeiro, c. 1926); CIFTA, *Relatorio da Directoria* (Rio de Janeiro, c. 1928); CIFTA, *Fiação e Tecelagem: Censo Organizado pelo Centro Industrial de Fiação e Tecelagem de Algodão* (Rio de Janeiro, 1935).

Specification 1 of table 7 indicates that, as predicted, there were negligible scale economies in the Brazilian cotton textile industry (the coefficient on firm size is negative, of small magnitude, and not statistically significant). The industry was, however, characterized by rapid productivity growth; the time trend was 6.1 percent a year. As expected, newer firms (those founded after 1905) had higher productivities than their older competitors (the coefficient translates into roughly an 8 percent TFP advantage for newer firms, everything else being equal).[26] Perhaps most striking is the sizable impact of the joint-stock corporate form. The coefficient of .226 on the joint-stock dummy translates into a 25 percent TFP advantage over non-joint-stock firms.

One might think that firms that were actively traded on an organized exchange might have been more efficient than joint-stock firms that were not traded. The notion is that firms that were regularly traded were monitored more closely by large investors. Ideally, we would add a traded dummy to specification 1, to measure the *marginal impact* of being publicly traded. Traded firms were, however, a subset of joint-stock firms, meaning that there is collinearity between the two variables. We therefore estimate the impact of being traded in specification 2 by substituting a traded dummy for the joint-stock dummy. We are able to reject the hypothesis that traded status explains the advantage that joint-stock firms had over their competitors; the coefficient is large and statistically significant, but it is of a smaller magnitude than that on joint-stock firms alone. It may have been the case that the secondary markets for equity were too thin to serve as efficient monitors. Or it may be the case

---

the contribution of the two inputs would have been accounted for by the estimates of β_1 and β_2.

26. Intercept coefficients can be translated into percentages through the following formula: $e^{\beta_1} - 1$.

that some of the most productive joint-stock companies' shares were closely held by their original investors.

What was the impact of being able to issue bonds on productivity growth? One view would hold that there should be a positive correlation between being able to sell debt and high levels and rates of growth of productivity. In this view, well-managed firms will be the most likely to succeed in selling debt to the investing public. In turn, this reduces their cost of capital and further increases their growth of productivity. An alternative view, associated with Brander and Spencer, is that if an owner-manager substitutes borrowed funds for equity, then the effort of the owner declines and the firm's output falls (because bondholders have less incentive than equity holders to monitor managers).[27] Specification 3 tests these hypotheses by introducing a dummy variable for firms whose bonds were traded on either the Rio de Janeiro or the São Paulo exchange. The magnitude of the coefficient is much smaller than that for a joint-stock company, indicating that although firms that issued bonds were roughly 10 percent more productive than the average firm, they were less efficient than joint-stock firms as a group.

One might argue that the differences in TFP between joint-stock and privately owned firms are due purely to regional productivity differences. Perhaps all of the low-TFP firms were located in isolated markets where transport barriers protected them from competition. Specifications 4 and 5 test this hypothesis. Specification 4 introduces a dummy variable for firms located in the highly integrated, rapidly growing, four-state market of Rio de Janeiro, the Distrito Federal, Minas Gerais, and São Paulo. The coefficient on region (.300) indicates that there were in fact sizable regional productivity differences. Specification 5 decomposes the effects of re-

27. James A. Brander and Barbara J. Spencer, "Moral Hazard and Limited Liability: Implications for the Theory of the Firm," *International Economic Review* 30, no. 4 (1989): 833–49.

gion and joint-stock status by introducing dummy variables for joint-stock firms outside of the competitive region, joint-stock firms in the region, and all other firms in the region.[28] The results indicate that, even if we control for regional effects, there was still a positive residual for firms that took the joint-stock form (note that the coefficient in 9B is of greater magnitude than 9A and that both are significant at the 1 percent level). The regressions also indicate that joint-stock firms outside the competitive region had a sizable productivity advantage against their privately owned competitors. The coefficient of .285 (line 6a, specification 5) translates into a 33 percent productivity differential.

What advantage was conferred on joint-stock firms that created such sizable productivity differences? One might imagine that joint-stock firms had higher capital-labor ratios and that this might have either allowed them to produce more cloth per worker or allowed them to specialize in high-value cloth, whose production required more capital-intensive techniques. Table 8 tests these hypotheses by substituting the volume of cloth produced (in meters) for the real value of output (specifications 1, 2, 3, 4, and 5 mirror specifications 1–5 of table 5, except that the proxy for output changes). With the exception of the time trend, the qualitative results of the relationship between vintage, region, capital-labor ratio, firm size, joint-stock status, and other relevant variables are similar to those obtained when we proxied output by real value. Joint-stock firms were more productive than their private competitors. Although there are a number of minor differences between the results in the two panels (such as the stronger impact of being publicly traded when output is proxied by volume), the only glaring difference is that, when

28. The fact that virtually all the joint-stock companies were located in the four-state region means that these variables are likely to be collinear. Thus, we cannot simultaneously introduce dummy variables for region and joint stock to measure the marginal impact of being traded, taking region into account.

output is proxied by meters of cloth, the time trend is negative. Thus, we can reject the hypothesis that joint-stock firms were able to produce more cloth per input than their private competitors.

The most reasonable interpretation of the variance of the time trend across the two panels is that joint-stock firms tended to produce more fine-weave, high-quality goods than private firms. Generally speaking, the production of such cloth requires that machines be run more slowly because fine yarns are more subject to breakage. The result is that firms need to purchase larger numbers of machines to produce the same volume of cloth, resulting in more machines per worker than in firms that produce low-value cloth. These results are consistent with information on the value of various types of output in the 1907 and 1915 censuses. The census data indicate that joint-stock firms tended to produce more high-value goods than their private counterparts.

A skeptical reader might respond that the use of physical inputs of capital and labor in the production functions means that, although public firms might have been more technically efficient, they were not necessarily more economically efficient. It might have been the case, for example, that the different techniques of production between joint-stock and private firms meant that joint-stock firms actually had higher unit costs because they had to purchase more-expensive skilled labor or because they had to purchase more-expensive types of raw cotton. Stigler's survivor method allows us to test this hypothesis. In a competitive market the most economically efficient firms survive and those firms that are economically inefficient go out of business. Firm types or firm sizes that are inefficient will therefore grow more slowly than firm types or sizes that are efficient.

The fastest-growing type of firm was limited-liability joint-stock companies, and the fastest-growing size category was small firms (capacity shares of less than 0.5 percent; see table 9). Fastest growing of all were small joint-stock firms. Over the thirty years from

TABLE 8

Alternate Specifications of Cobb-Douglas Production Functions, Brazilian Cotton Textile Industry, 1905–1927
(Unbalanced panel regressions on entire sample; total ordinary least squares; T statistics in parentheses)

Dependent Variable	LOG(METERS OF OUTPUT/WORKER)				
	Specification 1	Specification 2	Specification 3	Specification 4	Specification 5
1. Intercept	8.240 (48.685)	8.290 (49.408)	8.162 (49.651)	8.077 (51.001)	8.181 (46.686)
2. Ln(spindles/worker)—proxy for capital	0.307 (7.236)	0.301 (7.145)	0.322 (7.710)	0.299 (7.077)	0.289 (6.732)
3. Ln(workers)—proxy for firm size	−0.060 (−3.094)	−0.068 (−3.493)	−0.052 (−2.731)	−0.039 (−2.916)	−0.051 (−2.529)
4. Time	−0.008 (−3.103)	−0.008 (−3.012)	−0.007 (−2.921)	−0.007 (−2.916)	−0.007 (−2.953)
5. Vintage—dummy for firms founded on or after 1905	0.019 (0.475)	0.030 (0.755)	0.025 (0.625)	0.016 (0.421)	0.020 (0.500)
6. Joint stock—dummy for limited-liability joint-stock company	0.096 (2.432)				
a. Joint stock out—dummy for joint-stock firm outside competitive region					−0.052 (−0.459)
7. Traded—dummy for firms listed in stock exchange markets		0.147 (3.447)			
8. Bonds—dummy for bonded debt			0.080 (1.566)		

9. Region—dummy for firms in Minas Gerais, Rio de Janeiro, Distrito Federal, São Paulo	0.126 (3.323)				
a. Privately owned in Minas Gerais, Rio de Janeiro, Distrito Federal, São Paulo					0.088 (1.922)
b. Joint stock in Minas Gerais, Rio de Janeiro, Distrito Federal, São Paulo					0.153 (3.389)
N	785	785	785	785	785
Adjusted R^2	0.10	0.09	0.10	0.10	0.09

SOURCES: Agostino Vioto de Borja Castro, "Relatorio do segundo grupo," in Antonio José de Souza Rego, ed., *Relatorio da segunda Exposição Nacional de 1866* (Rio de Janeiro, 1869), pp. 3–73; Commissão [para] Exposição Universal [em] Philadelphia, *The Empire of Brazil at the Universal Exhibition of 1876 in Philadelphia* (Rio de Janeiro: Tipographia e Lithographia do Imperial Instituto Artistico, 1876), pp. 285–87 and statistical tables; Biblioteca da Associação Industrial, *Archivo da Exposição da Industria Nacional de 1881* (Rio de Janeiro: Tipographia Nacional, 1882), pp. xcvi–xcvii; Commissão de Inquerito Industrial, *Relatorio ao Ministerio da Fazenda* (Rio de Janeiro, 1882), p. 15; John C. Branner, "Cotton Factories in Brazil—1883," *Cotton in the Empire of Brazil*, U.S. Department of Agriculture, Miscellaneous Special Report No. 8 (Washington, D.C.: Government Printing Office, 1885); Consul W. Ricketts, *Report*, C4657, 1xv (1886), pp. 187–88 from British Consular Reports, *Consular Reports: Accounts and Papers* (London, 1870–1900) as cited by Stanley J. Stein, *The Brazilian Cotton Textile Manufacture: Textile Enterprise in an Underdeveloped Area* (Cambridge, Mass.: Harvard University Press, 1957), appendix I; Antonio Olyntho dos Santos Pires, *Relatorio apresentado ao Presidente da Republica dos Estados Unidos do Brasil pelo Ministerio de Estado dos Negocios da Industria, Viação e Obras Publicas* (Rio de Janeiro, 1896), pp. 24–25; José Carlos de Carvalho, "O Algodão: sua historia," and "O Cafe: sua historia," in *Sociedad Nacional de Agricultura, Fasciculo No. 7* (Rio de Janeiro, 1900); Cunha Vasco, "Industria de Algodão," *Boletim do Centro Industrial do Brasil*, Fasciculo 111 (Rio de Janeiro, 1905); Centro Industrial do Brasil, *O Brasil: suas riquezas naturaes, suas industrias, Industria de Transportes, Industria Fabril*, vol. 3 (Rio de Janeiro, 1909); Prefeitura do Distrito Federal, *Noticia sobre o desenvolvimento da industria fabril no Distrito Federal e sua situação actual* (Milano: Tipografia Fratelli Trevos, 1908); William Alexander Graham Clark, *Cotton Goods in Latin America, Part I, Cuba, Mexico, and Central America* (Washington, D.C.: Government Printing Office, 1909); Cunha Vasco, *Fabrica de fiação e tecelagem de Algodão* (Rio de Janeiro, 1908); Antonio F. Bandeira Junior, *A Industria no Estado de São Paulo* (São Paulo, 1908); Centro Industria do Brasil, *Relatorio da Directoria para ser Apresentado a Assemblea Geral Ordinaria do anno de 1915* (Rio de Janeiro, 1915); Centro Industria do Brasil, *O Centro Industrial na Conferencia Algodeira* (Rio de Janeiro, 1917); Centro Industrial de Fiação e Tecelagem de Algodão (hereafter, CIFTA), *Relatorio da Directoria 1921–1922* (Rio de Janeiro, 1922); CIFTA, *Exposição de Tecidos de Algodão* (Rio de Janeiro, 1923); CIFTA, *Relatorio da Directoria 1923* (Rio de Janeiro, 1924); CIFTA, *Relatorio da Directoria* (Rio de Janeiro, 1924); CIFTA, *Relatorio da Directoria do Centro Industrial de Fiação e Tecelagem de Algodão do Anno 1925* (Rio de Janeiro, c. 1925); CIFTA, *Fabricas filiadas* (Rio de Janeiro, c. 1926); CIFTA, *Relatorio da Directoria* (Rio de Janeiro, c. 1928); CIFTA, *Fiação e Tecelagem: Censo Organizado pelo Centro Industrial de Fiação e Tecelagem de Algodão* (Rio de Janeiro, 1935).

TABLE 9

Survivorship, by Capacity and Firm Type, 1895–1934

	NUMBER OF FIRMS (PERCENT IN PARENTHESES)		
	Joint stock	Private	Total
1905 Capacity (in percent)			
<.5	8 (9)	33 (37)	41 (46)
.5–1.00	3 (3)	15 (17)	18 (20)
1.01–3.00	6 (7)	15 (17)	21 (23)
3.01–5.00	6 (7)	3 (3)	9 (10)
>5.01	1 (1)	0 (0)	1 (1)
TOTAL	24 (27)	66 (73)	90 (100)
1915 Capacity (in percent)			
<.5	23 (14)	87 (51)	110 (65)
.5–1.00	19 (11)	16 (9)	35 (21)
1.01–3.00	16 (9)	5 (3)	21 (12)
3.01–5.00	2 (1)	1 (1)	3 (2)
>5.01	1 (1)	0 (0)	1 (1)
TOTAL	61 (36)	109 (64)	170 (100)
1925 Capacity (in percent)			
<.5	44 (24)	96 (52)	140 (77)
.5–1.00	10 (5)	8 (4)	18 (10)
1.01–3.00	16 (9)	5 (3)	21 (11)
3.01–5.00	3 (2)	0 (0)	3 (2)
>5.01	1 (1)	0 (0)	1 (1)
TOTAL	74 (40)	109 (60)	183 (100)

1934 Capacity (in percent)					
<.5	47	(23)	105	(52)	152	(75)
.5–1.00	11	(5)	13	(6)	24	(12)
1.01–3.00	20	(10)	5	(2)	25	(12)
3.01–5.00	1	(0)	0	(0)	1	(0)
>5.01	1	(0)	0	(0)	1	(0)
TOTAL	80	(39)	123	(61)	203	(100)

SOURCES: Agostino Vioto de Borja Castro, "Relatorio do segundo grupo," in Antonio José de Souza Rego, ed., *Relatorio da segunda Exposição Nacional de 1866* (Rio de Janeiro, 1869), pp. 3–73; Commissão [para] Exposição Universal [em] Philadelphia, *The Empire of Brazil at the Universal Exhibition of 1876 in Philadelphia* (Rio de Janeiro: Tipographia e Lithographia do Imperial Instituto Artistico, 1876), pp. 285–87 and statistical tables; Biblioteca da Associação Industrial, *Archivo da Exposição da Industria Nacional de 1881* (Rio de Janeiro: Tipographia Nacional, 1982), pp. xcvi–xcvii; Commissão de Inquerito Industrial, *Relatorio ao Ministerio da Fazenda* (Rio de Janeiro, 1882), p. 15; John C. Branner, "Cotton Factories in Brazil—1883," *Cotton in the Empire of Brazil*, U.S. Department of Agriculture, Miscellaneous Special Report No. 8 (Washington, D.C.: Government Printing Office, 1885); Consul W. Ricketts, *Report*, C4657, 1xv (1886), pp. 187–88 from British Consular Reports, *Consular Reports: Accounts and Papers* (London, 1870–1900) as cited by Stanley J. Stein, *The Brazilian Cotton Textile Manufacture: Textile Enterprise in an Underdeveloped Area* (Cambridge, Mass.: Harvard University Press, 1957), appendix I; Antonio Olyntho dos Santos Pires, *Relatorio apresentado ao Presidente da Republica dos Estados Unidos do Brasil pelo Ministerio de Estado dos Negocios da Industria, Viacão e Obras Publicas* (Rio de Janeiro, 1896), pp. 24–25; José Carlos de Carvalho, "O Algodão: sua historia," and "O Cafe: sua historia," in *Sociedad Nacional de Agricultura*, Fasciculo No. 7 (Rio de Janeiro, 1900); Cunha Vasco, "Industria de Algodão," *Boletim do Centro Industrial do Brasil*, Fasciculo 111 (Rio de Janeiro, 1905); Centro Industrial do Brasil, *O Brasil: suas riquezas naturaes, suas industrias. Industria de Transportes, Industria Fabril*, vol. 3 (Rio de Janeiro, 1909); Prefeitura do Distrito Federal, *Noticia sobre o desenvolvimento da industria fabril no Distrito Federal e sua situação actual* (Milano: Tipografia Fratelli Trevos, 1908); William Alexander Graham Clark, *Cotton Goods in Latin America, Part I, Cuba, Mexico, and Central America* (Washington, D.C.: Government Printing Office, 1909); Cunha Vasco, *Fabrica de fiação e tecelagem de Algodão* (Rio de Janeiro, 1908); Antonio F. Bandeira Junior, *A Industria no Estado de São Paulo* (São Paulo, 1908); Centro Industria do Brasil, *Relatorio da Directoria para ser Apresentado a Assemblea Geral Ordinaria do anno de 1915* (Rio de Janeiro, 1915); Centro Industria do Brasil, *O Centro Industrial na Conferencia Algodeira* (Rio de Janeiro, 1917); Centro Industrial de Fiação e Tecelagem de Algodão (hereafter, CIFTA), *Relatorio da Directoria 1921–1922* (Rio de Janeiro, 1922); CIFTA, *Exposição de Tecidos de Algodão* (Rio de Janeiro, 1923); CIFTA, *Relatorio da Directoria 1923* (Rio de Janeiro, 1924); CIFTA, *Relatorio da Directoria* (Rio de Janeiro, 1924); CIFTA, *Relatorio da Directoria do Centro Industrial de Fiação e Tecelagem de Algodão do Anno 1925* (Rio de Janeiro, c. 1925); CIFTA, *Fabricas filiadas* (Rio de Janeiro, c. 1926); CIFTA, *Relatorio da Directoria* (Rio de Janeiro, c. 1928); CIFTA, *Fiação e Tecelagem: Censo Organizado pelo Centro Industrial de Fiação e Tecelagem de Algodão* (Rio de Janeiro, 1935).

1905 to 1934, the number of joint-stock limited-liability companies more than tripled, while the number of private firms did not even double. The number of small joint-stock firms grew nearly fivefold (from eight in 1905 to forty-seven in 1934). These results corroborate the findings in tables 7 and 8 that scale economies were exhausted at small-sized firms. They also corroborate the findings that joint-stock companies, regardless of size, were more efficient than private firms. In short, technical efficiency and economic efficiency were one and the same in the case under study.

Conclusions and Implications

Changes in the regulations governing financial markets in Brazil allowed the capital markets to function more smoothly. It was not just that it was difficult to form a joint-stock company. Indeed, even after these restrictions were removed in 1882, capital did not quickly flow into the textile industry. Nor did legal restrictions on the operation of banks turn out to be important. Even after restrictions on the operations of banks were removed in 1890, there was little long-term investment by banks in the textile industry. Rather, the most important reforms were those related to limited liability and mandatory disclosure. These reforms lowered the costs of monitoring managers and eliminated the need for shareholders to monitor one another. This allowed entrepreneurs to mobilize capital from beyond their founding kinship and business groups. Indeed, secondary markets developed in Rio de Janeiro and São Paulo that made these investments liquid.

These institutional changes meant that many firms (and potential firms) were no longer capital constrained. Not every firm could tap the capital markets because it was necessary to either have a well-established reputation or have access to an intermediary who could signal investors that a firm was a good investment. Large numbers of firms, however, were able to take advantage of the joint-stock limited-liability form and mobilize capital from beyond their founding groups. The fall in the cost of capital meant that those firms had more flexibility in their choice of the capital-labor ratio. The result was an increase in the size of the industry and an increase in the rate of growth of productivity.

In short, had Brazil not undertaken the institutional reforms, the Brazilian textile industry would have been smaller and less efficient. To the extent that we can generalize from the case of textiles, the implication is that Brazil would have been even poorer than it actually was.

References

Atack, Jeremy. *Estimation of Economies of Scale in Nineteenth Century United States Manufacturing and the Form of the Production Function.* New York: Garland, 1985.

Bandeira Junior, Antonio F. *A Industria no Estado de São Paulo.* São Paulo, 1908.

Barjau Martinez, Luis, et al. "Estadísticas Económicas del Siglo XIX." *Cuadernos de Trabajo del Departamento de Investigaciones Históricas, INAH,* no. 14 (July 1976).

Bernard, A. B., and C. I. Jones. "Productivity across Industries and Countries: Time Series Theory and Evidence." *Review of Economics and Statistics* 78, no. 1 (1996): 135–46.

Bibliotheca da Associacão Industrial. *Archivo da Exposição da Industria Nacional de 1881.* Rio de Janeiro: Tipographia Nacional, 1982.

Borja Castro, Agostino Vioto de. "Relatorio do segundo grupo." In Antonio José de Souza Rego, ed., *Relatorio da segunda Exposição Nacional de 1866.* Rio de Janeiro, 1869, pp. 3–73.

Brander, James A., and Barbara J. Spencer. "Moral Hazard and Limited Liability: Implications for the Theory of the Firm." *International Economic Review* 30, no. 4 (1989): 833–49.

Branner, John C. *Cotton in the Empire of Brazil.* U.S. Department of Agriculture. Miscellaneous Special Report no. 8. Washington, D.C.: Government Printing Office, 1885.

Brazil. Commissão de Inquerito Industrial. *Relatorio ao Ministerio da Fazenda*. Rio de Janeiro, 1882.

———. Commissão [para] Exposição Universal [em] Philadelphia. *The Empire of Brazil at the Universal Exhibition of 1876 in Philadelphia*. Rio de Janeiro: Typ. e Lithographia do Imperial Instituto Artistico, 1876.

———. Instituto Brasileiro de Geografia e Estatística. *Estatísticas históricas do Brasil*. Rio de Janeiro, 1990.

———. Ministerio da Industria, Viação e Obras Publicas. *Relatorio, 1896*. Rio de Janeiro, 1896.

———. Prefeitura do Distrito Federal. *Noticia sobre o desenvolvimento da industria fabril no Distrito Federal e sua situação actual*. Milano: Tipografia Fratelli Trevos, 1908.

Calomiris, Charles W. "The Costs of Rejecting Universal Banking: American Finance in the German Mirror, 1870–1914." In Naomi Lamoreaux and Daniel Raff, eds., *The Coordination of Economic Activity within and between Firms*. Chicago: University of Chicago Press, 1994.

Carr, Jack L., and G. Frank Mathewson. "Unlimited Liability as a Barrier to Entry." *Journal of Political Economy* 96, no. 4 (1988): 766–84.

Centro Industrial de Fiação e Tecelagem de Algodão. *Estatisticas da industria, commercio e lavoura de Algodão relativos ao anno de 1927*. Rio de Janeiro, 1928.

———. *Exposição de Tecidos de Algodão*. Rio de Janeiro, 1923.

———. *Fabricas filiadas*. Rio de Janeiro, circa 1926.

———. *Fiação e Tecelagem: Censo Organizado pelo Centro Industrial de Fiação e Tecelagem de Algodão*. Rio de Janeiro, 1935.

———. *Relatorio da Directoria 1921–1922*. Rio de Janeiro, 1922.

———. *Relatorio da Directoria 1923*. Rio de Janeiro, 1924.

———. *Relatorio da Directoria*. Rio de Janeiro, 1924.

———. *Relatorio da Directoria do Centro Industrial de Fiação e Tecelagem de Algodão do Anno 1925*. Rio de Janeiro, circa 1925.

Centro Industrial do Brasil. *O Brasil: suas riquezas naturaes, suas industrias. Industria de Transportes, Industria Fabril*. Vol. 3. Rio de Janeiro, 1909.

———. *O Centro Industrial na conferencia algodeira*. Rio de Janeiro, 1917.

———. *Relatorio da Directoria para ser Apresentado a Assemblea Geral Ordinaria do anno de 1915*. Rio de Janeiro, 1915.

Clark, Gregory. "The Political Foundations of Modern Economic Growth, England, 1540–1800." *Journal of Interdisciplinary History* 26, no. 4 (1996): 563–88.

Clark, William A. Graham. *Cotton Goods in Latin America Part I: Cuba, Mexico, and Central America.* Washington, D.C., 1909.

Coatsworth, John H. "Obstacles to Economic Growth in Nineteenth-Century Mexico." *American Historical Review* 83, no. 1 (1978): 80–100.

Davis, Lance. "Capital Immobilities and Finance Capitalism: A Study of Economic Evolution in the United States, 1820–1920." *Explorations in Economic History* 1 (1963): 88–105.

————. "The Capital Markets and Industrial Concentration: The U.S. and U.K., a Comparative Study." *The Economic History Review* 19 (1966): 255–72.

————. "Sources of Industrial Finance: The American Textile Industry, a Case Study." *Explorations in Entrepreneurial History* 9 (1957): 189–203.

Davis, Lance E., and H. Louis Stettler III. "The New England Textile Industry, 1825–1860: Trends and Fluctuations." In *Conference on Research on Income and Wealth. Output, Employment, and Productivity in the United States after 1800.* New York: National Bureau of Economic Research; distributed by Columbia University Press, 1966.

de Carvalho, José Carlos. "O Algodão: sua historia." In *Sociedade Nacional de Agricultura.* Fasciculo No. 7. Rio de Janeiro, 1900.

————. "O Cafe: sua historia." In *Sociedade Nacional de Agricultura.* Fasciculo No. 7. Rio de Janeiro, 1900.

De Long, J. Bradford, et al. "Did J. P. Morgan's Men Add Value? An Economist's Perspective on Financial Capitalism." In Peter Temin, ed., *Inside the Business Enterprise: Historical Perspectives on the Use of Information. National Bureau of Economic Research Report.* Chicago and London: University of Chicago Press, 1991, pp. 205–36.

Diario Official da Federacão. Rio de Janeiro, 1890–1940.

Diario Official do Estado de São Paulo. São Paulo, 1891–1940.

dos Santos Pires, Antonio Olyntho. *Relatorio apresentado ao Presidente da Republica dos Estados Unidos do Brasil pelo Ministerio de Estado dos Negocios da Industria, Viacão e Obras Publicas.* Rio de Janeiro, 1896.

El Economista Mexicano. Mexico City, July 4, 1914.

Garcia Cubas, Antonio. *Cuadro Geográfico, Estadístico, Descriptivo é Histórico de los Estados Unidos Mexicanos.* Mexico City, 1884–1885.

————. *Mexico: Its Trade, Industries and Resources.* Mexico City, 1893.

Greif, Avner. "Micro Theory and Recent Developments in the Study of Economic Institutions through Economic History." In David M. Kreps and Kenneth F. Wallis, eds., *Advances in Economic Theory*. Vol. 2, Cambridge, Eng.: Cambridge University Press, 1997.

Griliches, Zvi, and Vidar Ringstad. *Economies of Scale and the Form of the Production Function: An Econometric Study of Norwegian Manufacturing Establishment Data*. Amsterdam: North Holland Publishing, 1971.

Haber, Stephen H. "Business Enterprise and the Great Depression in Brazil: A Study of Profits and Losses in Textile Manufacturing." *Business History Review* 66, no. 2 (1992): 335–63.

————. "Financial Markets and Industrial Development: A Comparative Study of Governmental Regulation, Financial Innovation, and Industrial Structure in Brazil and Mexico, 1840–1930." In Stephen Haber, ed., *How Latin America Fell Behind: Essays on the Economic Histories of Brazil and Mexico, 1800–1914*. Stanford: Stanford University Press, 1997.

————. "Industrial Concentration and the Capital Markets: A Comparative Study of Brazil, Mexico, and the United States, 1830–1930." *Journal of Economic History* 51, no. 3 (1991): 559–80.

————. *Industry and Underdevelopment: The Industrialization of Mexico, 1890–1940*. Stanford: Stanford University Press, 1989.

Haber, Stephen H., ed. *How Latin America Fell Behind: Essays on the Economic Histories of Brazil and Mexico, 1800–1914*. Stanford: Stanford University Press, 1997.

Hanley, Anne. "Capital Markets in the Coffee Economy." Ph.D. diss., Stanford University, 1995.

Jornal do Commercio. Rio de Janeiro, 1880–1940.

Kane, N. F. *Textiles in Transition: Technology, Wages, and Industry Relocation in the U.S. Textile Industry, 1880–1930*. New York: Greenwood Press, 1988.

Kuznets, Simon. *Economic Growth of Nations: Total Output and Production Structure*. Cambridge, Mass.: Belnap Press of Harvard University Press, 1971.

Lamoreaux, Naomi. "Banks, Kinship, and Economic Development: The New England Case." *Journal of Economic History* 46 (1986): 647–67.

Leff, Nathaniel. "Economic Development in Brazil, 1822–1913." In Haber, ed., *How Latin America Fell Behind*.

————. *Underdevelopment and Development in Brazil*. London: George Allen & Unwin Publishers, 1982.

Levy, Maria Bárbara. *História da bolsa de valores do Rio de Janeiro*. Rio de

Janeiro, Brazil: IBMEC (Instituto Brasileiro de Mercados de Capitais), 1977.

McGouldrick, Paul F. *New England Textiles in the Nineteenth Century.* Cambridge, Mass.: Harvard University Press, 1968.

McKinnon, Ronald I. *Money and Capital in Economic Development.* Washington, D.C.: Brookings Institution, 1973.

Mexico. Archivo General de la Nación. "Extracto de las Manifestaciones presentadas por los fabricantes de hilados y tejidos de algodón para el semestre de enero a junio de 1912." Caja 5, Exp. 4, Mexico City, n.d.

———. Archivo General de la Nación. "Extracto de las Manifestaciones presentadas por los fabricantes de hilados y tejidos de algodón para el semestre de enero a junio de 1913." Caja 31, Exp. 2, Mexico City, n.d.

———. Dirección General de Estadística. *Anuario Estadístico de la República Mexicana 1893–94.* Mexico, 1894.

———. Gobierno del Estado de México. *Estadística del Departamento de México.* Mexico: Biblioteca Enciclopedica del Estado de Mexico, 1980.

———. Ministerio de Fomento. *Memoria 1865.* Mexico, 1866.

———. Secretaría de Fomento, Colonización e Industria. *Memoria que la Dirección De Colonización e Industria presentó al Ministerio De Relaciones en 17 de Enero de 1852, sobre el estado de estos Ramos en el Año Anterior.* Mexico, 1852.

———. Secretaría de Fomento. *Boletin Semestral de la República Mexicana.* Mexico City, 1890.

———. Secretaría de Hacienda y Crédito Público (SHCP). *Documentos para el Estudio de la Industrialización de México, 1837–1845.* Mexico City, DF: Secretaría de Hacienda y Credito Publico: Nacional Financiera, 1977.

———. Secretaría de Hacienda. *Estadística de la República Mexicana.* Mexico, 1896.

———. Secretaría de Hacienda. *Estadísticas de la República Mexicana.* Mexico City, 1880.

———. Secretaría de Hacienda. *Memoria de la Secretaría de Hacienda.* Mexico, 1896.

———. Secretaría del Estado. *Memoria de la Secretaría del Estado y del Despacho de Fomento, Colonización, Industria y Comercio de la República Mexicana.* Mexico, 1857.

———. SHCP. *Boletín de la Secretaría de Hacienda y Crédito Público.* Mexico City, 1917–1932.

————. SHCP. Departamento de Estadística. "Estadísticas del Ramo de Hilados y Tejidos de Algodón y de Lana." Obras Raras Collection. Library of Banco de Mexico. Mexico City, n.d.

Neuhaus, Paulo. *História monetária do Brasil, 1900–45.* Rio de Janeiro, Brazil: Instituto Brasileiro de Mercado de Capitais, 1975.

North, Douglass C. *Institutions, Institutional Change, and Economic Performance.* New York: Cambridge University Press, 1990.

O Estado de São Paulo. São Paulo, 1888–1921.

Patrick, Hugh. "Financial Development and Economic Growth in Underdeveloped Countries." *Economic Development and Cultural Change* 14 (1966): 174–89.

Peláez, Carlos Manuel, and Wilson Suzigan. *História monetária do Brasil: análise da política, comportamento e institucões monetárias.* Rio de Janeiro, Brazil: IPEA/INPES (Instituto de Planejamento Economico e Social, Instituto de Pesquisas), 1976.

Pérez Hernandez, José Maria. *Estadística de la República Mexicana.* Guadalajara, 1862.

Retrospecto Commercial do Jornal do Comercio. Rio de Janeiro, 1911–30.

Ricketts, W. *Report.* C4657, 1xv, 1886, pp. 187–88, from British Consular Reports, *Consular Reports: Accounts and Papers* (London, 1870–1900).

Ridings, Eugene. *Business Interest Groups in Nineteenth Century Brazil.* New York: Cambridge University Press, 1994.

Rodrigues Bastos, Ana Marta, and Elisabeth von de Weid. *Fio da meada: Estrategia de expansao de uma industria textil: Companhia America Fabril, 1878–1930.* Rio de Janeiro: FCRB, 1986.

Rosenthal, Jean Laurent. *The Fruits of Revolution: Property Rights, Litigation, and French Agriculture, 1700–1860.* Cambridge, Eng.: Cambridge University Press, 1992.

Saes, Flávio Azevedo Marques de. *Crédito e bancos no desenvolvimento da economia paulista, 1850–1930.* São Paulo, Brazil: Instituto de Pesquisas Economicas, 1986.

Semana Mercantil. Mexico City, various dates.

Smith, George David, and Richard Sylla. "The Transformation of Financial Capitalism: An Essay on the History of American Capital Markets." *Financial Markets, Institutions and Instruments* 2, no. 2 (1993): 1–61.

Sokoloff, Kenneth L. "Was the Transition from the Artisanal Shop to the Non-Mechanized Factory Associated with Gains in Efficiency? Evidence from the U.S. Manufacturing Censuses of 1820 and 1850." *Explorations in Economic History* 20 (1984): 351–82.

Stein, Stanley J. *The Brazilian Cotton Textile Manufacture: Textile Enterprise in an Underdeveloped Area.* Cambridge, Mass.: Harvard University Press, 1957.

Summerhill, William R. "Transport Improvements and Economic Growth in Brazil and Mexico." In Haber, ed., *How Latin America Fell Behind.*

Suzigan, Wilson. *Indústria brasileira: origem e desenvolvimento.* São Paulo: Editora Brasiliense, 1986.

Sylla, Richard E. *The American Capital Market, 1846–1914.* New York: Arno Press, 1975.

Topik, Steven. *Political Economy of the Brazilian State, 1889–1930.* Austin: University of Texas Press, 1987.

Triner, Gail D. "Brazilian Banks and the Economy, 1906–1918," M.A. thesis, Columbia University, 1990.

Vasco, Cunha. "A industria do Algodão." *Boletim do Centro Industrial do Brasil,* December 30, 1905.

———. *Fabrica de fiação e tecelagem de Algodão.* Rio de Janeiro, 1908.

Vilela Luz, Nicia. *A luta pela industrialização do Brasil.* São Paulo: Editora Alfa Omega, 1978.

Latin America and Foreign Capital in the Twentieth Century: Economics, Politics, and Institutional Change

Economic Growth and Foreign Capital in Latin America since 1900

To the extent that studies of long-run economic growth have touched on Latin America, it has usually been to depict a peripheral region that has experienced *divergence* rather than *convergence* in terms of its income level relative to the core economies.[1] Inevitably,

Prepared for the conference "Institutional Change and Latin American Economic Growth: Empirical Studies in the New Institutional Economics," Hoover Institution, Stanford University, February 1998. I wish to thank Alan Dye, Stephen Haber, Anne Krueger, Douglass North, and Barry Weingast for their comments, and I am grateful to all the conference participants for valuable criticisms on an earlier draft. Any remaining deficiencies in the chapter are solely my responsibility.

1. The premodern origins of this relative backwardness are discussed in J. H. Coatsworth, "Economic Retardation and Growth in Latin America and Southern Europe Since 1700," Harvard University, December 1993, photocopy; and in J. H. Coatsworth, "Economic and Institutional Trajectories in Pre-Modern Latin America," in J. H. Coatsworth and A. M. Taylor, eds., *Latin America and the World Economy in the Nineteenth and Twentieth Centuries: Explorations in Quantitative Economic History* (Cambridge, Mass.: Harvard University Press, 1998); and in the volume by S. Haber, ed., *How Latin America Fell Behind: Essays on the Economic Histories of Brazil and Mexico, 1800–1914* (Stanford: Stanford University Press, 1997). For a discussion of the persistence of this backwardness in the mid to late twentieth century, see A. M. Taylor, "On the Costs of Inward-Looking Development: Price Distortions, Growth, and Divergence in Latin America," *Journal of Economic History* 58 (March 1998): 1–28.

the region—like the rest of the periphery—could not match the core during the initial burst of the Industrial Revolution in early nineteenth century Europe and North America. But as global markets developed in the nineteenth century, and as labor, capital, and technology migrated between countries ever more freely, some economies at the periphery seemed poised to experience a long-awaited catching up.[2] Unfortunately, after 1914, the experience of two world wars and a Great Depression wrecked much of that global economy and with it, some argue, the chances for convergence that seemed so likely before 1914. Only recently has a rebuilt global economy started to reemerge from the various crises and aftershocks of the twentieth century.[3]

It is one task of economic historians to document these times and provide some measure of explanation for the economic, political, and institutional changes that defined them. For variety and volatility of economic experience in this century, no region can surpass—and therefore perhaps no region can be more instructive—than Latin America. Latin America began the twentieth century as a follower, a relatively poor region on the periphery of the world

2. A good example would be Argentina, perhaps the most infamous case of economic development potential unfulfilled. See A. M. Taylor, "External Dependence, Demographic Burdens and Argentine Economic Decline after the *Belle Époque*," *Journal of Economic History* 52 (December 1992): 907–36; Taylor, "Tres fases del crecimiento económico argentino," *Revista de Historia Económica* 12 (Otoño 1994): 649–83; Taylor, "Three Phases of Argentine Economic Growth," Working Paper series on Historical Factors in Long Run Growth, No. 60, National Bureau of Economic Research, October 1994.

3. See M. Abramovitz, "Catching Up, Forging Ahead, and Falling Behind," *Journal of Economic History* 46 (June 1986): 385–406; W. Baumol, "Productivity Growth, Convergence and Welfare: What the Long-Run Data Show," *American Economic Review* 76 (December 1986): 1072–85; A. Maddison, *Dynamic Forces in Capitalist Development: A Long-Run Comparative View* (Oxford: Oxford University Press, 1991); J. D. Sachs and A. M. Warner, "Economic Reform and the Process of Global Integration," *Brookings Papers on Economic Activity*, 1995, pp. 1–118; and J. G. Williamson, "Globalization, Convergence, and History," *Journal of Economic History* 56 (June 1996): 277–306.

economy, but it ended the twentieth century even further behind the leaders (see table 1 and figure 1). Today's best estimates of historical trends in income show that in 1900 Latin America's average level of income per capita was well below that of the leading economies of the core—the countries in Europe, North America, and the modern Organization for Economic Cooperation and Development (OECD). Some countries in the region were much richer than others, however, and countries with nascent industrial sectors and other signs of modernization had a narrower income gap. Among them were the settler economies of Chile and Argentina, and Mexico, which, after sluggish growth for much of the nineteenth century, grew rapidly during the Porfiriato (1876–1911).[4]

The overall picture of Latin American development began to change after 1929 and more dramatically after 1950 and during the postwar period.[5] The region's economies started to experience

---

4. As noted by Coatsworth, "Economic Retardation and Growth" and "Economic and Institutional Trajectories," it is inappropriate to speak of Latin America's falling behind in the eighteenth and nineteenth centuries as a uniform and homogeneous feature of the region. Some countries fell far behind, such as Mexico and Brazil, motivating the title of Haber (1997), *How Latin America Fell Behind*. Others had decent growth performance compared to much of Europe, if not to the "exceptionalism" of the United States, and even caught up with the core economies, Argentina being just the finest example. Thus, the idea that colonial institutions or factor endowments ensured some deterministic, path-dependent, or path-influenced descent into underdevelopment for the region as a whole requires careful consideration when pursued on a country-by-country basis. Spatial and temporal variations in economic performance were considerable (S. L. Engerman and K. L. Sokoloff, "Factor Endowments, Institutions, and Differential Paths of Growth among New World Economies: A View from Economic Historians of the United States," in Haber, *How Latin America Fell Behind*; D. C. North, *Institutions, Institutional Change, and Economic Performance* [Cambridge, Eng.: Cambridge University Press, 1990]). The same is true of the twentieth century, when still more candidates for causes of underdevelopment can be identified, such as the rejection of openness in trade and capital markets as discussed below, despite the region's open stance since the colonial era.

5. The standard reference is C. F. Díaz Alejandro, "The 1940s in Latin America," in M. Syrquin, L. Taylor, and L. E. Westphal, eds., *Economic Structure and Perfor-*

TABLE 1
Income per Capita, 1900–1990

	GDP PER CAPITA IN 1980 INTERNATIONAL DOLLARS					
	1900	*1913*	*1929*	*1950*	*1973*	*1987*
Argentina	$1,284	$1,770	$2,036	$2,324	$3,713	$3,302
Brazil	436	521	654	1,073	2,504	3,417
Chile	956	1,255	1,928	2,350	3,309	3,393
Colombia	610	801	975	1,395	2,318	3,027
Mexico	649	822	835	1,169	2,349	2,667
Peru	624	819	890	1,349	2,357	2,380
Latin American average	760	998	1,220	1,610	2,758	3,031
Asian average	485	539	601	505	1,061	1,952
NICs average*	492	532	690	545	1,939	4,444
Organization for Economic Cooperation and Development (OECD) average	1,817	2,224	2,727	3,553	7,852	10,205

*NICs refers to newly industrialized countries; in Maddison's data base Taiwan and South Korea.
SOURCE: A. Maddison, *The World Economy in the 20th Century* (Paris: OECD, 1989).

slower rates of growth on average as compared to the rest of the world, notably relative to the core and to certain fast-growing Asian economies; these differential growth rates implied a falling behind, or divergence, in levels of income per capita. In 1900, the Latin American income level was well above that in Asia and stood at 41 percent of the OECD core. In 1950, Latin American gross domestic product (GDP) per capita was 45 percent of the OECD core level

mance: Essays in Honor of Hollis B. Chenery (Orlando, Fla.: Academic Press, 1984) and "Latin America in the 1930s," in R. Thorp, ed., *Latin America in the 1930s: The Role of the Periphery in World Crisis* (New York: St. Martin's Press, 1984), who identified 1929 as the major turning point, though not the only one. For an analysis that extends to the present day, see Taylor, "On the Costs of Inward-Looking Development."

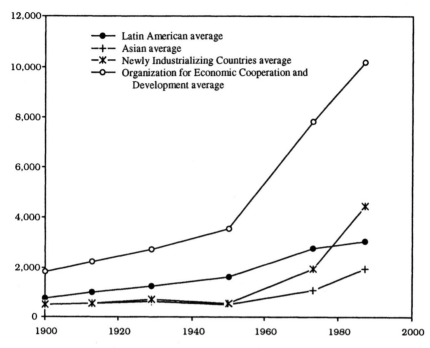

Figure 1   Convergence and Divergence of Income per Capita, 1900–1990 (in 1980 international dollars) *Source:* A. Maddison, *The World Economy in the 20th Century* (Paris: Organization for Economic Cooperation and Development, 1989).

and more than three times the Asian average. But by the 1980s Latin America had fallen back to less than one-third the OECD level and was being approached and overtaken by parts of Asia. This twentieth-century relative retardation and slump in living standards is Latin America's burden of history and remains a central, burning issue in the region's political, social, and economic landscape. In countries that have fallen a great distance in economic terms, such as Argentina—one of the richest economies in the world circa 1900—the burden is great indeed. Unraveling this history and identifying the lessons for today are key challenges for social scientists studying the region.

One obvious way to approach the study of Latin America's growth performance is via the theory and empirics of economic growth. My preference here is to begin with the simplest, and, its proponents still say, the most relevant model of growth as applied to modern experience: the neoclassical theory of growth according to Robert Solow.[6] This theory centers on the accumulation of capital; a low level of income per person is essentially a result of capital scarcity. The production function for output is of the form $Y = AK^aL^{1-a}$. For a given technology A, and labor force L, improvements in output per worker $(Y/L) = (K/L)^a$ are driven by increases in the capital-labor ratio (K/L). This process of *capital deepening* requires, in conventional cases of constant or expanding labor force L, some capital accumulation (increases in K, $\Delta K > 0$). Accumulation occurs via investment ($\Delta K =$ Investment), that is, by the expansion in the quantity of machines, equipment, durable producer goods, land improvements, infrastructure, and so on.[7]

The neoclassical growth model remains one of the most robust explanations for economic growth in the twentieth century, both for wide cross sections of countries, and for Latin America itself.[8] I

6. The seminal piece is R. M. Solow, "A Contribution to the Theory of Economic Growth," *Quarterly Journal of Economics* 70 (February 1956): 65–94. For a survey of endogenous growth and its empirical relevance, see P. M. Romer, "The Origins of Endogenous Growth," *Journal of Economic Perspectives* 8 (winter 1994): 3–22; and H. Pack, "Endogenous Growth: Intellectual Appeal and Empirical Shortcomings," *Journal of Economic Perspectives* 8 (winter 1994): 55–72. Proponents of the neoclassical model include N. G. Mankiw, "The Growth of Nations," *Brookings Papers on Economic Activity* 1 (1995): 275–310; and R. J. Barro and X. Sala-i-Martin, *Economic Growth* (New York: McGraw-Hill, 1995).

7. It is simple to extend the neoclassical model to embrace the notion of human capital accumulation, including skills, knowledge, and research.

8. Influential empirical papers supporting the model came from S. Dowrick and D.-T. Nguyen, "OECD Comparative Economic Growth 1950–85: Catch-Up and Convergence," *American Economic Review* 79 (December 1989): 1010–30; and N. G. Mankiw, D. Romer, and D. N. Weil, "A Contribution to the Empirics of Economic Growth," *Quarterly Journal of Economics* 107 (May 1992): 407–37. For a large body of empirical results, see Barro and Sala-i-Martin, *Economic Growth*. A

especially want to appeal to its relevance in a global economy context, however, with potentially open economies embedded in world markets. Although in its original form the model applied to a closed economy, where investment equals savings, its implications for an open economy are easily derived.[9] In an open economy we must direct our attention to two sources of capital. Accumulation of capital requires either the mobilization of domestic capital through savings or large inflows of foreign capital.[10] In simple terms,

Investment = Domestic savings + Foreign savings;

that is, every dollar used in investment for the future has to be financed one way or another, either by domestic agents sacrificing

thorough sensitivity analysis was offered by R. Levine and D. Renelt, "A Sensitivity Analysis of Cross-Country Growth Regressions," *American Economic Review* 82 (September 1992): 942–63, emphasizing the robustness of the investment-growth relationship. I have found the neoclassical approach useful as a means to study long-run economic growth in the case of Argentina (Taylor, "Three Phases of Argentine Economic Growth," and "Tres fases del económico argentino") and the region as a whole (Taylor, "On the Costs of Inward-Looking Development"), with similar emphasis on investment as a major source of growth.

9. A basic open economy model is presented in O. J. Blanchard and S. Fischer, *Lectures on Macroeconomics* (Cambridge, Mass.: MIT Press, 1989).

10. A national income identity implies that gross national product (GNP), or output (Q), and imports (M) may be allocated for private consumption spending (C), private investment spending (I), government spending (G), and exports (X). Thus $Q + M = C + I + G + X$. Adding to both sides of this equality net factor income from abroad—for simplicity interest payments (rB) from net claims on foreigners (B) bearing interest (r) and rearranging—we obtain an expression for gross domestic product (GDP), (Y), $Y = Q + rB = C + I + G + (X - M) + rB$. The latter two terms are the external balance, or balance on the current account, $CA = (X - M) + rB$, equal to the trade balance plus nontrade net income from abroad. Rearranging, we obtain the current account identity, where $CA = S - I$, and S is national savings, $S = Y - C - I - G$. An inflow of capital occurs when CA is negative, and we may define foreign savings (or net foreign investment) as $S_F = NFI = -CA$. Thus, $I = S + S_F$.

TABLE 2

Foreign Investment in Latin America and Asia, 1900–1990

	FOREIGN INVESTMENT/GROSS DOMESTIC PRODUCT							
	1900	*1914*	*1929*	*1938*	*1950*	*1970*	*1980*	*1990*
Argentina	4.15	2.60	1.12	0.87	0.12	0.14	0.23	0.64 *
Brazil	2.55	2.96	0.92	0.70	0.18	0.17	0.32	0.36
Chile	1.88	2.11	1.56	1.63	0.49	0.38	0.27	0.40
Colombia	0.74	0.27	0.34	0.35	0.24	0.19	0.13	0.21
Mexico	1.55	1.83	1.28	0.79	0.17	0.12	0.23	0.32
Peru	1.78	1.21	0.64	0.46	0.22	0.22	0.32	0.48
Uruguay	3.14	1.62	0.67	0.59	0.18	0.13	—	0.31 *
Venezuela	2.52	0.98	1.05	0.73	0.55	0.36	0.32	0.47
India	0.25	0.34	0.30	0.45	0.08	0.18	0.11	0.25
Indonesia	0.62	0.95	1.11	1.29	—	0.29	0.66	1.68
Malaysia	—	1.48	1.04	0.79	—	0.33	0.29	0.58
Philippines	—	0.17	0.22	—	—	0.34	0.29	0.58
Thailand	—	0.38	0.35	0.30	—	0.16	0.21	0.33

SOURCE: M. J. Twomey, "Patterns of Foreign Investment in the Third World in the Twentieth Century," in J. H. Coatsworth and A. M. Taylor, eds., *Latin America and the World Economy in the Nineteenth and Twentieth Centuries: Explorations in Quantitative Economic History* (Cambridge, Mass.: Harvard University Press, 1989).

*Data shown are from 1989.

consumption and generating an investable surplus of savings or by foreigners being willing to do likewise.

Thus, if we can explain changes in investment via changes in the incentives or barriers for accumulation, and so account for the responses of domestic and foreign savings, we have a potentially useful theory of long-run growth in a world of open, or even imperfectly open, economies. The simplest data from Latin America's twentieth-century history offer at least prima facie evidence that the degree of integration in world capital markets (or, conversely, the extent of barriers or imperfections in such markets) was some-

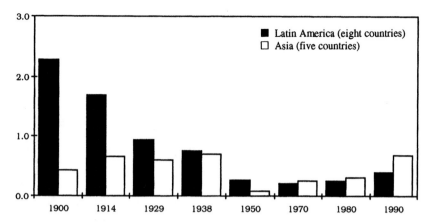

Figure 2   Foreign Investment in Latin America and Asia, 1900–1990 (as a share of GDP) *Source:* Simple unweighted averages, as listed in table 2. M. J. Twomey, "Patterns of Foreign Investment in the Third World in the Twentieth Century," in J. H. Coatsworth and A. M. Taylor, eds., *Latin America and the World Economy in the Nineteenth and Twentieth Centuries: Explorations in Quantitative Economic History* (Cambridge, Mass.: Harvard University Press, 1989).

how related to economic growth performance[11] (see table 2 and figure 2). For example, during a period of respectable economic performance before the Great Depression, Latin America's capital inflows were large by global standards: very large before 1914, and still substantial even up to the 1930s. But after the 1930s, Latin America received relatively less foreign capital than other peripheral regions—the Asian economies, for example, most of whom, as we saw above, exhibited much faster postwar economic growth than did the Latin American group.

11. For an exhaustive study of long-run movements of capital flows in the world economy, we are indebted here to the work of M. J. Twomey, "Patterns of Foreign Investment in the Third World in the Twentieth Century," in J. H. Coatsworth and A. M. Taylor, eds., *Latin America and the World Economy in the Nineteenth and Twentieth Centuries: Explorations in Quantitative Economic History* (Cambridge, Mass.: Harvard University Press, 1998).

From this introductory review of the macroeconomic historical evidence two things stand out: First, since the early years of the century Latin American growth performance has been disappointing, exhibiting retardation relative to the core, especially after the 1930s. Second, we also find evidence that foreign capital, though it retreated in importance in many countries in the autarkic years after the 1930s, apparently retreated further and faster in the case of Latin America. What remains to be asked is what causal connections exist between these two correlated events. My analysis centers on an examination of interventions in international markets that affected the integration of Latin America in the global economy. Since my focus is the capital market, it is natural to begin with a discussion of the emergence of explicit capital controls. In the next section I trace the emergence of capital controls in the 1930s and their subsequent evolution and pervasive effects on investment prices and quantities—and thus growth—in the postwar period.

The Great Depression as a Watershed in Capital Markets

The Great Depression is conventionally depicted as a turning point in Latin America for commercial policy and protectionism and as marking the onset of import substitution and a long-run increase in barriers in international *goods markets*. This perspective is evident in almost all works, and the discussion of trade distortions is now standard textbook material.[12] I will not argue that this description is

12. See, for example, A. Fishlow, "Origins and Consequences of Import Substitution in Brazil," in L.E.D. Marco, ed., *International Economics and Development: Essays in Honor of Raúl Prebisch* (New York: Academic Press, 1971); R. Thorp, "A Reappraisal of the Origins of Import-Substituting Industrialisation: 1930–1950," in T. Halperín Donghi, ed., *The Colonial and Post-colonial Experience: Five Centuries of Spanish and Portuguese America*, Quincentenary Supplement, *Journal of Latin American Studies* (Cambridge: Cambridge University Press, 1992); E. Cardoso and A. Fishlow, "Latin American Development: 1950–1980," *Journal of Latin American Studies* 24 (1992): 197–218; E. Cardoso and A. Helwege, *Latin America's Economy: Diver-

incorrect. Instead, I maintain it is incomplete; a complementary analysis exists with a quite different emphasis on capital markets. Moreover, in terms of economic theories of long-run growth, this new emphasis offers what I will argue is a clearer and more plausible explanation for the dynamic losses involved in the relative slowdown and divergence of the region's economies.[13]

Thus, this chapter argues that the policy response of the 1930s, and the subsequent economic retardation, can be better understood as the cause and effect of the creation of long-run barriers in international *capital markets*. The argument proceeds in the present section in three parts.

First, I discuss the emergence of capital controls in the 1930s as the prototypical or archetypal market intervention that set the stage for later distortions in the capital market price system in Latin American economies. This requires an understanding of the gold standard system that collapsed in the 1930s and the macropolicy responses that characterized government reactions throughout the region and, for comparison, the world.

Second, I trace the region's subsequent postwar distortions that descended from the interventions of the 1930s and evolved within a macropolicy framework that had a high tolerance for price distortions at the international level. The evidence here reviews data on the black markets for currency, tariffs, and investment goods prices to get a general picture of barriers to accumulation.

Third, I review analyses of the growth or welfare implications of these distortions. The overall aim here is to show not only that

---

sity Trends and Conflicts (Cambridge, Mass.: MIT Press, 1992); S. Edwards, *Crisis and Reform in Latin America: From Despair to Hope* (New York: Oxford University Press, 1995); and V. Bulmer-Thomas, *The Economic History of Latin America since Independence* (Cambridge, Eng.: Cambridge University Press, 1994); "The Latin American Economies in the 1930s," in L. Bethell, ed., *The Cambridge History of Latin America*, vol. 6 (Cambridge, Eng.: Cambridge University Press, 1996).

13. In contrast, trade theories offer only an explanation for static losses.

distortions existed but that they had negative effects that were quantitatively and statistically significant. Here I have time for only a brief survey of the enormous literature on this topic.

Capital Controls in the 1930s

One almost universal feature of the global economy of the late nineteenth century was the virtually complete absence of capital controls. Indeed free migration of labor, and, for the most part, a liberal regime of low trade barriers, was the norm, albeit with some exceptions. This laissez-faire economic orthodoxy reached full expression in capital markets, in the financial world, and in the form of monetary standards built around the gold standard, fixed exchange rates, free convertibility, and unfettered movement of capital.[14] In this "golden age" did Keynes's stereotypical pajama-clad investor consume breakfast in bed in London while telephoning a broker to bid his investments move hither and yon around the world without let or hindrance.[15]

Governments believed their credibility rested on their ability to adhere to and sustain this system, so that, even during World War I, the general belief was that a return to gold was paramount and that the capital controls enacted by various countries, especially the belligerents, were merely a temporary expedient.[16] The literature on

14. See M. Edelstein, *Overseas Investment in the Age of High Imperialism* (New York: Columbia University Press, 1982); B. J. Eichengreen, *Golden Fetters: The Gold Standard and the Great Depression, 1919–1939* (Oxford, Eng.: Oxford University Press, 1992); *Globalizing Capital: A History of the International Monetary System* (Princeton, N.J.: Princeton University Press, 1996).

15. Keynes, quoted in L. B. Yeager, *International Monetary Relations: Theory, History, and Policy*, 2d ed. (New York: Harper and Row, 1976).

16. P. Einzig, *Exchange Control* (London: Macmillan, 1934); Eichengreen, *Golden Fetters* and *Globalizing Capital*; M. Obstfeld and A. M. Taylor, "The Great Depression as a Watershed: International Capital Mobility in the Long Run," in M. D. Bordo, C. D. Goldin, and E. N. White, eds., *The Defining Moment: The Great Depression and the American Economy in the Twentieth Century* (Chicago: University of Chicago Press, 1998).

the collapse of the interwar gold standard indicates that various forces—including crises of expectations, asymmetries in the equilibrating mechanism, recent memories of hyperinflation in some countries, increased speculation in expanding future markets, and temptations for competitive devaluation—all rendered the gold standard "unsafe for use" in the 1920s and 1930s, at least when governments came under increased pressure after 1929 to engage in macroeconomic management to stave off the threat of deflation and depression.[17]

In such an imploding world economy, countries on the brink of a crippling gold outflow had no choice but to "break the rules of the game" (or lose all their gold reserves and have the decision made for them sooner or later). They could turn to a blunt and noninstantaneous instrument like devaluation to salvage their external balances, or, in more desperate straits, they could end gold drain by fiat, by imposing capital controls. This breakdown of the old regime began in the core (with Britain's departure from gold) in late 1931. As other countries followed, some chose devaluation, mostly the countries of northwest Europe and its new world offshoots; some chose controls, chiefly Germany and its trading partners in central and eastern Europe. In Latin America, as elsewhere in the periphery, the crisis struck much earlier, and many economies had abandoned the gold standard with devaluations in 1928 and 1929, as their terms of trade collapsed and payments problems became severe. By the early 1930s, as problems continued, many were ready to go further and combine devaluations with capital control measures.

For the timing of capital controls in Latin America in the 1930s, see table 3. A clear dichotomy exists between a group of controllers, including many of the larger countries of the region, notably the

17. Eichengreen, *Golden Fetters* and *Globalizing Capital*; P. Temin, *Lessons from the Great Depression* (Cambridge, Mass.: MIT Press, 1989).

TABLE 3

Latin America's Adoption of Capital Controls as of 1939

Country	EXCHANGE CONTROL, 1930–39			FREE MARKET ACTIVITY			
	None	Begun	Abolished	Toler-ated	Con-trols	None	Black Market
Argentina		1931			•		
Bolivia		1931			•		•
Brazil		1931				•	
Chile		1931			•		
Colombia		1931				•	•
Costa Rica		1932			•		
Cuba	•			•			
Dominican Republic	•			•			
Ecuador		1933	1937	•			
El Salvador	•			•			
Guatemala	•			•			
Haiti	•			•			
Honduras		1934				•	
Mexico	•			•			
Nicaragua		1932			•		
Panama	•			•			
Paraguay		1932					
Peru	•			•			
Uruguay		1932				•	
Venezuela		1936		•			

SOURCE: H. M. Bratter, "Foreign Exchange Control in Latin America," *Foreign Policy Reports* 14 (1939): 274–88.

southern cone (Argentina, Brazil, and Chile) and a set of smaller countries in the region, especially in Central America, all of whom eschewed controls. This division is often referred to as the partition of the region into *reactive* and *passive* countries, as they were termed by Díaz Alejandro.

Usually this classification is seen as being principally derived from a response to *external* political and economic forces.[18] For example, consider a small Caribbean or Central American country subject to U.S. foreign policy pressure, perhaps in the form of gunboats, and heavily reliant on U.S. export markets and finance. That country might be afraid to devalue and enact controls, fearing retaliatory action by the dominant military and economic power in the hemisphere. Indeed, the past experience of many countries had shown the lengths to which the United States might go to protect its overseas economic interests. Conversely, larger countries, or those more distant from the United States (hence, more powerful and independent), could more easily make the choice to break the rules and deviate from the orthodoxy, even before the United States itself did in 1933.

This depiction of Latin American outcomes as being heavily dependent on external forces is surely relevant in a setting of small, open economies at the periphery, all of whom have little power to affect global political or economic conditions, most of which they must take as given.[19] For some countries the external political costs of policy deviation were, indeed, substantial—for example, Cuba or Mexico or Central America under the influence of U.S. foreign and economic policy. As I argue later, however, leaving the story here may be too restrictive and may lean too far toward monocausality in emphasizing external forces as the main determinant of outcomes in the region.

Postwar Distortions

Events of the 1930s interest us when considering the determinants of long-run economic performance in Latin America because

18. Díaz Alejandro, "Latin America in the 1930s."
19. One can envisage a few exceptions; for example, Brazil might have some market power in coffee.

the immediate responses to those events were not merely reactions to transient external economic shocks, but were also responses that revealed some other characteristics of these countries.

That the responses were persistent we can detect from the nature of postwar distortions in these economies. After the 1930s the structure of exchange controls varied greatly, and in some places tariffs replaced or complemented multiple exchange-rate regimes. The extent of controls is therefore best evaluated using multiple criteria relevant to the capital market that pick up various kinds of distortions, such as black market premiums on the currency, the extent of tariffs, distortions to relative capital prices, and currency depreciation.

I claim that, even late in the postwar period and despite numerous policy changes along the way by various countries, the basic passive-reactive categorization proposed by Díaz Alejandro for the 1930s remained relevant. Still decades later the larger and more southerly countries tended to be the ones with large distortions and interventions; typically, the passive countries of the 1930s—the smaller and more northerly group of countries—had the smaller distortions. The quantitative evidence appears in table 4, drawn from another paper.[20]

The persistence in policy response is not surprising if the response, instead of being merely a reaction to fleeting adverse *external* conditions in the crisis of the 1930s, reflected deeper characteristics of the polity in each country, that is, *internal* conditions less subject to change. Clear candidates in the sphere of domestic political conditions include a country's degree of democracy; the acces-

---

20. However, this finding does not contradict earlier quantitative and historical descriptions of the nature of policy choices in Latin America since the onset of inward-looking strategies in the 1950s. Always in the vanguard of such policies were countries such as the southern cone group.

TABLE 4

Distortions in Latin America and Elsewhere, 1970–1990

	Black Market Premium on Currency	Own-Weight Tariff Incidence	Log Relative Price of Capital Goods	Rate of Depreciation of Currency
All countries	0.27	0.17	0.44	0.10
Asia Pacific	0.06	0.13	0.23	0.02
Latin America	0.26	0.22	0.27	0.37
Southern cone	0.32	0.27	0.19	0.60

SOURCE: A. M. Taylor, "On the Costs of Inward-Looking Development: Price Distortions, Growth, and Divergence in Latin America," *Journal of Economic History* 58 (March 1998): 1–28.

sibility or plurality of the government system, especially for weak or marginal groups; the centralization of power; the general education of the populace as it might affect demands for representation; and so on. All these factors could accentuate political pressure for active intervention.

Moreover, we have reason to suspect that all these characteristics more or less fit into the story, within and beyond Latin America. Arguably, the southern cone countries, by the early twentieth century, did tend to resemble the core countries more closely, with more developed educational systems, a more developed democratic tradition, and a broader franchise. In countries like Argentina, Chile, and Brazil these populist social and political pressures have figured heavily. Yet such pressures should also have had economic consequences, especially in the policy vacuum of the 1930s following the collapse of the gold standard and, we guess, in line with the theories already suggested for these forces as they worked in the core. Conversely, conventional wisdom suggests, countries in Central America experienced much less populist pressure, had on average less broadly representative government, and so on—predicting, based on our working theoretical hypotheses, that they would have had less inclination toward interventions and controls to temper external forces in the capital market.

Let us take the argument a stage further, for a global comparison, and use an extreme example for illustration. We can recognize a marked contrast between the populist pressure generated in, say, post-1945 Argentina by the *descamisados*, assorted unions and corporatist groups, and all the other lobbies, compared with, say, the almost complete absence of protests, populism, and political turmoil in a state such as Singapore. The same contrast might well hold for almost any comparison of the reactive, and even some in the passive, group in Latin America and the East Asian fast-growing economies (South Korea, Taiwan, Hong Kong, and Singapore). Thus the perspective advanced here also has the potential to explain policy outcomes in Latin America as compared to its usual developing-country benchmark, the more economically successful and more outward-oriented countries of East Asia.

What remains is to see how feasible it is to try to measure and quantify these differences in politics and regimes and to see whether the putative relationship with policy outcomes has empirical content. But, first, we will spend a moment confirming the ultimate claim that these interventions and distortions, as they resulted from the domestic political process, did indeed have implications for economic performance.

Growth Implications

The discussion of the role of capital market interventions and their resulting price distortions would be irrelevant if it could not show that such policies had implications for historical development experience. The literature on the role of such distortions as a detriment to growth is now extensive and does not require full recapitulation here.[21] Suffice it to state here the relevant results as applied to the Latin American case. In another paper devoted to this topic, and covering experience since the 1930s, I have examined the size of distortions and, for the 1970s and 1980s, used econometric estimations to figure their importance for investment and economic growth.[22]

The comparative data show that Latin America's distortions were much higher than the Asian group in almost all areas (see table 4). In the same paper I also showed that this went along with lower investment rates and growth rates in Latin America versus Asia; for example, between 1970 and 1990, investment rates in the two regions were 16 percent versus 23 percent, and growth rates of per capita income, 0.5 percent versus 3.4 percent. Econometric counterfactual analysis (not repeated here) showed that distortions had a paramount and robust role in depressing Latin America's rate of accumulation of capital and, hence, the rate of growth. All the differences in investment rates can be explained by this exercise and, thus, about half the implied differences in growth rates.[23]

The purpose of this brief section is merely to motivate the search for the underlying determinants of these detrimental policies in the political and institutional environment of the countries themselves.

21. See, for example, J. B. De Long and L. H. Summers, "Equipment Investment and Economic Growth," *Quarterly Journal of Economics* 106 (May 1991): 445–502; W. Easterly, "How Much Do Distortions Affect Growth?" *Journal of Monetary Economics* 32 (1993): 187–212; S. Edwards, "Trade Orientation, Distortions and Growth in Developing Countries," *Journal of Development Economics* 39 (1992): 31–57; and C. I. Jones, "Economic Growth and the Relative Price of Capital," *Journal of Monetary Economics* 34 (1994): 359–82. All these studies find a strong negative correlation between price distortions on the one hand and investment or growth on the other.

22. See Taylor, "On the Costs of Inward-Looking Development."

23. It bears repeating that I am not in search of a monocausal explanation here, but I do claim any factors that can explain between 50 and 100 percent of Latin America's retardation in the growth of output and capital demand at least some attention.

It matters because the reference group, the Asian group, though initially subject to a similar inward-looking response as almost every other economy in the 1930s, 1940s, and 1950s, did eventually reform and embrace policies favoring integration into the global economy. Latin American countries, almost without exception, did not.[24] Objective distortion measures for the Asian group were little different than the Latin group in the early postwar period.[25] But after 1970 the differences were marked, as were the different economic outcomes. The bigger question is how to identify the institutional obstacles that prevented Latin America from taking the same route to early economic reforms, reforms that are now happening belatedly and, some critics suggest, only halfheartedly.[26]

Given space constraints, this section has reviewed the evidence on distortions and growth since the Great Depression. The hope was to persuade the reader, first, that distortions existed and, second, that they mattered for long-run economic outcomes. A purely economic analysis might end here, with an appeal to theory, and further appropriate testing for robustness, to claim that distortions were somehow causally responsible for the growth outcome. Indeed, because this has been the ending point for many such studies, the point is widely accepted.[27]

Such an end point is still unsatisfying, for it begs further questions: why did such distortions emerge in the first place, and why

---

24. It is the exception that proves the rule, perhaps. The exception might be Chile, which did engage in free market reforms in the 1970s. However, this was under a military dictatorship that aimed to squash populist pressures and resembling, therefore, the more centralized and autocratic pressures at work in Asian regimes.

25. See Taylor, "On the Costs of Inward-Looking Development."

26. See Edwards, *Crisis and Reform in Latin America.*

27. See, for example, the earlier cited studies: De Long and Summers (1991); Easterly, "How Much Do Distortions Affect Growth?"; Edwards, "Trade Orientation"; and Jones, "Economic Growth."

did they persist in the long run? These implicitly comparative puzzles, of course, have great bearing on the question of why Latin America's twentieth-century economic institutions have evolved in such a peculiar fashion as compared to other regions of the world. To answer them, we need to fashion some tool for exploring the political economy of policy choice during the Great Depression and the decades that followed.

Political Factors in the Core and Periphery

Beginning with the collapse of the gold standard, Latin America's macropolicy response began its long and wayward course, so it is natural to start there. In fact, macroeconomic historians have already proposed some models for understanding the nature of macropolicy responses in the 1930s. Those models revolve around a simple policy "trilemma" that confronts policymakers facing pressures from different constituencies to achieve three mutually inconsistent goals: exchange-rate stability, free capital mobility, and macroeconomic stability (e.g., full employment). So far the models have been used mostly to understand the response of the core economies, notably Britain, Germany, France, and the United States, plus certain other European and New World economies.[28]

The conjecture I wish to advance is that the political economy of institutional changes in the 1930s *in the periphery* might be understood in more or less the same terms economic historians have used to discuss the macroeconomic crisis of the gold standard *in the core*. Such a political-economy model might thus have universal, global (rather than core-specific) value if it can predict the reactive and passive responses by periphery countries to external shocks.

---

28. See Eichengreen, *Globalizing Capital;* and Obstfeld and Taylor, "The Great Depression as a Watershed."

The conjecture seems like a desirable but difficult goal, though in this chapter I can only sketch some ideas and implications and fall far short of proof. Should the conjecture apply, it would lend more credibility and applicability to the theory and would have intrinsic methodological appeal, as we place a premium on models that apply to a class of different cases, rather than requiring a different story for each and every situation.

The model is simply laid out. At the start, under a fixed exchange-rate system, such as the gold standard, and in an open economy with free capital mobility, policymakers have no power to use monetary policy as an instrument for manipulating the domestic economy. Essentially, monetary policy is endogenous, as domestic interest rates are set by the world market and via the arbitrage actions of the capital. Any attempt to move the interest rate is futile; it would entail the loss (or gain) of reserves for a temporary (if any) decline (respectively, rise) in domestic interest rates. Thus was monetary policy depoliticized under the gold standard; no objectives were attainable so the instrument was never touched.

For the core at least, all this changed, it is argued, with the onset of the Great Depression and, preceding it, a gradual but profound change in the power of various constituencies in the political process, notably the influence of working-class groups and parties. Gold standard orthodoxy had satisfied the interests of bankers, financiers, and others but ill-served the working class; in times of boom abroad or bust at home, the authorities could make no attempt to temper the force of recession by easy monetary policy. Consequently, unemployment in crises could be severe yet be dismissed as beyond the scope of national economic policy. Such a view is not taken today because, in the 1930s, governments broke the rules of the game and allowed monetary policy into their tool kit. This happened in two ways: capital controls could be admitted, allowing monetary policy discretion without risk of capital movement, or a floating exchange-rate system could be introduced, allowing monetary policy to act freely without a need to defend the parity.

In Europe and the United States, the applicability of this kind of model to historical events in the core economies is now accepted, based on the seminal work of authors such as Peter Temin and Barry Eichengreen.[29] Democratic political institutions and the new broadening of the franchise were realities in the early twentieth century, likewise the growing influence of the poor and working-class groups. Only a few economies—the gold bloc of France, Netherlands, and Belgium—clung to the gold standard longer than was necessary in the 1930s, and they paid a heavy price in a world of deflation and economic collapse. By 1936, all core economies had given up the parity.[30]

But what can we say about events at the periphery? Might such a model, if it were more general, also illuminate the various responses of different countries outside the core? In particular, can it help us understand the evolution of policies and economic growth in Latin America? The idea is in marked contrast to explanations based on external conditions; older schools of thought, such as dependency theory and structuralism, have looked almost exclusively at external macroeconomic forces as being behind the ruin of the periphery.[31] More-recent historical critiques have challenged these approaches, not just for theoretical and empirical shortcomings, but also for a lack of attention to microeconomic, institutional, and political developments *internal* to Latin America as an explanation for

29. For more detail see Eichengreen, *Golden Fetters*; and Temin, *Lessons from the Great Depression*.

30. See Eichengreen, *Globalizing Capital*; and Obstfeld and Taylor, "The Great Depression as a Watershed."

31. See Cardoso and Helwege, *Latin America's Economy*, for an overview of such ideas associated with the Structuralists.

economic outcomes in the long run.[32] A reordering of research directions is warranted, some argue, to portray Latin American economic history more accurately as a process conditioned by both internal and external forces.

In this spirit, I suggest that we reconsider the history of macroeconomic policy in the same way and try to understand the 1930s policy responses of the economies as being potentially driven by internal forces. As we have seen, a theory we can take off the shelf applies the same analytic devices to describe the core economies and suggests that the path chosen by policymakers is explicable in terms of domestic politics. Thus, for example, the theory predicts that rising democratic and pluralistic forces raised the likelihood of deviation from the gold standard.[33] The question for Latin America is, can we detect such a link between domestic politics and policy outcomes? And does it matter for only the 1930s, or can it also explain policy persistence?

To explore this hypothesis, we need to quantify two features of economic developments and political institutions since the 1930s. First, we need measures of policy response at various junctures, such as capital controls, black market activity, and price distortions. Second, the much more subjective measures of political institutions will tell us something about how susceptible economic policies were to broad democratic forces in general, and the influence of less-privileged groups in particular. To make the challenge harder, we

---

32. For a trenchant critique, see S. Haber, "Introduction: Economic Growth and Latin American Economic Historiography," in Haber, *How Latin America Fell Behind*.

33. An example would be France in the 1920s, and the demands of various class groups that the fiscal burden be shifted, producing stalemate and delaying a return to the gold standard. Another example would be Britain in the 1920s, and the miners' strikes and general strikes in response to the strictures of a tight monetary policy designed to deflate the price level towards its purchasing-power-parity level, with the pound overvalued at resumption.

need these measures for many countries at many different points in time.

In terms of measuring policies we have already seen a wide range of data. We can see which countries enacted controls in the 1930s and how these policies evolved into multifaceted distortions by the 1950s, 1960s, and beyond.[34] Thus we can provide measures of policy response. In terms of measuring political institutions we are on more difficult ground, as expected. However, the results of the Polity project can be employed here.[35] The Polity database supplies annual data series on regime type and political authority for 177 countries since 1800—series that include measures of democracy, autocracy, the breadth of the political process and its accessibility to various groups, and so on. Combining all the political and economic data, we can try to explore how political conditions shaped macropolicy response in the 1930s and afterward.

Looking first at the 1930s, if we seek evidence that the core type of gold standard political economy model might function as a model for the periphery, then we need evidence that passive and reactive states were distinguished by very different internal domestic politi-

34. The application of the trilemma idea to Latin America may appear not so straightforward. We have noted already that for many countries in the region, an initial attempt to resolve the trilemma through devaluation proved insufficient, and many then turned to controls as an auxiliary device. In general, the trilemma must be seen as encompassing "mixed strategies" of this sort; partial use of both devaluation and capital control tools may, jointly, suffice to relieve tensions. It is a matter of judgment; then, to decide which constraint is really binding and, therefore, which policy move was critical. Implicitly, I am taking the position that if, in the 1930s, the floating rate proved insufficient to solve the tensions (perhaps because it was a dirty float as was often the case, and controls were in the end necessary), then this constituted a controls-based strategy, as opposed to a true floating rate strategy with free capital mobility.

35. See K. Jaggers and T. R. Gurr, "Tracking Democracy's Third Wave with the Polity III Data," *Journal of Peace Research* 32 (1995): 469–82. The data were downloaded from ICPSR, file 6695.

cal characteristics. Since reactive in Latin America is synonymous with capital controls, it suffices to look for systematic differences between control and noncontrol countries in Latin America. Table 5, panel (a), shows a difference between the two groups that is consistent with the theory. The passive noncontrol countries were more autocratic and centralized and had less constraint on executive power, less regular and competitive participation in the political process, and less democratic regimes. All of this left them less exposed to populist pressure. Conversely, the reactive group had much more scope for popular pressure to feed into the political and economic decision-making process.

Panel (b) confirms the relationship by looking not at means but at correlations among the variables in the Latin American sample. The correlations tell a similar story and help us identify strongly collinear characteristics (e.g., autocracy is almost exactly opposite to democracy in many cases). Panel (b) also looks at the correlation of the political variables with the economic policy outcomes, both controls of the extent of devaluation. For the most part, the clearer correlations are between political variables and control outcomes. This is not surprising, as almost all countries were forced to devalue; it was only with respect to capital controls that differences emerged.

Panel (c) examines the statistical fit of the relationship for the most promising candidates, the variables *parcomp* and *democ*. *Democ*, a democracy measure, fares poorly, but *parcomp* does better, especially in explaining the imposition of controls—the definitive policy of the reactive group of countries. This is good news for the theory, for in the Polity III database the *parcomp* variable measures "the extent to which non-elites are able to access institutional structures of political expression." I think this variable succinctly summarizes the sociopolitical tensions that lie at the heart of the Eichengreen model of reaction against the gold standard in core

TABLE 5
Politics and Capital Controls in Latin America in the 1930s

(A) POLITICAL VARIABLES FOR CONTROL AND NONCONTROL COUNTRIES IN LATIN AMERICA

Control	Autoc	Democ	Xconst	Parreg	Parcomp	Cent
0	4.00	1.63	2.50	2.63	1.88	1.25
1	3.25	2.92	3.33	3.33	3.17	1.17

(B) CORRELATIONS OF POLITICAL VARIABLES WITH CONTROLS AND DEVALUATION IN LATIN AMERICA

	Autoc	Democ	Xconst	Parreg	Parcomp	Cent	Control	Deval
Autoc	1.000							
Democ	−0.712	1.000						
Xconst	−0.721	0.730	1.000					
Parreg	0.217	0.322	0.345	1.000				
Parcomp	−0.419	0.588	0.554	0.588	1.000			
Cent	0.064	−0.185	0.000	−0.016	0.091	1.000		
Control	−0.156	0.251	0.289	0.339	0.496	−0.068	1.000	
Deval	−0.413	−0.052	0.112	−0.593	0.338	0.322	−0.092	1.000

(C) REGRESSION MODEL: CONTROLS AND DEVALUATION WITH POLITICAL VARIABLES IN LATIN AMERICA

	Control	Control	Deval	Deval
Parcomp	0.19	—	3.78	—
	(2.42)		(1.14)	
Democ	—	0.05	—	−0.24
		(1.10)		(0.16)
R squared	.246	.063	.114	.003

SOURCE: The économic variables are from Bratter (*Control*) and the League of Nations Yearbooks (*Deval*). Controls takes the value 1 if controls were applied in the 1930s, 0 otherwise. *Deval* is equal to the percentage devaluation of the currency relative to gold parity as of January 1935.

NOTES: Political variables are for 1929 and are taken from the Polity III database. *Autoc* is a measure of autocracy, from 0 to 10; *democ* is a measure of democracy, from 0 to 10; *xconst* is a measure of constraints on the executive from 1 (unlimited authority) to 7 (executive party or subordination); *parreg* is a measure of the regulation of participation in the political process, from 0 (unregulated) to 5 (institutionalized); *parcomp* is a measure of the competitiveness of participation, from 0 (unregulated) to 5 (competitive); *cent* is a measure of centralization of state authority, from 1 (unitary) to 3 (federal).

TABLE 6

Politics and Distortions in Latin America and the Asian NICs in 1970

	Democ70	Par-comp70	Par-comp29	Bmp70	Owti	Owqi	Ppi70dev
NIC3	1.00	2.00	—	0.05	0.08	0.16	−0.17
Latin Passive	2.64	2.45	1.88	0.21	0.17	0.22	−0.02
Latin Reactive	3.75	3.00	3.17	0.34	0.23	0.28	0.20

NOTES AND SOURCES: For classification, NIC3 is South Korea, Taiwan, and Singapore (Hong Kong is omitted as political variables are not available for this nonsovereign state); Latin Passive are the group of countries who did not enact controls in the 1930s; Latin Reactive is the group that did based on Bratter. Democ70 is the democracy measure (0 to 10) for 1970; Parcomp70 and Parcomp29 are the competitiveness of participation measures (0 to 5) for 1970 and 1929; these three variables are from Polity III. Bmp70 is the black market premium in 1970, Owti the tariff incidence, Owqi the quota incidence, and Ppi70dev the percentage deviation of the relative price of investment goods from the world level, and these distortion measures are from Sachs and Warner.

economies as driven by newly enfranchised groups ready and able to challenge the old orthodoxy.

The finding here is that similar forces are also discernible in a set of peripheral economies. Although quantitative, and although statistical significance appears weak at present, the results are novel in that they support this well-established theory from the core in a new geographical setting, and they might be viewed as surprisingly good since the political data are essentially so subjective and prone to error. It is also reassuring that, although the political variables were collected for a project tracking democracy and peace, they do in fact have some relation to other political outcomes, here in the realm of economic policy.

It might be satisfactory if the story ended here, but we can ask the data to tell us much more. We know that the reactive policies of the 1930s persisted for decades. A tougher test is whether the political data can give any prediction of economic policy outcomes in the postwar era. Table 6 suggests they can and still be in line with the theory. Moreover, at the later date we can start to make some inter-regional comparisons. Three groups of countries are of interest circa 1970. First, we have the three successful fast-growing Asian newly industrialized countries (NICs). Then we have the historically passive Latin American group and finally the reactive Latin American group, with the distinction here based on 1930s policy response. Reactive policies tended to persist; the various distortion measures are clearly higher for the reactive group. Distortions are very low in the NIC3 group, as expected. As for the relationship of these economic policy outcomes, it is apparent that the subsamples more prone to populist pressures do experience more distortions. Less democratic and less competitive participation in the political process of the NICs is the accompaniment to noninterventionist policy. Passive Latin American countries come next with more populist pressures and more intervention. Lastly the reactive group has high levels of democracy and competitive participation in the political process. Following our previous finding it is tempting now to see whether this same pattern holds vis-à-vis the 1930s political situation. Choosing one variable—competitive participation—we do find a similar result (in the 1930s none of the NICs existed so this finding applies only to passive-versus-active Latin America).

The results of this section are, of course, tentative. Few of the relationships will safely submit to more sophisticated testing, as we push the limit of small sample size and subjective data construction. For the most part, I focus on means and levels of variable, not on a specific econometric model. It is enough to illustrate, I hope, the potential for a political economy model of macropolicy applied to the periphery just as it has been applied by economic historians studying the core.

Lessons for Today

This chapter tries to carve out a new area of understanding in twentieth-century Latin American economic history, focusing on the great shift in policy objectives after the Great Depression. I argue that peripheral economies were subject to the same kinds of populist pressures seen in the core and, accordingly, that policy outcomes depended to some extent on the political institutional framework that prevailed at the time of the interwar crisis. This is revealed by the heterogeneity of policy response within Latin America and in the persistence of that response in the postwar period. Even in the 1960s and 1970s, the same patterns were visible in reactive and passive economies, and a comparison with East Asian outcomes only underscores the result.

Sufficient gaps in this analysis, however, make it only provisional. More research is surely needed on a case-by-case basis to identify the links between external constraints, populist pressure, and the mechanics of policy choice. I would also stress that the macroeconomic focus of the chapter should not be read as implying an absence of concern for microeconomic foundations. All the aggregate distortions seen, and the policies behind them, are ultimately built on sets of specific interventions designed to raise transactions costs or otherwise throw sand in the wheels of markets, contracts, and free trading. These fundamental issues echo the literature on transactions costs, incentive structures, and the persistence of imperfect institutions due to interest-group action, rent seeking, path dependence, and so on. Finally, a major issue, beyond the scope of the chapter but exceedingly important nonetheless, concerns the origins of pre-1929 political institutions in determining subsequent outcomes. We must look back further in the political history of Latin America to understand better why the particular forms of democracy, elections, centralization, and representation evolved to where they were in the 1920s and why they varied as they did across space and time.[36] In this regard we should also mention the problem of distinguishing the present approach from a traditional view based on U.S. foreign policy strength as an external determinant of policy reactions in the 1930s; it is true that the more undemocratic and passive countries tend to be those closest to U.S. influence.

Even with all these caveats, this chapter makes a first attempt at extending some ideas of core economic history to the periphery. We must, however, recognize some important distinctions, given the focus on capital markets; in the capital-scarce periphery individuals, groups, and states faced very different costs and benefits from interventions in the capital market. For this reason, the analysis suggested here is in some ways at odds with the core model.[37]

A first implication of the hypothesis suggested here is that we need to revise our understanding of the balance of internal and external economic and political forces as they affected the evolution of Latin American macropolicies after 1930. But the intent is not to replace a monocausal *externally* oriented theory with a monocausal *internally* oriented theory. A role for both is needed. Although small semiopen economies such as those in the region will never be able

36. On groups, politics, institutions, and growth see M. Olson Jr., *The Logic of Collective Action: Public Goods and the Theory of Groups* (New York: Schocken Books, 1968); *The Rise and Decline of Nations: Economic Growth, Stagflation, and Social Rigidities* (New Haven, Conn.: Yale University Press, 1982); and North, *Institutions*. North has emphasized the long-run impact of centralized, undemocratic Spanish colonial institutions on Latin American development. As we see by the twentieth century, a populist form of politics had evolved in some countries that was important in determining later twentieth-century outcomes. See R. Dornbusch and S. Edwards, eds., *The Macroeconomics of Populism in Latin America* (Chicago: University of Chicago Press, 1991).

37. In the postwar period it would seem that, say, Europe was as susceptible to populist pressure given its democratic foundations. Did postwar Europe fail economically like Latin America? No. But that pressure, as mediated via the trilemma, could not offer vital supplies of foreign capital as in a periphery situation—though by creating other rigidities it could have had important growth-reducing implications in some areas of the economy. See Olson, *Logic of Collective Action*.

to escape the implications of global economic forces entirely, it is not necessarily true that economic outcomes are shaped entirely by outside forces. To a great extent, macropolicies since the 1930s have evolved in line with Díaz Alejandro's passive-reactive categorization, but this evolution is traceable in large part to the nature of domestic political institutions in the various countries. The more reactive economies were those more subject to the kinds of populist pressures that generated greater deviations from the gold standard in the 1930s in the core, suggesting a universal theory of policy reaction in the depression years in both the core and the periphery. Latin America differed in that this policy response persisted into the 1970s and 1980s, whereas some other developing countries (for example, the Asian group) were able to reform these policies much sooner.

A second implication is that economists, historians, and political scientists can use the laboratory of economic history to assess the interaction of democratic political tensions and policy outcomes. This is a controversial subject, with influential work from economists such as Alberto Alesina, Dani Rodrik, and Robert Barro. Barro's alarming claim that too much democracy may be bad for economic growth is certainly echoed in history and in more than just a partial correlation of democracy indicators and growth outcomes. Indeed, investigations along the lines of the model suggested here can take us beyond the surface level findings of reduced-form growth empirics and into some of the more detailed mechanisms by which political structure affects policy choices and hence growth.

History is also a key testing ground and affords a more detailed picture of such a process at work. The policy response of the core in the 1930s was certainly driven by populist pressures demanding an end to the gold standard and the laissez-faire macroeconomic economic orthodoxy of the day, as emphasized by Temin and Eichengreen.[38] The present chapter argues that no less affected in this way were the economies of the periphery. Critical here was an analysis that did not end in the 1930s but that followed the response in the postwar era. Reactive policies were successful in averting depression in the 1930s, both in the core and periphery.[39] But the legacy of the Great Depression persisted up to fifty or more years in Latin America, and this chapter suggests that populism in the realm of domestic politics was a key cause.[40]

It would be an exaggeration, not to say dangerous, to suggest that these results in any way devalue the worth of a democratic society, which has so many nonpecuniary welfare benefits. But history suggests we should not get overoptimistic about the irreversibility of the current wave of economic reform and global integration, both in the core and in the periphery. We need a true understanding of the potential power of popular will and political means to derail the process, as happened in the 1930s. Recent reforms aim to undo the last sixty years of isolation and reintegrate Latin America into the global economy, but they are not guaranteed to succeed and face many of the same challenges. For example, in seeking price stability via fixed exchange rates and gold standard–type currency

38. See Eichengreen, *Golden Fetters*; and Temin, *Lessons from the Great Depression.*
39. See J. M. Campa, "Exchange Rates and Economic Recovery in the 1930s: An Extension to Latin America," *Journal of Economic History* 50 (September 1990): 677–82; and B. J. Eichengreen and J. D. Sachs, "Exchange Rates and Economic Recovery in the 1930s," *Journal of Economic History* 45 (December 1985): 925–46.
40. A. Alesina et al., "Political Instability and Economic Growth," Working Paper series no. 4173, National Bureau of Economic Research, 1992; R. J. Barro, "Democracy and Growth," Working Paper series no. 4909, National Bureau of Economic Research, October 1994; D. Rodrik, "Getting Interventions Right: How South Korea and Taiwan Grew Rich," *Economic Policy*, no. 20 (April 1995): 55–72; "Coordination Failures and Government Policy: A Model with Applications to East Asia and Eastern Europe," *Journal of International Economics* 40 (1996): 1–22; "Trade Strategy, Investment and Exports: Another Look at East Asia," *Pacific Economic Review* 2 (February 1997): 1–24.

boards, the economies of Latin America, and now East Asia, are exposing themselves to the full brunt of the macroeconomic trilemma.

Economists have warned for many years of the constraints on growth and efficiency caused by the closure of an economy to outside influences. This message about the *constraints of closedness* seems to have been appreciated of late by politicians and the public; economic reforms have advanced and the world economy has achieved greater integration. But in the present climate have the *constraints of openness* been adequately understood by politicians and the public? History teaches us that the choice to embrace globalization, and all the benefits and costs that such a choice entails, has always meant hard choices in times of crisis, and in the present day we should expect no different. Collapsing financial systems, hard monetary rules, and freely mobile capital were all ingredients of an antiglobalization reaction six decades ago. In the end, and under popular pressure, policymakers untied their hands in the 1930s and have been using them ever since.

That said, few would say the democratic political process should be sacrificed to evade those tensions. Instead, this chapter indicates that policymakers, and their constituencies, face a responsibility to find an informed position to understand the short- and long-term implications of their actions and that here economic history has its part to play.

References

Abramovitz, M. "Catching Up, Forging Ahead, and Falling Behind." *Journal of Economic History* 46 (June 1986): 385–406.

Alesina, A., et al. "Political Instability and Economic Growth." Working Paper series no. 4173, National Bureau of Economic Research, 1992.

Barro, R. J. "Democracy and Growth." Working Paper series no. 4909, National Bureau of Economic Research, October 1994.

Barro, R. J., and X. Sala-i-Martin. *Economic Growth.* New York: McGraw-Hill, 1995.

Baumol, W. "Productivity Growth, Convergence and Welfare: What the Long-Run Data Show." *American Economic Review* 76 (December 1986): 1072–85.

Blanchard, O. J., and S. Fischer. *Lectures on Macroeconomics.* Cambridge, Mass.: MIT Press, 1989.

Bratter, H. M. "Foreign Exchange Control in Latin America." *Foreign Policy Reports* 14 (1939): 274–88.

Bulmer-Thomas, V. *The Economic History of Latin America since Independence.* Cambridge, Eng.: Cambridge University Press, 1994.

———. "The Latin American Economies in the 1930s." In L. Bethell, ed., *The Cambridge History of Latin America.* Vol. 6. Cambridge, Eng.: Cambridge University Press, 1996.

Campa, J. M. "Exchange Rates and Economic Recovery in the 1930s: An Extension to Latin America." *Journal of Economic History* 50 (September 1990): 677–82.

Cardoso, E., and A. Fishlow. "Latin American Development: 1950–1980." *Journal of Latin American Studies* 24 (1992): 197–218.

Cardoso, E., and A. Helwege. *Latin America's Economy: Diversity Trends and Conflicts.* Cambridge, Mass.: MIT Press, 1992.

Coatsworth, J. H. "Economic Retardation and Growth in Latin America and Southern Europe since 1700." Harvard University, December 1993. Photocopy.

Coatsworth, J. H. "Economic and Institutional Trajectories in Pre-Modern Latin America." In J. H. Coatsworth and A. M. Taylor, eds., *Latin America and the World Economy in the Nineteenth and Twentieth Centuries: Explorations in Quantitative Economic History.* Cambridge, Mass.: Harvard University Press, 1998.

De Long, J. B., and L. H. Summers. "Equipment Investment and Economic Growth." *Quarterly Journal of Economics* 106 (May 1991): 445–502.

Díaz Alejandro, C. F. "The 1940s in Latin America." In M. Syrquin, L. Taylor, and L. E. Westphal, eds., *Economic Structure and Performance: Essays in Honor of Hollis B. Chenery.* Orlando, Fla.: Academic Press, 1984.

———. "Latin America in the 1930s." In R. Thorp, ed., *Latin America in the 1930s: The Role of the Periphery in World Crisis.* New York: St. Martin's Press, 1984.

Dornbusch, R., and S. Edwards, eds. *The Macroeconomics of Populism in Latin America.* Chicago: University of Chicago Press, 1991.

Dowrick, S., and D.-T. Nguyen. "OECD Comparative Economic Growth 1950–85: Catch-Up and Convergence." *American Economic Review* 79 (December 1989): 1010–30.

Easterly, W. "How Much Do Distortions Affect Growth?" *Journal of Monetary Economics* 32 (1993): 187–212.

Edelstein, M. *Overseas Investment in the Age of High Imperialism.* New York: Columbia University Press, 1982.

Edwards, S. "Trade Orientation, Distortions and Growth in Developing Countries." *Journal of Development Economics* 39 (1992): 31–57.

———. *Crisis and Reform in Latin America: From Despair to Hope.* New York: Oxford University Press, 1995.

Eichengreen, B. J. *Golden Fetters: The Gold Standard and the Great Depression, 1919–1939.* Oxford, Eng.: Oxford University Press, 1992.

———. *Globalizing Capital: A History of the International Monetary System.* Princeton, N.J.: Princeton University Press, 1996.

Eichengreen, B. J., and J. D. Sachs. "Exchange Rates and Economic Recovery in the 1930s." *Journal of Economic History* 45 (December 1985): 925–46.

Einzig, P. *Exchange Control.* London: Macmillan, 1934.

Engerman, S. L., and K. L. Sokoloff. "Factor Endowments, Institutions, and Differential Paths of Growth among New World Economies: A View from Economic Historians of the United States." In S. Haber, ed., *How Latin America Fell Behind: Essays on the Economic Histories of Brazil and Mexico, 1800–1914.* Stanford: Stanford University Press, 1997.

Fishlow, A. "Origins and Consequences of Import Substitution in Brazil." In L.E.D. Marco, ed., *International Economics and Development: Essays in Honor of Raúl Prebisch.* New York: Academic Press, 1971.

Haber, S. "Introduction: Economic Growth and Latin American Economic Historiography." In S. Haber, ed., *How Latin America Fell Behind: Essays on the Economic Histories of Brazil and Mexico, 1800–1914.* Stanford: Stanford University Press, 1997.

Haber, S., ed. *How Latin America Fell Behind: Essays on the Economic Histories of Brazil and Mexico, 1800–1914.* Stanford: Stanford University Press, 1997.

Jaggers, K., and T. R. Gurr. "Tracking Democracy's Third Wave with the Polity III Data." *Journal of Peace Research* 32 (1995): 469–82.

Jones, C. I. "Economic Growth and the Relative Price of Capital." *Journal of Monetary Economics* 34 (1994): 359–82.

Levine, R., and D. Renelt. "A Sensitivity Analysis of Cross-Country Growth Regressions." *American Economic Review* 82 (September 1992): 942–63.

Maddison, A. *The World Economy in the 20th Century.* Paris: Organization for Economic Cooperation and Development, 1989.

———. *Dynamic Forces in Capitalist Development: A Long-Run Comparative View.* Oxford, Eng.: Oxford University Press, 1991.

Mankiw, N. G. "The Growth of Nations." *Brookings Papers on Economic Activity* 1 (1995): 275–310.

Mankiw, N. G., D. Romer, and D. N. Weil. "A Contribution to the Empirics of Economic Growth." *Quarterly Journal of Economics* 107 (May 1992): 407–37.

North, D. C. *Institutions, Institutional Change, and Economic Performance.* Cambridge, Eng.: Cambridge University Press, 1990.

Obstfeld, M., and A. M. Taylor. "The Great Depression as a Watershed: International Capital Mobility in the Long Run." In M. D. Bordo, C. D. Goldin, and E. N. White, eds., *The Defining Moment: The Great Depression and the American Economy in the Twentieth Century.* Chicago: University of Chicago Press, 1998.

Olson, M., Jr. *The Logic of Collective Action: Public Goods and the Theory of Groups.* New York: Schocken Books, 1968.

———. *The Rise and Decline of Nations: Economic Growth, Stagflation, and Social Rigidities.* New Haven, Conn.: Yale University Press, 1982.

Pack, H. "Endogenous Growth: Intellectual Appeal and Empirical Shortcomings." *Journal of Economic Perspectives* 8 (winter 1994): 55–72.

Rodrik, D. "Getting Interventions Right: How South Korea and Taiwan Grew Rich." *Economic Policy,* no. 20 (April 1995): 55–72.

———. "Coordination Failures and Government Policy: A Model with Applications to East Asia and Eastern Europe." *Journal of International Economics* 40 (1996): 1–22.

———. "Trade Strategy, Investment and Exports: Another Look at East Asia." *Pacific Economic Review* 2 (February 1997): 1–24.

Romer, P. M. "The Origins of Endogenous Growth." *Journal of Economic Perspectives* 8 (winter 1994): 3–22.

Sachs, J. D., and A. M. Warner. "Economic Reform and the Process of Global Integration." *Brookings Papers on Economic Activity* (1995): 1–118.

Solow, R. M. "A Contribution to the Theory of Economic Growth." *Quarterly Journal of Economics* 70 (February 1956): 65–94.

Taylor, A. M. "External Dependence, Demographic Burdens and Argentine Economic Decline after the *Belle Époque*." *Journal of Economic History* 52 (December 1992): 907–36.

———. "Three Phases of Argentine Economic Growth." Working Paper series on Historical Factors in Long Run Growth, No. 60, National Bureau of Economic Research, October 1994.

———. "Tres fases del crecimiento económico argentino." *Revista de Historia Económica* 12 (Otoño 1994): 649–83.

———. "On the Costs of Inward-Looking Development: Price Distortions, Growth, and Divergence in Latin America." *Journal of Economic History* 58 (March 1998): 1–28.

Temin, P. *Lessons from the Great Depression.* Cambridge, Mass.: MIT Press, 1989.

Thorp, R. "A Reappraisal of the Origins of Import-Substituting Industrialisation: 1930–1950." In T. Halperín Donghi, ed., *The Colonial and Postcolonial Experience: Five Centuries of Spanish and Portuguese America.* Quincentenary Supplement, *Journal of Latin American Studies.* Cambridge, Eng.: Cambridge University Press, 1992.

Twomey, M. J. "Patterns of Foreign Investment in the Third World in the Twentieth Century." In J. H. Coatsworth and A. M. Taylor, eds., *Latin America and the World Economy in the Nineteenth and Twentieth Centuries: Explorations in Quantitative Economic History.* Cambridge, Mass.: Harvard University Press, 1998.

Williamson, J. G. "Globalization, Convergence, and History." *Journal of Economic History* 56 (June 1996): 277–306.

Yeager, L. B. *International Monetary Relations: Theory, History, and Policy.* 2d ed. New York: Harper and Row, 1976.

Schooling, Suffrage, and the Persistence of Inequality in the Americas, 1800–1945

The importance of institutions in economic growth has come to be more fully appreciated in recent years, by both scholars and policymakers.[1] Schools are widely acknowledged as among the most fundamental of such institutions. Increases in a society's levels of schooling and literacy have been related theoretically as well as empirically to many socioeconomic changes conducive to growth, including higher labor productivity, more rapid technological change, and higher rates of commercial and political participation.[2] Moreover, in addition to promoting growth, they also have a powerful influence on the distribution of the benefits of growth. Schooling and literacy attainment can be salient avenues for individuals to realize upward mobility, and limiting access to education has been shown to be an effective barrier to advancement by those affected.[3] Although we know that substantial differences in the prevalence of schooling and literacy across countries may have contributed to disparities in their patterns of economic growth, we lack a basic under-

---

1. Douglass North, *Structure and Change in Economic History* (New York: Norton, 1981).
2. Theodore W. Schultz, *The Economic Value of Education* (New York: Columbia University Press, 1963).
3. Robert Higgs, *Competition and Coercion: Blacks in the American Economy, 1865–1914* (Cambridge, Eng.: Cambridge University Press, 1977).

standing of how these differences first emerged and evolved over time.

This chapter examines the experience in the Americas after colonization by the Europeans. The New World is an interesting case for the study of investment in schooling and literacy in that many societies arising out of European colonization were so prosperous that they clearly had the material resources to support the establishment of institutions of primary education.[4] Only a relatively small number, however, made such investments on a scale sufficient to serve the general population before the twentieth century. At a general level, such contrasts in institutional development across the Americas have often been attributed to differences in wealth, national heritage, culture, or religion, but systematic comparative studies are rare or nonexistent. Even those that have been conducted typically neglect how the institutions developed over the long run, confining their focus to cross-sectional variations in the contemporary world.

One striking feature of the development of educational institutions in the Americas is the major investment in primary education made by the United States and Canada early in their histories. Virtually from the time of initial settlement, North Americans seem generally to have been convinced of the value of providing their children with a basic education, including the ability to read and write, and established schools to accomplish that goal. In colonial New England, schooling was frequently organized at the village or town level and funded through a variety of sources: charity, lotteries, license fees for dogs, taverns, marriages, and traders in slaves, sales of public lands, as well as the so-called *rate bill*, whereby all

4. Stanley L. Engerman and Kenneth L. Sokoloff, "Factor Endowments, Institutions, and Differential Paths of Growth among New World Economies: A View from Economic Historians of the United States," in Stephen Haber, ed., *How Latin America Fell Behind* (Stanford: Stanford University Press, 1997).

but designated paupers would be charged when they had children enrolled. Instruction by family members, neighbors, or private tutors often filled in where formal schools were not convenient or available. The United States probably already had the most literate population in the world by the beginning of the nineteenth century, but the "common school movement," getting under way in the 1820s, put the country on a new path of investment in educational institutions. Between 1825 and 1850 nearly every northern state that had not already done so enacted a law strongly encouraging or requiring localities to establish "free schools," open to all children and supported by general taxes. Although the movement made slower progress in the South, schooling had spread to the point that, by the middle of the nineteenth century, more than 40 percent of the school-age population in the United States overall was enrolled and nearly 90 percent of white adults were literate. In early nineteenth-century Canada schools were also common, and even though this northernmost English colony lagged behind the United States by several decades in establishing tax-supported primary schools with universal access, its literacy rates were nearly as high.

The rest of the hemisphere trailed far behind the United States and Canada in education and literacy. Despite enormous wealth, the British colonies in the Caribbean basin, with the possible exception of Barbados, were very slow to organize schooling institutions that would serve broad segments of the population. Indeed, it was evidently not until the British Colonial Office took a direct interest in the promotion of schooling, late in the nineteenth century, that significant steps were taken in this direction. Similarly, even the most progressive Latin American countries, such as Argentina and Uruguay, were more than seventy-five years behind the United States and Canada in providing primary schooling and attaining high levels of literacy. Most of Latin America was unable to achieve these standards until well into the twentieth century, if then. This relative backwardness in the organization of institutions of primary

education could have significantly affected the long-run development of these other nations of the Americas, and thus the question
of what accounts for this pattern is especially intriguing. Differences
in the resources available to invest in schooling, as reflected in, say,
per capita income, is perhaps the first possibility that comes to mind
as to why the rest of the hemisphere lagged behind the United
States and Canada, but the latter do not appear to have been much
advantaged in that dimension at the time they began to move ahead
in the promotion of education.

Religion is another potentially significant factor, and some have
suggested that societies in which Catholics predominated may have
been slow to invest in public schools, either because the Church
valued education, at least for ordinary people, less than their Protestant counterparts, or because it stifled individual or community
initiatives to organize private or public schools. Although plausible
and consistent with the greater prominence of Catholicism in Latin
America, this view has to contend with the relatively high levels of
schooling and literacy in French Canada, as well as the modest
levels among the British (and largely Protestant) colonies in the
Caribbean basin. A third possibility is that differences in ethnicity
or national heritage played an important role in determining which
societies made major investments in schooling early in the process
of development and which did not. This sort of explanation encom-
passes arguments that Native Americans did not consider the establishment of schools an attractive use of resources because of their
association with Western ways of thinking or that populations with
English backgrounds had a greater appreciation of education than
those of Spanish descent. Yet another hypothesis is that the long
tradition of centralized structures of government in Latin American
countries may have impeded the organization of schools on a widespread basis. For example, local or provincial governments, which
had the authority to take the lead in organizing primary schools in

the United States and Canada, may have effectively or legally been constrained in carrying out such initiatives elsewhere.

Finally, another hypothesis is that the long-standing greater degree of inequality in Latin America, as compared to the United States or Canada, may play a role in explaining the differential records in establishing education institutions. Several mechanisms could have led extreme levels of inequality to depress investments in schooling institutions. First, in a setting where private schooling predominated, or where parents paid user fees for their children, greater wealth or income inequality would generally reduce the fraction of the school-age population enrolled—holding per capita income constant. Second, greater inequality may also have exacerbated the collective action problems associated with the establishment and funding of universal public schools because the distribution of benefits across the population would be quite different from the incidence of taxes and other costs or because population heterogeneity made it more difficult for communities to reach consensus on public projects. Given that early public schooling systems were almost universally organized and managed at the local level, these problems may have been especially relevant. Where the wealthy enjoyed disproportionate political power, elites could procure private schooling services for their own children and resist being taxed to underwrite or subsidize services to others. Extreme inequality in wealth or income might also lead to low levels of schooling on a national basis if it were associated with substantial disparities across communities or geographic areas. As long as schools had to be supported by local resources, poor districts might not have been able to sustain an extensive system of primary education. Only the populations of wealthy districts, presumably small in number, would then have easy access to schooling.

Our original motivation for undertaking this comparative examination was an interest in whether and how the extent of inequality in wealth, human capital, and political power might have influenced the evolution of educational institutions and thus the path of economic growth and the persistence of inequality over time. Indeed, this concern with the impact and persistence of the extreme inequality characterizing much of the New World is largely responsible for the organization of the chapter. In the next two sections we survey the record of schooling and literacy in the Americas, highlighting salient patterns and discussing the general consistency of the history with some of the explanations for divergence that have been suggested. In the third section we systematically analyze relevant evidence and find that, although investment in schooling is strongly and positively correlated with per capita income over time and across countries, much variation remains to be accounted for. Moreover, the extent of inequality in political power, as reflected in the proportion of the population who vote, does seem to be associated with lower literacy and schooling rates. Although the comparison between the experiences of the United States (especially) and Canada with those of other countries in the hemisphere serves as our reference point, we are also concerned with the variation within the latter group. Argentina, Uruguay, Cuba, Costa Rica, Chile, and Barbados may have lagged behind the U.S. and Canada, but they made earlier and greater progress at educating their populations than did their neighbors. Other explanations for the variation across the Americas in levels of investment in education may ultimately prove as powerful as ones derived from differences in the degree of inequality, but this comparative examination should nevertheless help improve our understanding of the differential paths of development observed in the New World. Whatever tended to reduce or delay investments in schooling institutions fostered inequality in the distribution of human capital and likely retarded economic growth over the long run.

I

Not long after permanent settlements on the northern part of the North American mainland were established by Europeans, educational institutions began to be organized. Foremost among them were primary schools that drew students from local communities who administered as well as supported them. Massachusetts is frequently celebrated as the leader, but other colonies in New England conceded little in their enthusiasm for basic and widespread education.[5] Indeed, all of the region's states had made some provision for public education by 1800, generally requiring towns beyond a certain size to support a primary or grammar school. Despite resistance to the levying of school taxes slowing the responses to these governmental initiatives, New Englanders already enjoyed relatively broad access to primary education and had attained high rates of literacy through a combination of local public schools, private institutions, and home instruction. Elsewhere in the United States, schooling was not so widespread; private schools generally predominated in the Middle Atlantic and the South. Aside from New York, few governments in these regions had gone beyond requiring public schooling to be provided to the children of paupers until the early 1800s. Access to schools was especially limited in the South, even among the free population.

The first major breakthrough in the expansion of schooling occurred during the second quarter of the nineteenth century with a series of political battles—known as the "common school movement"—that took place throughout the country for tax-supported, locally controlled "free schools." Such schools were to be open to all who wished to attend, supported primarily through local taxes (often, however, receiving some aid from state governments), and

5. Ellwood P. Cubberley, *The History of Education* (Boston: Houghton Mifflin, 1920).

managed by local authorities (state-appointed officers typically provided some oversight to the multitude of local school systems that operated within the respective states). Although there had previously been scattered successes, principally in New England, at achieving the goal of universal access to a primary education, the movement is usually dated as beginning about 1825 and ending about 1850, by which time virtually every northern state had passed and implemented laws to encourage townships or counties to establish such common schools.

This twenty-five-year period was marked by intense political struggle in state after state, with especially strong support for free schools coming from urban dwellers, members of labor organizations, and residents of western states—reflecting the drive for democratization that occurred during the Jacksonian era. Opposition is said to have come from religious and private school interests as well as from the wealthier classes who might have expected to bear disproportionate increases in taxes.[6] Entirely free schools were obtained only gradually, however, as the progression of laws and township policies chipped away incrementally at the traditional use of permanent endowments, licensing fees, lotteries, and "rate bills" (tuition or user fees) to finance the schools and replaced them with general taxes. Resistance to raising rates or levying new taxes was always a factor to be overcome, and state governments often offered inducements like financial aid for schools tied to decisions by districts to agree to tax themselves; even some northern states continued to rely on a combination of taxes and rate bills to fund the schools as late as 1871 (New Jersey). Although some southern states passed legislation allowing for free schools as early as the 1830s,

---

6. For a discussion of the "common school movement," see Cubberley, *History of Education*. Also see Lee Soltow and Edward Stevens, *The Rise of Literacy and the Common School in the United States* (Chicago: University of Chicago Press, 1981).

there was limited progress in establishing them until after the Civil War.[7]

Historians of education typically highlight the fact that the common school movement was one of a number of campaigns for democratization in various social and economic policies that coincided with, or followed shortly after, widespread extension of the suffrage.[8] Despite the sentiments popularly attributed to the Founding Fathers, voting in the United States was largely a privilege reserved for white men with significant amounts of property until early in the nineteenth century. By 1815, only four states had adopted universal white male suffrage, but as the movement to do away with political inequality gained strength, they were joined by the rest of the country as virtually all new entrants to the Union extended voting privileges to all white men, and older states revised their laws. The shift to full white manhood suffrage was largely complete by the late 1840s, with only minor restrictions in a few states enduring beyond 1850.[9] Overall, the timing of the movements for extending the suffrage and for common schools, with the latter following the former, is consistent with the view that increasing equality in political influence helped realize the increased investments in public schooling, along with the corresponding extension of access to a primary education. That the southern states were generally the laggards in both broadening the electorate and starting common schools, while New England and the western states were leaders in both, likewise provides support for this view. Since doing away with property restrictions on the franchise enhanced the political voice of the groups that would benefit most from the establishment of tax-supported free schools, it should not be surprising if the

7. Cubberley, *History of Education.*
8. Ibid.
9. Spencer D. Albright, *The American Ballot* (Washington, D.C.: American Council on Public Affairs, 1942).

achievement of greater equality in political influence led to the institutional changes that contributed to greater equality in the distribution of human capital.

Although both the French and English areas of Canada had relatively few schools and low levels of literacy in 1800, as compared to their neighbor to the south, this northernmost country in the hemisphere made major investments in extending institutions of primary education to the general population early. By the end of the nineteenth century, Canada ranked second in the world, only behind the United States, in terms of literacy and the fraction of its school-aged population actually enrolled. Despite being influenced by political developments in both Britain and France, there was a pronounced impact on Canada arising from extensive economic contacts with the northeastern part of the United States. Whatever the source, Canadian concern with the establishment of a broad system of public schools began increasing at the beginning of the nineteenth century. The organization, management, and financing of education was carried out primarily at the district level, but some supervision and financial aid was provided by provincial governments. The second quarter of the nineteenth century was a period of expanding school systems and growing support from public resources, as in the United States. Tax-supported free primary schools, however, were not fully realized on a widespread basis until the third quarter of the nineteenth century.[10] Compulsory education legislation followed over the 1870s (Ontario [1871], British Columbia [1873], and Manitoba [1876], but Quebec did not pass such legislation until 1943. Under the Union Act of 1841 and the British North America Act of 1865, allowance was made for separate

10. See, for example, Charles E. Phillips, *The Development of Education in Canada* (Toronto: W. J. Gage, 1957); and J. Donald Wilson, Robert M. Stamp, and Louis-Philippe Audet, *Canadian Education: A History* (Scarborough, Ont.: Prentice-Hall of Canada, 1970).

secular and religious schools, both of which would be state financed, for those provinces who wanted them. Most important here was Quebec, which maintained, in addition to a secular school system, separate Catholic and Protestant schools. Canada was clearly behind the United States in both schooling and literacy for most of the nineteenth century but managed to virtually close the gap by 1895 in terms of the ratio of students in school to the population aged five to nineteen (0.60 to 0.62 respectively). As in the United States, the progress of the movement for tax-supported public schools coincided generally in time with, or followed soon after, extensions of the franchise.[11]

Many elements seem to have contributed to the early spread of tax-supported primary schools in the United States and Canada. The two societies may have been quicker to invest in institutions of primary schooling because of the English belief in the value of education, which was perhaps rooted in religious views. In seventeenth-century New England at least, the organization of primary schools was often rationalized as necessary for ensuring that all members of the population were able to read the Bible. Rough quantitative estimates of their prevalence suggest that only modest shares of the population could have attended such schools, and it is also clear that literacy rates in the New England and Middle Atlantic colonies were much higher than those in the southern colonies as well as those in Europe at that time. This would seem to cast doubt on the notion that the high rates of primary schooling and literacy were due solely to either English heritage or religion, especially in conjunction with the records of British colonies in the Caribbean. Indeed, the arguments for public schooling during the common

11. For a discussion of how and why the franchise was extended in the West more generally, see Daron Acemoglu and James A. Robinson, "Why Did the West Extend the Franchise?" (University of Southern California; Massachusetts Institute of Technology, 1998, manuscript).

school movement focused on the economic and civic importance of education, rather than the religious. Schooling would help equip men for self-governance and participation in a democracy and provide an avenue for self-improvement and upward mobility. It was, however, to be provided to girls as well, and a comparison of the scattered estimates of literacy from the late 1700s through the 1850s suggests that although all benefited from the expansion of common schools, they helped females close a gender gap.

Among all of the economies in the New World, whether established by Britain or other European countries, the United States and Canada had made greater commitments to public schooling and attained higher literacy rates than any other country in the Americas by the early nineteenth century. This pattern is all the more striking when one recognizes that these societies were not generally considered to have been the most prosperous of those in the Americas at the time.[12] The idea that their distinctiveness in this regard may have something to do with differences in ethnic heterogeneity or in the degree of inequality is both intuitive and consistent with what we know.[13] For example, the much greater economic equality and ethnic homogeneity present in the northern United States and Canada, as compared to elsewhere in the Americas, would be expected in principle to have led to a relatively even sharing of costs and benefits and thus to reduce the severity of collective action problems and to increase the likelihood of a community taxing itself to finance universal primary schools. Further support for this notion of the significance of equality (in this case, political equality) comes from the coincidence in time between the common school movement of the 1820s and 1830s in the United States and the broadening of the

12. Engerman and Sokoloff, "Factor Endowments."
13. See Claudia Goldin and Lawrence F. Katz, "Human and Social Capital: The Rise of Secondary Schooling in America, 1910 to 1940" (Harvard University, 1997, manuscript) for a discussion of this idea in another context.

franchise during that same era, and from similar associations between suffrage reform and the passage of measures to support public schools in both Canada and England.[14] Moreover, within the United States, there is also a cross-sectional correspondence across states between leadership in broadening the franchise and leadership in the establishment of universal common schools.

Whatever the source, the United States and Canada were clearly far ahead of their neighbors in the Americas in providing basic schooling to their populations throughout the 1800s and well into the 1900s (see table 1). By 1870, more than 80 percent of the population aged ten or above in both the United States and Canada were literate, more than triple the proportions in countries such as Argentina, Chile, Costa Rica, and Cuba and four times the proportions in Brazil and Mexico. These stark contrasts were partly due to high literacy in the United States and Canada, which had the most literate populations in the world at that time. But much of the explanation seems to be in the poor performance of the other societies in the Americas. Even during the era of European colonization—when their levels of per capita income were comparable—these other societies obviously trailed the colonies that were to become the United States and Canada in developing institutions of primary education and literate populations. Moreover, even those that were more successful at realizing economic growth, such as Argentina in the late nineteenth and early twentieth centuries, were much slower to establish systems of public schooling that reached broad segments of their populations. For example, the nonwhite population in the United States had literacy rates comparable to, or higher than, those in Argentina in 1870, 1890, and 1910.

Overall, the United States and Canada appear to have been the only nations in the hemisphere to attain high levels of literacy by

14. For discussions of the connection between extensions of suffrage and public schooling in many countries and contexts, see Cubberley, *History of Education*.

TABLE 1
Literacy Rates in the Americas, 1850–1950

	Year	Ages	Rate (in percent)
Argentina	1869	6+	23.8%
	1895	6+	45.6
	1900	10+	52.0
	1925	10+	73.0
Barbados	1946	10+	92.7
Bolivia	1900	10+	17.0
Brazil	1872	7+	15.8
	1890	7+	14.8
	1900	7+	25.6
	1920	10+	30.0
	1939	10+	57.0
British Honduras (Belize)	1911	10+	59.6
	1931	10+	71.8
Chile	1865	7+	18.0
	1875	7+	25.7
	1885	7+	30.3
	1900	10+	43.0
	1925	10+	66.0
	1945	10+	76.0
Colombia	1918	15+	32.0
	1938	15+	56.0
	1951	15+	62.0
Costa Rica	1892	7+	23.6
	1900	10+	33.0
	1925	10+	64.0
Cuba	1861	7+	23.8 (38.5, 5.3)*
	1899	10+	40.5
	1925	10+	67.0
	1946	10+	77.9
Guatemala	1893	7+	11.3
	1925	10+	15.0
	1945	10+	20.0
Honduras	1887	7+	15.2
	1925	10+	29.0

TABLE 1
(continued)

	Year	Ages	Rate (in percent)
Jamaica	1871	5+	16.3
	1891	5+	32.0
	1911	5+	47.2
	1923	5+	67.9
	1943	10+	76.1
Mexico	1900	10+	22.2
	1925	10+	36.0
	1946	10+	48.4
Paraguay	1886	7+	19.3
	1900	10+	30.0
Peru	1925	10+	38.0
Puerto Rico	1860	7+	11.8 (19.8, 3.1)*
Uruguay	1900	10+	54.0
	1925	10+	70.0
Venezuela	1925	10+	34.0
Canada	1861	All	82.5
English-majority counties	1861	All	93.0
French-majority counties	1861	All	81.2
United States			
Northern whites	1860	10+	96.9
Southern whites	1860	10+	56.4
All	1870	10+	80.0 (88.5, 21.1)*
	1890	10+	86.7 (92.3, 43.2)*
	1910	10+	92.3 (95.0, 69.5)*

SOURCES: For the countries in South America, Central America, and the Caribbean, see Carlos Newland, "La Educación Elemental en Hispanoamérica: Desde la Independencia hasta la Centralización de los Sistemas Educativos Nacionales," *Hispanic American Historical Review* 71, no. 2 (May 1991), and "The Estado Docente and Its Expansion: Spanish America Elementary Education, 1900–1950," *Journal of Latin American Studies* 26, no. 2 (May 1994); Aline Helg, *La Educación en Colombia, 1918–1957: Una historia social, económica y política* (Bogotá, Colombia: Fondo Editorial, CEREC, 1987); George W. Roberts, *The Population of Jamaica* (Cambridge, Eng.: Cambridge University Press for the Conservation Foundation, 1957); John A. Britton, ed., *Molding the Hearts and Minds: Education, Communications, and Social Change in Latin America* (Wilmington, Del.: Scholarly Resources, 1994); West Indian Census, *General Report on the Census of Population 9th April, 1946* (Kingston: Government Printing Office, 1950). For the United States, see U.S. Bureau of the Census, 1967 (Washington, D.C.: Government Printing Office), chapter 4. For Canada, see Marc Egnal, *Divergent Paths: How Culture and Institutions Have Shaped North American Growth* (New York: Oxford University, 1996), p. 81.

* The figures for whites and nonwhites are reported respectively within parentheses.

the middle of the nineteenth century. In contrast, not until late in the 1800s were two other sets of New World societies able to raise literacy rates much above the relatively modest level of 30 percent. The first group consisted of a number of British colonies in the Caribbean basin, where investments in public schooling institutions date back to the British emancipation of slaves in 1834, when provisions were made for grants to each colony for the education of blacks. These funds were cut off in 1845, after which each colony was responsible for its own educational policies and expenditures. Only Barbados seems to have maintained, if not increased, this early support for primary schools, with costs being covered by a mixture of local taxes, charity, school fees, and aid generally provided to both religious as well as secular schools. The British Colonial Office continued to support the expansion of public schooling, however, arguing (for example) that compulsory education was needed more in the West Indies than in advanced societies.

Compulsory schooling laws were introduced, first in British Guiana in 1876, with Saint Lucia and the Leeward Islands following in 1889 and 1890, respectively, but they were ineffectively enforced. Although a wide variety of policies came to be pursued by the various colonies, yielding a diverse pattern of schooling and literacy rates, the efforts of the Colonial Office, coupled with the availability of more resources from colonial taxation, may be responsible for the general pattern of marked progress in the extension of primary schooling and the diffusion of literacy during this period. Barbados was the major success story, with estimated literacy rates placing it among the more developed nations of the world. In other colonies, such as British Honduras and Jamaica, however, improvements were steady but slower, with the most striking increases in literacy occurring after 1891. Rates of literacy for blacks were generally lower in most of the British colonies in the Caribbean than in the United States but were comparable to or above those of most countries in South and Central America.

The other group of New World societies that began to realize rapid and substantial increases in literacy, paralleling major extensions of public schooling, during the late 1800s consists of a subset of former Spanish colonies. Argentina and Uruguay were the clear leaders among them (although still far behind the United States and Canada), with more than half their populations (age ten or older) literate by 1900. Chile and Cuba trailed somewhat behind, with roughly 40 percent literacy, and Costa Rica further still, at 33 percent. These five countries, which varied considerably in many important respects, had attained literacy rates greater than 66 percent by 1925. In contrast, a broad range of other Latin American countries, including Mexico, Brazil, Venezuela, Peru, Colombia, Bolivia, Guatemala, and Honduras, were not able to move much beyond 30 percent literacy until after 1925.

II

Although virtually all New World economies enjoyed high levels of per capita income by the standards of the period, the United States and Canada had pulled far ahead of their Latin American neighbors in the establishment of schools and literacy attainment by the beginning of the nineteenth century. This dramatic contrast with the North is perhaps the most salient feature of the Latin American record in the development of education institutions overall, but it should not be allowed to obscure the important differences across countries in literacy rates and schooling (see tables 1 and 2). There were no significant movements toward public provision of primary education anywhere in Latin America until late in the nineteenth century, but literacy rose quickly in those countries that had taken the lead in promoting schooling. By 1900, Argentina, Chile, and Uruguay had literacy rates of over 40 percent, followed by Costa Rica with 33 percent. These figures are low relative to those of the United States and Canada but much higher than those of the two

TABLE 2

Students as a Percentage of Population in Selected Latin American Countries
(ca. 1896)

Country	Population	Students	Students as a Percentage of Total Population
Costa Rica	243,205	21,829	8.98%
Uruguay	800,000	67,878	8.48
Argentina	4,086,492	268,401	6.57
Paraguay	329,645	18,944	5.75
Mexico	11,395,712	543,977	4.77
Guatemala	1,460,017	65,322	4.47
Venezuela	2,323,527	100,026	4.30
Nicaragua	282,845	11,914	4.21
Ecuador	1,271,861	52,830	4.15
El Salvador	777,895	29,427	3.78
Chile	3,267,441	95,456	2.92
Peru	2,700,945	53,276	1.97
Colombia	3,878,600	73,200	1.89
Brazil	14,002,335	207,973	1.49
Bolivia	2,300,000	24,244	1.05

SOURCE: Oficina National de Estadística, *Resúmenes Estadísticos: Años 1883–1910* (San José, Costa Rica: Imprenta Nacional, 1912).

largest Latin American societies, Mexico and Brazil, with only 22 and 25 percent, respectively. Moreover, countries such as Bolivia, Guatemala, and Honduras fell even further behind, with literacy rates ranging from 11 to 17 percent. When one considers that these countries had similar government structures (federations) and a common institutional heritage (Spanish or Portuguese in the case of Brazil), the question of the sources of these substantial differences seems both intriguing and relevant to understanding what conditions were conducive to early investment in educational institutions like primary schools.

The local governments established under Spanish rule reflected the corporate quality of Latin American society, characterized by a hierarchical structure where only *vecinos* (neighbors) were considered citizens. Such sharp distinctions in social class endured after independence, and neighbors continued to dominate the political order throughout the nineteenth century by way of political systems based on indirect elections and restrictions on voting that included income/wealth and literacy requirements. With this sort of extreme inequality in the distributions of income, human capital, and political power, it is perhaps not surprising that Latin American local governments typically failed to organize schools that were tax supported and open to all in what were generally very heterogeneous populations. This pattern stands in stark contrast with the experience in the United States and Canada, where local and state governments were the pioneers in establishing such schools. In Latin America national governments often had to get involved before substantial progress was made. Indeed, it is the timing of when national governments chose or were able to directly intervene in promoting education institutions that is often crucial in accounting for the differences between countries in their records of providing their populations with literacy and other basic skills. The greater importance of national government policy in Latin America and some of the conditions that influenced when national governments got involved are illustrated in our review below of four cases: Argentina, Chile, Costa Rica, and Mexico.

Argentina

After Argentina had established itself as a state and a national and stable government had been set up, the 1853 constitution directed that primary education was to be provided by the provincial governments and that Congress had the right to introduce guidelines for general and university education. In 1881, the National Council of Education was created to act as the governing body for Buenos Aires and the national territories; educational policy outside those federal districts continued to be made by provincial authorities. The federal government would intervene in the educational affairs of provinces, however, when elementary school systems proved inadequate or provincial resources for education were scarce. Nevertheless, provincial government control over primary education remained unchallenged, as a matter of law, until 1904 when the Lainez Law eroded local jurisdiction over educational matters by allowing the federal government to establish elementary schools anywhere in the country in order to raise school standards. One of the most important pieces of education legislation during the nineteenth century was the 1420 Law, the final leg in the drive toward mass education started in 1860 under President Sarmiento. This 1884 law made primary education free and compulsory for all children between the ages of six and fourteen, instituted lay education, set limits on the maximum distance that a student could travel to attend school, and required one school for every 1,500 inhabitants in any given town.

Argentinean educational attainment was impressive by Latin American standards; the average literacy rate in the country went from 22.1 percent in 1869 to 65.0 percent in 1914.[15] Nonetheless, the school system in Argentina was concentrated in the more prosperous regions and in areas with greater economic importance, such as urban centers (see table 3), particularly the area around Buenos Aires, as well as regions with a greater number of foreign-born. This pattern of much higher rates of literacy in urban centers than in the rest of respective countries was typical of Latin American societies that lagged in the establishment of educational institutions, but not of the United States or Canada.

The fact that the 1853 constitution conferred the responsibility of providing education to the provinces can partly explain this situ-

15. Leslie Bethell, ed., *The Cambridge History of Latin America*, 5 vols. (Cambridge, Eng.: Cambridge University Press, 1984).

TABLE 3
Literacy Rates in Selected Cities

City	Year	Male	Female	Total	Country Literacy Rate
Boston, Massachusetts	1850			91.1	95.1 *
New York City, New York	1850			93.6	93.9 *
Philadelphia, Pennsylvania	1850			93.2	93.1 *
Santiago, Chile	1854	52.4	43.3	47.1	13.3
Buenos Aires, Argentina	1855	56.0	48.0	52.0	23.8 (1869)
San Juan, Puerto Rico (white)	1860	67.4	79.4	71.8	19.8
San Juan, Puerto Rico (colored)	1860	22.5	15.4	18.2	3.1
San Juan, Puerto Rico (all)	1860	52.3	43.0	47.9	11.8
Havana, Cuba (white)	1861	58.4	55.6	57.5	38.5
Havana, Cuba (colored)	1861	8.2	6.7	7.4	5.3
Havana, Cuba (all)	1861	45.9	34.1	41.3	23.8
San Jose, Costa Rica	1864	57.0	23.0	40.2	23.6 (1892)
Buenos Aires, Argentina	1869	55.0	47.0	52.2	23.8
Kingston, Jamaica	1871			40.4	16.3
Santiago, Chile	1875	37.0	33.3	34.4	25.7
São Paulo, Brazil	1882			42.0	15.3 (ca. 1882)
Kingston, Jamaica	1891			59.2	32.0
Buenos Aires, Argentina	1895	75.0	64.0	71.8	45.6

SOURCES: Newland, "La Educación Elemental"; Leslie Bethell, ed., *The Cambridge History of Latin America*, vols. 4 and 5 (Cambridge, Eng.: Cambridge University Press, 1984); Roberts, *The Population of Jamaica*, p. 78; U.S. Bureau of Census, *Seventh Census of the United States: 1850* (Washington, D.C.: Government Printing Office, 1853).

*Literacy level is for the state, not the country, that is, Massachusetts, New York, Pennsylvania. Also, literacy rates correspond to population over the age of twenty.

ation; poor provinces were less able to raise the resources necessary to make substantial improvements in schooling, and the 1881 law set a limit to federal government aid to provinces while making it solely responsible for funding schools in the capital and federal territories. Although virtually all regions in Argentina substantially

TABLE 4

Provincial Government Expenditures on Primary Education in Argentina
(per capita)

	ANNUAL EXPENDITURES (IN NOMINAL PESOS)	
Province and City	*1874*	*1896*
Buenos Aires	0.30	1.16
Littoral	0.37	0.56
Santa Fé	0.47	0.67
Entre Ríos	0.12	0.50
Corrientes	0.56	0.48
Central	0.11	0.29
Córdoba	0.09	0.29
San Luis	0.29	0.42
Santiago del Estero	0.06	0.24
Andina	0.38	0.60
Mendoza	0.71	0.72
San Juán	0.55	0.78
La Rioja	0.10	0.34
Catamarca	0.14	0.48
Norteña	0.36	0.46
Tucumán	0.50	0.49
Salta	0.18	0.38
Jujuy	0.07	0.38
TOTAL	0.28	0.68

SOURCE: Juan Carlos Vedoya, *Cómo fue la enseñanza popular en la Argentina* (Buenos Aires: Plus Ultra, 1973), p. 89.

NOTE: The 1896 data were converted into pesos fuertes ($1 peso = $0.35 peso fuerte) to make figures comparable. Per capita figures were obtained by dividing provincial budgets for education for the years 1874 and 1896 and by census figures for the population for 1869 and 1895.

boosted their per capita investments between 1875 and 1896, the province of Buenos Aires, which included the city of Buenos Aires, as well as the most productive farmlands in the country, did so at a pace that was nearly twice the national average, 300 percent (see table 4). By 1895, the literacy rate in Buenos Aires was 71.8 percent, while the rest of the country had a literacy rate of only 45.6 percent.[16] In 1914 the national literacy rate was 64.8 percent; in the eastern provinces of Buenos Aires, Santa Fé, Entre Ríos, and Corrientes, it reached 73.1 percent, but in the rest of the country the literacy rate was only 42.4 percent. Heavy immigration at the end of the nineteenth century induced many changes, however.[17]

Immigration had a major positive impact on literacy. The foreign-born were not only relatively more literate than the native population but more demanding of better public services such as education, and national governments were concerned with their incorporation into society. The Argentine government was aware that the provision of public education served as a means of encouraging immigration and of socializing immigrants, and legislation to promote schooling, such as the 1420 Law and the 1904 Lainez Law, was thus partly influenced by the inflow of people. Other evidence suggesting a conscious policy of using schools to foster assimilation is a 1920 law establishing that the primary educational system should create state schools without ethnic or religious discrimination, giving it an integrative character. The positive effect of immigration on literacy in Argentina can be seen in table 5; in 1895 and 1914 the average literacy rate of those who were foreign-born was 55 and 59 percent, respectively; whereas that of natives was 25 and 40 percent. Interestingly, the difference between literacy rates for foreign and native children between the ages of six and fourteen was quite small in 1909 (57 and 56 percent respectively; see table 5). This implies that the gap between the foreigners and natives was solely due to adults and that the growth of primary schooling was substantial enough that more than half of school-age children were then able to attain literacy—regardless of their place of birth.

16. See table 3.
17. From "Resúmen de la República" (Buenos Aires: República Argentina), table 13.

TABLE 5

Literacy Rates for Argentina by Province and Country of Birth: 1895, 1909, and 1914

Province and City	FOREIGN BORN (IN PERCENT)			NATIVES (IN PERCENT)		
	1895 (All ages)	1909 [a] (6–14)	1914 (All ages)	1895 (All ages)	1909 [a] (6–14)	1914 (All ages)
Buenos Aires	68%	71%	74%	53%	78%	65%
Martin García Island	n.a.	100	71	n.a.	61	72
Littoral: East						
Buenos Aires	60	57	64	37	60	50
Santa Fé	60	52	63	30	59	46
Entre Ríos	57	52	64	27	50	42
Corrientes	41	52	55	18	45	33
Central						
Córdoba	58	51	67	27	51	43
San Luis	70	58	74	27	49	46
Santiago del Estero	71	52	63	11	33	26
Andina: West						
Mendoza	53	45	54	31	49	42
San Juán	56	52	51	32	54	42
La Rioja	65	48	63	22	39	39
Catamarca	68	59	69	21	40	39
Norteña						
Tucumán	64	56	56	19	50	38
Salta	41	55	53	18	64	36
Jujuy	25	42	24	17	43	30
Territories						
North						
Misiones	20	38	38	17	45	34
Formosa	31	44	39	20	50	33
Chaco	51	52	56	15	50	35
Los Andes [b]	n.a.	8	47	n.a.	28	26
Center						
La Pampa	61	44	67	18	41	34
West						
Neuquén	23	47	42	8	39	22

TABLE 5
(continued)

Province and City	FOREIGN BORN (IN PERCENT)			NATIVES (IN PERCENT)		
	1895 (All ages)	1909 [a] (6–14)	1914 (All ages)	1895 (All ages)	1909 [a] (6–14)	1914 (All ages)
Territories (continued)						
South						
Río Negro	44	46	54	20	43	28
Chubut	77	63	67	28	56	36
Santa Cruz	73	n.a.	77	26	n.a.	45
Tierra del Fuego	84	67	78	39	61	54
TOTAL	55	57	59	25	56	40

SOURCES: For years 1895 and 1914, *Resúmen de la República* (República de Argentina). The numbers represent the literate foreign (native) population divided by the total foreign (native) population. For the year 1909, *Censo General de Educación* (1909) (Buenos Aires: República de Argentina, 1910). The number represents the literate foreign (native) population divided by the foreign (native) population between the ages of six and fourteen.

[a] The 1909 figure for the total is a weighted average.

[b] Los Andes existed transitorily between the years 1900 and 1943. Its surface was then divided between the provinces of Catamarca and Jujuy. We therefore classify it among the northern territories.

The expansion of the public schools in Argentina was not part of a general movement for democratization as it was in the United States. Major Argentine electoral reforms did not precede the first big push at establishing more and better-funded public schools as they had in the United States. Indeed, the 1853 constitution had not restricted the right to vote based on income/wealth or literacy, but that did not mean that there was general political equality in late-nineteenth-century Argentina. Some provinces maintained income/wealth or literacy requirements for suffrage, and the ease of political expression for the poor and illiterate was likely also constrained by a limited number of polling places and the absence of a secret ballot. Although partly due to a puzzling lack of propensity for foreign-born to apply for citizenship and thus obtain the right to vote, the fraction of the population who voted remained very low (less than 2 percent in 1896, for example) until 1912, when the Sáenz Peña Law ushered in the secret ballot. Although Argentina was one of the outstanding achievers in matters of education in Latin America, its high level of literacy tended to be concentrated in the littoral area (Buenos Aires, Santa Fé, Entre Ríos, Corrientes) and among the immigrants who not only contributed to the increase in the level of literacy but promoted active government policy in matters of education.

Chile

As in Argentina, immigration played an important role in increasing the relative levels of education in Chile. The rate of literacy in 1854 was 13.3 percent for the country as a whole but 46.3 for the foreign-born.[18] Problems of regional disparity prevailed in Chile as well; between the years 1885 and 1914 an increase in nitrates led to an economic boom that mainly benefited the cities. The consequent growth of cities led to an expansion in public services, of which schooling was among the most important. Between 1885 and 1910, literacy increased from 28.9 percent for the population as a whole to more than 50 percent, with the literate population heavily concentrated in Chile's three large cities: Santiago, Valparaíso, and Concepción. The Chilean experience is puzzling in that the country was able to maintain a relatively high level of education when compared with the rest of Latin America despite its large number of private schools and what appeared to be relatively strict voting laws. A closer examination, however, shows that Chile was one of the few countries that provided subsidies to private schools[19] and that

18. Carlos Newland, "La Educación Elemental en Hispanoamérica: Desde la Independencia hasta la Centralización de los Sistemas Educativos Nacionales," *Hispanic American Historical Review* 71, no. 2 (May 1991).

19. Carlos Newland, "The Estado Docente and Its Expansion: Spanish America

the laws governing elections during the nineteenth century were less constraining in Chile than in the rest of Latin America.

One of the first laws to govern elections was the 1833 constitution, which established income and property requirements that could easily be met by artisans, salaried workers, miners, petty merchants, public employees (such as army officers and policemen), and the 60,000 men in the national guard, for whom the government purposefully set low income requirements in 1840.[20] Veterans of the wars of independence were exempted from the income and literacy requirements. In 1874, suffrage was expanded to include all literate males, regardless of income since "whoever [could] read and write [had] the income that the law require[d]."[21] A sufficient test of literacy was whether a person could write his own name, starkly different from other Latin American countries, where individuals had to show a "literary" or professional title in order to fulfill the literacy requirement.[22] As a result of the 1874 law the number of registered voters tripled: from 49,047 in 1872 to 148,737 in 1878. The only group to significantly grow in numbers, both in absolute and relative terms, were registrants listing agriculture as their only occupation, from 16,698 in 1872 to 70,966 in 1878. Thus political power may not have been as unequally distributed in Chile as it was in the rest of Latin America. This does not necessarily mean that there was higher political participation than in other Latin American countries. If political power had been held by a broader spectrum of the population, it is possible that local government would have been

---

Elementary Education, 1900–1950," *Journal of Latin American Studies* 26, no. 2 (May 1994).

20. J. Samuel Valenzuela, "Building Aspects of Democracy before Democracy: Electoral Practices in Nineteenth Century Chile," in Eduardo Posada-Carbó, ed., *Elections before Democracy: The History of Elections in Europe and Latin America* (New York: St. Martin's Press, 1996).

21. Ibid., p. 224.

22. See, for example, the 1857 constitution in Mexico.

less reticent to provide public education and that collective-action problems may have been dampened.

Costa Rica

Costa Rica has long been considered a relatively egalitarian society. Historians have attributed part of this equality to its endowments: a sparsely populated land, with a small indigenous population, and a predominance of free peasantry in the central valley. The lack of precious minerals as well as the difficulty of realizing scale economies in agriculture owing to a mountainous terrain also likely contributed to relative equality in incomes. One fundamental characteristic of Costa Rica's political organization, once it became independent from Spain in 1821, were *ayuntamientos* (city councils), which had been set up by the Cádiz constitution between 1812 and 1814 as a basic governmental structure. During the conflicts between Guatemala and León (in Nicaragua) over control of the newly independent states in Central America, these councils assumed many functions typical of a national state, such as defense, and until 1823 they rotated the seat of government every three months between the four principal cities: Cartago, San José, Alajuela, and Heredia. After the newly independent nation of Costa Rica was established, the government recognized the authority of the *ayuntamientos* for the provision and control of education, originally conferred on them by the Cádiz constitution.[23]

The role of the municipalities in overseeing schools was bolstered during the 1820s when the national government implemented a series of measures that helped the municipal govern-

---

23. Luis Fernando Sibaja, "Ayuntamientos y Estado en los Primeros Años de Vida Independiente de Costa Rica (1821–1835)," in *Actas del III Congreso de Academias Iberoamericanas de la Historia: El Municipio en Iberoamérica (Cabildos e Instituciones Locales)* (Montevideo, Uruguay: Instituto Histórico y Geográfico del Uruguay, 1995).

ments to raise more revenue for educational expenses.[24] In 1849, education boards, composed of leading local civil, political, and ecclesiastical figures, were set up to supervise local school systems. The 1869 constitution made primary education obligatory for both sexes and tuition-free, with municipalities in charge of its general direction and the federal government in charge of inspection. Because of the problems municipal governments had in raising revenue, however, the Treasury assumed responsibility for paying teachers' salaries. All other expenses were left to the municipalities, including the costs of infrastructure, which demanded substantial funds and exacerbated the fiscal problems faced by local governments. This situation remained unchanged until 1885, when a new administration issued two laws, the Fundamental Law of Public Instruction (1885) and the General Law of Common Education (1886), that set the basis for reform from the bottom up. The new laws relied on two basic premises: that the executive power had absolute control over matters related to primary education and that this power was to be exercised through the government's direct delegates and administered through the local authorities. Citizens in each district were required to pay for infrastructure expenses in public schools. In addition, the laws increased the federal allocation for education, and the national government began buying school supplies in bulk and selling them to the local boards of education at a discount. In August 1888, Congress approved a federal loan for education of $300,000 pesos at 9 percent interest. Although the districts that benefited most from this loan were those that had enough revenue to cover the interest payments, localities with lower

---

24. Astrid Fischel, *Concenso y Represión: una interpretación socio-política de la educación costarricense* (San José, Costa Rica: Editorial Costa Rica, 1987). Local taxes included taxes on cutting up cattle (the largest source of revenue), fines (including those charged for not attending school), money from the commutation of a sentence, taxes for the sale of tobacco and liquor, donations and contributions, vacant inheritances, and taxes on heads of family.

revenues were entitled under the law to receive government aid if they could not raise sufficient funds by taxing their constituents. An important reason for the success of these reforms was that the minister of public instruction, Mauro Fernández, was also the minister of finance at this time; this made it easier to coordinate the educational reforms and the reforms concerning local public finances.

The increased government funds assigned to primary education in the 1885 and 1886 laws reflected an interest and support for public schooling in Costa Rica. Unlike any of the other Latin American countries, Costa Ricans attributed particular significance to primary education, which was seen as the basis for a democracy. During the 1881 economic crisis, when the price of coffee fell and a fiscal crisis ensued, subsidies from the federal government to the school system were suspended for secondary and higher education (including normal schools) but not for primary education.[25] In contrast, Chile committed roughly equivalent amounts to primary, secondary, and higher education in 1875, despite there being many more students in primary school. In 1900, Mexico spent $104.79 per secondary school student and $126.42 per higher education student, while devoting only $0.20 to primary students.

Mexico

In Mexico, even under Spanish rule, schooling was seen as important (it was originally used by the Catholic Church as a means of converting the indigenous population to Catholicism). By the end of the eighteenth century the Bourbon dynasty had set up a system that encouraged the expansion of schooling by giving *cabildos* (town councils) control over all matters relating to primary education. The 1812 Cádiz constitution established a General Director of Studies to oversee all matters of education in the colonies and instructed the colonial government to create primary schools in which children

25. Ibid.

would be taught to "read, write and count, and catechism," while retaining localities' rights over education.[26] This municipal prerogative was recognized after independence in the 1824 constitution, which protected the right of the new federal entities to organize education according to their specific needs. Schooling was declared "necessary for all citizens" in the provisional constitution of 1814, and, after independence, the 1833 constitution declared schooling obligatory for men, women, and children.[27] The ten years of civil war before independence, together with almost fifty years of persistent deadlock between conservatives and liberals, however, led to a climate of uncertainty and constant changes in government that undoubtedly complicated the task of raising resources to support an extensive system of public schools. Not until after the reform wars and the end of the French intervention (1867) was a legal outline of the public school system drafted (1861) and enacted (1867 and 1869) as laws of public instruction. It took another decade for the society to invest the necessary resources in the project, during the period of President Porfirio Díaz's government.[28]

In contrast with the Costa Rican experience, the Mexican government did not divide the tasks of control and administration between itself and the municipalities. The 1867 and 1869 laws of pub-

26. Antonio Annino, "The Ballot, Land and Sovereignty: Cadiz and the Origins of Mexican Local Government, 1812–1820," in Eduardo Posada-Carbó, ed., *Elections before Democracy: The History of Elections in Europe and Latin America* (New York: St. Martin's Press, 1996). Even though most of the articles in the Cádiz constitution were not implemented as law, owing to the wars of independence (1810–21), it began a process of decentralization by creating more *cabildos*. These town councils were used as a political instrument aimed at weakening insurgency but in fact gave towns greater local autonomy and reinforced insurgency from the periphery to the center.

27. Fernando Solana, Raúl Cardiel Reyes, and Raúl Bolaños Martínez, coordinators, *Historia de la educación pública en México* (Mexico: Fondo de Cultura Economica, 1981).

28. The period of the Porfiriato starts in 1876 when Porfirio Díaz assumes the presidency for the first time; it ends in 1910 with the Mexican revolution.

lic instruction—intended to reorganize public education at a national level and to unify tuition-free primary schools in the country—began the tendency toward centralizing all matters relating to education. Due to the federal nature of the country, however, their implementation was limited to the capital city (Distrito Federal, hereafter, DF) and the federal territories (Baja California, Quintana Roo, and Tepic), even though some states issued similar laws afterward. A similar situation arose with the 1869 law, which suppressed religious education and set out in detail the number of schools required, as well as study plans and school calendars that were to be used throughout the country. Consequently, conflicts about educational policy arose early between different levels of government. For example, the Díaz administration proposed the Federal Law of Public Instruction of 1888, which created a unified federally directed primary school system, and urged states to adopt the law. The result was a de facto congressional veto, which was essentially overturned when, in 1890, the minister of public instruction called two national education congresses and got them to agree on a uniform national school system.[29] Because Congress opposed the loss of state and municipal power in educational matters, from 1896 onward the Díaz government implemented all legislation relating to education by presidential decree. This strategy of bypassing Congress, or using parallel institutions to override it, was repeated by the central government even after the revolution (1910) that followed Díaz's rule.

Nevertheless, the federal government undertook to establish a system of tuition-free primary schools with the 1888 Federal Law of Primary Instruction. By 1900, many state governments had passed similar laws subsidizing and administering municipal schools, which up to this point had been inadequately supported, and creating a unified state policy in matters of education. During the 1920s

---

29. Mary Kay Vaughan, *The State, Education, and Social Class in Mexico, 1880–1928* (Dekalb: Northern Illinois University Press, 1982).

President Calles set up federal delegates in charge of education and gave them the power to administer the federal funds in each district. This created parallel bureaucracies for education in each state—one associated with the state and one with the federal government. The 1920s also marked the creation of the Ministry of Education (1921) and the first national campaigns (called cultural missions) to implant literacy nationwide by the two most prominent secretaries of education in Mexican history: José Vasconcelos (1921–1924) and Moises Sáenz (1928). Those campaigns coincided with the largest increase in the federal budget for education at that time: 15 percent of the total federal budget for the year 1923, which by 1930 then fell to its prerevolutionary level of 7 to 9 percent. In sum, although the federal government promoted the expansion of the school system, it was at the expense of local government control, and thus national and provincial governments gradually took over the responsibilities of municipalities in matters of education.[30]

Mexico's history in matters of education raises two distinct issues: What factors led the country toward a centralized administration of education? and When centralization did occur, what were the results? that is, Was centralization beneficial in stimulating the expansion of public schools? Who benefited? and How costly was it to let the states, and ultimately the national government, conduct all policy relating to schooling?

In municipalities and provinces with great inequality or population heterogeneity, elites who would have borne a greater than proportionate share of the costs and received a less than proportionate share of the benefits, would have been inclined to use their disproportionate political influence to oppose raising and disburs-

---

30. Ibid. State expenditures on schooling went from 10.52 percent in 1878 to 23.08 in 1910, becoming the largest item in states' budgets. Combined expenditures in education for both the federal and the state governments during the Porfiriato increased at an impressive pace: $26,767,224 in 1878 and $126,177,950 in 1910—a rise of more than 370 percent.

ing funds for public schools. In such cases, the federal government could step in as a third party to solve collective action problems or compel an implicit redistribution of resources. When the federal government first began to pursue an active educational policy, however, during the Porfiriato, the gap between the expenditures of the federal government and those of the states widened, and by 1910 $6.92 was spent per inhabitant in the DF and federal territories, while an average of $0.36 was spent by the state governments.[31] This was because the federal government was constrained to focus on districts over which it had unambiguous authority in educational matters and reflected the limited support of public schools in most states. This was not true throughout Mexico, however. The generally more prosperous states of northern Mexico, such as Coahuila, Sonora, Nuevo León, Tamaulipas, and Chihuahua, together with the state of Yucatán (the major henequen producer), had among the highest expenditures on education in the country (see table 6).

The northern states had demonstrated early on a commitment to public schooling; indeed, in some areas public schools with broad access were established at the beginning of the nineteenth century, not unlike the pattern in the United States and Canada. Like their northern neighbors, the cities and towns of northern Mexico had relatively homogeneous populations of largely European descent who had isolated or exterminated the indigenous groups of the region in order to occupy the territory. This tended to produce communities with relative equality in income and human capital (as in Canada and the United States). The city of Chihuahua, founded in 1709, opened its first primary public school in 1786 when its population reached 18,288 inhabitants, and in 1797 efforts were undertaken to create a system of public schools in every large town in the state. By 1808 there were public primary schools in five different

31. See table 6.

localities.[32] But the centralization of the control and administration of resources left such localities impoverished and unable to set their own priorities in matters of education. Efforts to reduce this problem—such as those undertaken under the Díaz administration, which gave preferential treatment to some municipalities (in this case, Nuevo León and Coahuila, two of the northern states) by giving them the responsibility of administering primary school expenditures in their states—proved unsuccessful. In other words, although the intervention of the federal government stimulated the spread of public schooling in the country at large, some of the more progressive states' school systems may have actually deteriorated because of a redistribution of resources across states, or toward the center, by federal taxation.

As our brief review of the four case countries illustrates, the pattern common to the northern part of North America, wherein local or state populations mobilized early on to establish primary schools accessible to everyone, was rare in Latin America. Moreover, those relatively few areas where this did occur, such as in parts of northern Mexico and Costa Rica, resembled the United States and Canada in having relatively homogeneous populations.[33] This seems consistent with the idea that, given some base level of per capita income, the ease with which collective efforts to coordinate, organize, or provide public goods, such as universal access to primary schools, varied across communities with the degrees of population homogeneity and equality in economic and political circumstances. From this perspective, it is not surprising that the highly

32. Luis Alboites, *Breve Historia de Chihuahua* (Mexico: Colegio de Mexico, 1994).

33. To say that the population of northern Mexico was homogeneous is not strictly accurate. Although precise figures are not available, it seems likely that many Native Americans were living in isolated rural areas. The towns and more densely settled districts, however, had relatively homogeneous populations of European descent.

TABLE 6
Combined State and Municipal Revenue and Primary School Expenditures
during the Porfiriato (in pesos per capita)

State	Combined State and Municipal Revenue 1888	Combined State and Municipal Revenue 1907	Increase in per Capita Revenue 1888–1907	Expenditures in Primary Education 1874	Expenditures in Primary Education 1907	Increase in Primary School Expenditures 1874–1907
Northwest						
Baja California*						
Baja California Sur*						
Nayarit*						
Sinaloa	4.44	4.65	4.73%	0.31	0.60	93.55%
Sonora	3.67	6.56	78.75	0.38	0.98	157.89
North						
Chihuahua	2.96	6.98	135.81	0.02	0.98	4800
Coahuila	3.47	6.66	91.93	0.25	1.12	348
Durango	1.15	2.47	114.78	0.10	0.53	430
Zacatecas	2.62	2.87	9.54	0.08	0.52	550
Northeast						
Nuevo León	1.40	3.31	136.43	0.36	0.68	88.89
Tamaulipas	1.34	5.66	322.39	0.07	0.77	1000
Central West						
Aguascalientes	1.40	4.24	202.86	0.11	0.38	245.45
Guanajuato	1.74	2.01	15.52	0.24	0.19	−20.83
Jalisco	1.09	2.53	132.11	0.05	0.34	580
Querétaro	1.49	2.45	64.43	0.09	0.18	100
San Luis Potosí	2.63	2.53	−3.80	0.17	0.28	64.71
Gulf						
Tabasco	3.26	5.35	64.11	0.25	0.52	108
Veracruz	4.82	4.05	−15.98	0.19	0.46	142.11
Central South						
Distrito Federal*						
Hidalgo	2.10	2.80	33.33	0.18	0.39	116.67
México	1.24	2.93	136.29	0.24	0.31	29.17
Morelos	3.20	4.04	26.25	0.27	0.51	88.89
Puebla	2.15	3.64	69.30	0.20	0.30	50
Tlaxcala	1.12	2.09	86.61	0.16	0.35	118.75

TABLE 6
(continued)

State	Combined State and Municipal Revenue 1888	Combined State and Municipal Revenue 1907	Increase in per Capita Revenue 1888–1907	Expenditures in Primary Education 1874	Expenditures in Primary Education 1907	Increase in Primary School Expenditures 1874–1907
South						
Chiapas	0.66	2.43	268.18	0.03	0.23	666.67
Colima	2.25	4.45	97.78	0.21	0.61	190.48
Guerrero	1.58	1.25	−20.89	0.22	0.18	−18.18
Michoacán	1.16	1.56	34.48	0.07	0.12	71.43
Oaxaca	0.77	1.59	106.49	0.09	0.24	166.67
Southeast						
Campeche	3.16	7.24	129.11	0.18	1.00	455.56
Quintana Roo*						
Yucatán	2.35	11.51	389.79	0.17	0.80	370.59
TOTAL	38.17	68.69		3.12	7.39	
AVERAGE	2.01	3.62	95.58	0.16	0.39	185.58

SOURCE: Mary Kay Vaughan, *The State, Education, and Social Class in Mexico, 1880–1928* (Dekalb: Northern Illinois University Press, 1982).

NOTES: The federal government spent $1.37 per inhabitant on education in 1878, and $6.92 in 1910. The regional division for Mexico is based on Angel Bassols's (UNAM, Department of Economics) economic classification of states, based on the physical characteristics of the region.
*Funded by the federal government.

stratified societies of Latin America lagged far behind the United States and Canada in establishing schooling institutions and attaining high rates of literacy.

We have emphasized two closely related reasons why population homogeneity might favor the successful completion of collective action projects such as the establishment of universal schools. First, where citizens are alike in values, endowments, and behavior, they should find it easier to agree on whether and how to carry out such an enterprise. Second, when the benefits and especially the costs of a project are unequally distributed, and in fact serve as a means of redistributing substantial resources from rich to poor, those who bear a highly disproportionate share of the costs will likely attempt to block the project. Particularly in cases where this group also enjoys disproportionate political power, such projects often fail. This type of situation is seen throughout Latin America in the restrictions on the conduct of elections—who had the right to vote and whether ballots were secret or public. Income (or wealth) and literacy requirements for suffrage were common, but it was mainly a lack of literacy that limited the population who could participate politically. In this way, elite individuals who were generally among the small group who could vote, and who stood to bear a much higher share of the costs than they would reap of the benefits, would resist public enterprises such as the provision of universal schools supported by tax revenue. Thus, the inequality in the distributions of income, human capital, and political power that arose out of the conditions of early settlements tended to persist over time—perpetuated at first by the institutions of imperial Spain and then by those that evolved (or failed to evolve) in the newly formed states after independence.

With independence from Spain, the new nations had more liberty to shape their social and economic institutions, and great contrasts across the paths they came to follow are evident. None of them generated universal primary schools on any widespread basis from local or state levels, as had much of the United States and Canada. When major progress came on this front, it was typically because of interventions from national governments at the end of the nineteenth century or later. In Costa Rica, one of the most progressive nations, a more equal distribution of resources and a relatively homogeneous population may have made resistance to public schools less enduring and more easily overcome, but the national government played a major role by infusing needed resources to the municipalities. In Argentina and Chile, the effects of exogenous factors such as immigration, coupled with more equality in political power (as compared to other Latin American countries), helped spur the respective national governments to push for the expansion of public schools. In Mexico, however, whose highly heterogeneous and unequal society was perhaps more typical of Latin America overall, the political climate was adverse for major investments in public education, and a sharp break with past institutions was necessary to establish an extensive public school system.

III

Although other factors such as per capita income were important, our review suggests that the extent of inequality in the Americas, especially as reflected in the distribution of political power, may well have been influential in accounting for the magnitude of investments in schooling early in the development process. Both in the United States and in Canada, large numbers of distinct political jurisdictions chose to introduce universal primary schools supported by general taxes not long after major extensions of the suffrage. A similar pattern of expansions of primary schools following suffrage reform is also evident in nineteenth-century Britain. Within Latin America, those countries that were leaders in public provision of education, and in the attainment of high rates of literacy—Argentina, Costa Rica, and Chile (to a perhaps lesser degree)—generally had relatively greater equality in the distributions of income, human capital, and political power, probably throughout their histories since European colonization. Societies that had quite heterogeneous populations and much less equality, such as Mexico, were, in contrast, slower to establish or expand public schools. Overall, the evidence across countries on the proportions of the population that were literate and that enjoyed the right to vote is consistent with these characterizations.

Although the theories of how the extent of inequality might affect the social decision to invest in public institutions of primary education are reasonable, and receive considerable support from the outlines of the historical experience, one would like to subject the idea to a more systematic test of consistency with the evidence. This is not easy, however. First, estimates of inequality in income or wealth during the nineteenth century exist for only a few countries, and data are scarce for other relevant variables as well. Second, and fundamental in a conceptual sense, it is difficult to identify clear lines of causation because the provision of universal primary schooling has a powerful effect on the degree of inequality in each of the various dimensions we focus on (wealth/income, human capital, and political power). When variables are mutually reinforcing or simultaneously determined, discerning what is exogenous and what is endogenous is not transparent.

The problem is that, throughout the nineteenth century, citizenship and the right to vote were linked to literacy in most of the Americas. Indeed, as seen in table 7, virtually all Latin American countries maintained, with minor exceptions, both literacy and wealth requirements for the franchise through the early twentieth century. Some examples include Bolívar's constitution, which required the capacity to read and write to obtain citizenship; the Cádiz constitution of 1812, which required citizens to be literate by 1830 (this condition applied to the remaining colonies such as Cuba and Puerto Rico); the Peruvian constitution of 1823, which made literacy a binding condition for citizenship by the year 1840 (three years later, a new constitution made the literacy requirement binding immediately); and Mexico's policy, in which each state decided on the date when literacy would become a binding requirement for citizenship (most states set the dates between 1836 and 1850).[34] Furthermore, because the education system taught most individuals to read first and write later, many of the definitions of citizenship in the

34. Dorothy Tanck de Estrada, "Las Cortes de Cádiz y el desarrollo de la educación en México," *Historia Mexicana* 29, no. 1 (1979): 17.

newly independent Latin American countries made reading and writing separate requirements; an individual had to read *and* to write in order to obtain full citizenship rights. These restrictions on the right to vote seem to have been enforced, with some exceptions.[35] As evident from both tables 7 and 8, the proportions of the population voting in Latin American elections varied substantially among countries and were generally very low by international standards—especially in those with low literacy rates (see table 1). This suggests both that such countries had highly heterogeneous populations and that groups with low literacy rates had limited political power and found it difficult to secure increases in resources targeted at the expansion of schools (among other public services they might have desired). The obstacle to mobilizing support for public schools with open access was made all the more formidable by the fact that those who enjoyed the right to vote were likely those who would have paid most of the taxes for operating new schools and yet reaped few of the direct benefits. In such a situation, where inequality in human capital and political power reinforce each other, it is easy to understand how both forms of inequality could persist over time in societies that began with extreme inequality—as many of the New World economies other than the United States and Canada did.

A basic test of the hypothesis that inequality in political power may have worked toward delaying investments in the establishment of broad systems of public schooling in many New World societies is to examine whether there were great imbalances in who had the right to vote and how they varied across countries.

35. In Chile, a voting registry was created in which political parties sought to enroll most of their supporters; one logical choice of supporters for the ruling parties was the National Guard. To enfranchise the National Guard, the government had to lower income restrictions and slacken literacy requirements (a person was required to read and write their name) and, by doing so, it enfranchised most of the population. See Valenzuela, "Building Aspects of Democracy."

TABLE 7
Laws Governing the Franchise and the Extent of Voting
in Selected American Countries, 1840–1940

		Secret Ballot	Wealth Require- ment	Literacy Require- ment	Voting Population (in percent)
1840–80					
Chile	1869	Y	Y	Y	1.6%
	1878	Y	N	N [a]	—
Costa Rica	1890	N	Y	Y	—
Ecuador	1848	N	Y	Y	0.0
	1856	N	Y	Y	0.1
Mexico	1840	N	Y	Y	—
Peru	1875	N	Y	Y	—
Uruguay	1840	N	Y	Y	—
	1880	N	Y	Y	—
Venezuela	1840	N	Y	Y	—
	1880	N	Y	Y	—
Canada	1867	N	Y	N	7.7
	1878	Y	Y	N	12.9
United States	1850 [b]	Y	N	N	12.9
	1880	Y	N	N	18.3
1881–1920					
Argentina	1896	N	Y	Y	1.8 [c]
	1916	Y	N	N	9.0
Brazil	1894	N	Y	Y	2.2
	1914	N	Y	Y	2.4
Chile	1881	Y	N	N	3.1
	1920	Y	N	Y	4.4
Colombia	1918 [d]	Y	N	N	6.9
Costa Rica	1912	N	Y	Y	—
	1919	N	N	N	10.6
Ecuador	1888	Y	Y	Y	2.8
	1894	Y	N	Y	3.3
Mexico	1920	Y	N	N	8.6
Peru	1920	N	Y	Y	—
Uruguay	1900	N	Y	Y	—
	1920	Y	N	N	13.8
Venezuela	1920	N	Y	Y	—
Canada	1911	Y	N	N	18.1
	1917	Y	N	N	20.5

TABLE 7
(*continued*)

		Secret Ballot	Wealth Require- ment	Literacy Require- ment	Voting Population (in percent)
United States	1900	Y	N	Y [e]	18.4%
	1920	Y	N	Y	25.1
1921–40					
Argentina	1928	Y	N	N	12.8
	1937	Y	N	N	15.0
Bolivia	1951	?	Y	Y	4.1
Brazil	1930	N	Y	Y	5.7
Colombia	1930	Y	N	N	11.1
	1936	Y	N	N	5.9
Chile	1920	Y	N	Y	4.4
	1931	Y	N	Y	6.5
	1938	Y	N	Y	9.4
Costa Rica	1940	Y	N	N	17.6
Ecuador	1940	Y	N	Y	3.3
Mexico	1940	Y	N	N	11.8
Peru	1940	Y	N	Y	—
Uruguay	1940	Y	N	N	19.7
Venezuela	1940	Y	Y	Y	—
Canada	1940	Y	N	N	41.1
United States	1940	Y	N	Y	37.8

[a] After eliminating wealth and education requirements in 1878, Chile instituted a literacy requirement in 1885, which seems to have been responsible for a sharp decline in the proportion of the population that was registered to vote.

[b] Three states, Connecticut, Louisiana, and New Jersey, still maintained wealth requirements in 1840 but eliminated them soon afterward. All states except Illinois and Virginia had implemented the secret ballot by the end of the 1840s.

[c] This figure is for the city of Buenos Aires and likely overstates the proportion who voted at the national level.

[d] The information on restrictions refers to national laws. The 1863 constitution empowered provincial state governments to regulate electoral affairs. Afterward, elections became restricted (in terms of the franchise for adult males) and indirect in some states. It was not until 1948 that a national law established universal adult male suffrage throughout the country. This pattern was followed in other Latin American countries, as it was in the United States and Canada to a lesser extent.

[e] Eighteen states, seven southern and eleven nonsouthern, introduced literacy requirements between 1890 and 1926. These restrictions were directed primarily at blacks and immigrants.

TABLE 8
International Comparisons of Laws Relating to Suffrage, and the Extent of Voting

Country	Year Secret Ballot Attained	Year Women Gained the Vote	Year Universal Equal Male Suffrage Attained	Proportion of Population Voting 1900 (in percent)
Austria	1907	1919	1907	7.9%
Belgium	1877	1948	1919	22.0
Denmark	1901	1918	1918	16.5
Finland	1907	1907	1907	4.6
France	1831	1945	1848	19.4
Germany	1848	1919	1872	15.5
Italy	1861	1946	1919	6.8
Netherlands	1849	1922	1918	12.0
Norway	1885	1909	1921	19.5
Sweden	1866	1921	1921	7.1
Switzerland	1872	1971	1848	22.3
United Kingdom	1872	1918	1948	16.2
Canada	1874	1917	1898 [a]	17.9
United States	1849 [b]	1920	1870 [c]	18.4
Argentina	1912	1947	?	1.8 [d]
Bolivia	?	?	1956	—
Brazil	1932	1932	1988	3.0
Chile	1833	1949	1970	4.2
Costa Rica	1925	1949	1913	—
Ecuador	1861	1929	1978	3.3
El Salvador	1950	1939	1950	—
Guatemala	1946 [e]	1946	1965	—
Peru	1931	1955	1979	—
Uruguay	1918	1932	1918	—
Venezuela	1946	1945	1946 [f]	—

[a] By 1898, all but two Canadian provinces had instituted universal equal suffrage for males.

[b] By the end of the 1840s, all states except Illinois and Virginia had adopted the secret ballot.

[c] Eighteen states, seven southern and eleven nonsouthern, introduced literacy requirements between 1890 and 1926. These restrictions were directed primarily at blacks and immigrants.

[d] This figure is for the city of Buenos Aires and likely overestimates the national figure.

[e] Illiterate males did not obtain the secret ballot until 1956; females did not obtain it until 1965.

[f] The 1858 constitution declared universal direct male suffrage, but this provision was dropped in later constitutions. All restrictions on universal adult suffrage were ended in 1946, with the exception of different age restrictions for literate and illiterate persons.

Differential access to the right to cast a vote is one of the most direct, and easily measurable, channels through which an elite can exercise disproportionate political influence. Summary information about the policies governing who had the right to vote in various countries of the Americas during the late nineteenth and early twentieth centuries is reported in table 7. The display indicates that, although the right to vote was generally reserved to adult males, the United States and Canada were the clear leaders in doing away with restrictions based on wealth and literacy and thus had much higher fractions of their populations voting than anywhere else in the New World. Not only did they attain the secret ballot and extend the franchise even to the poor and illiterate much earlier (a right that was to a significant degree withdrawn at the expense of blacks in much of the southern United States during the 1890s and for an extended period), but the United States and Canada were about a half century ahead of even the most democratic countries of Latin America (Uruguay, Argentina, and Costa Rica) in the proportions of the population voting. Through 1940, they routinely had proportions voting that were 50 to 100 percent higher than did their most progressive neighbors to the south, three times higher than in Mexico, and up to ten times higher than in countries such as Brazil and Bolivia.

This pattern suggests that there was at least some relationship between the extents of literacy and of the right to vote—or between inequality in human capital and in political power. The United States and Canada had no restrictions on white male universal suffrage, were early in establishing universal public schools, and enjoyed high levels of literacy; in contrast, nearly all their neighbors in the hemisphere maintained literacy requirements and other restrictions on the franchise until the beginning of the twentieth century or later. Moreover, within Latin America, it was typically those countries that had the broadest franchise and were the first to extend the right to vote—such as Argentina, Uruguay, and Costa

Rica—that led Latin America in expanding the public school system and raising literacy rates late in the nineteenth century. This empirical association is consistent with our hypothesis, but several alternative interpretations might be offered. One is to simply dismiss the low proportions of the voting population as a consequence of the prevalence of literacy requirements in societies with low rates of literacy. But this begs the question of why it was that those countries with low literacy rates were much more likely to maintain the literacy requirements, or why countries that dropped such restrictions were more likely to establish public schools and realize large advances in literacy during the nineteenth and early twentieth centuries. Although others might try to account for the empirical association as largely a result of the legacy of British institutions, one should be skeptical of this approach as well. Not only does it ignore the variation noted within Latin America, but few of the many other (including former) British colonies in the Americas came close to matching the records of the United States and Canada in literacy attainment until the British Colonial Office got involved in promoting public schooling late in the nineteenth century.

The extension of suffrage in the United States and Canada, as well as its relation to the respective movements for the establishment of tax-supported public primary or common schools, helps establish a path of causation from a change in the extent of one form of inequality to a change in the extent of another. Although not excluding the possibility of other factors influencing social decisions to expand public schooling, at least in some of the countries in the Americas, a change in the extent of political inequality acted as a salient stimulus. The achievement of universal white male suffrage in the United States was the product of a long series of hard-fought political battles over the first decades of the nineteenth century—not a commitment on the part of those who drafted the Constitution. Historians of education have judged it no coincidence that this movement triumphed in the 1820s in the United States at the same time that the movement for "common schools"—tax supported, publicly controlled and directed, and free to all—got started. Other prominent occurrences of the extension of suffrage being implemented just before major expansions of schooling include the passage in England of the landmark Elementary Education law of 1870 (and a series of further laws through 1891 expanding access to primary schools) not long after the Second Reform Act of 1867.[36]

By providing an even broader international perspective, table 8 highlights how slow most of the New World societies, despite being nominal democracies, were to extend the franchise to the bulk of their populations. The great majority of European nations, as well as the United States and Canada, achieved secrecy in balloting and universal adult male suffrage long before countries in Latin America or the Caribbean, and the proportions of the population voting in the former were always higher and often four to five times those in the latter. Although many factors may have contributed to the relatively low vote totals in Latin America and the Caribbean, the political decisions to maintain wealth and literacy requirements (evidently binding constraints) on the franchise appear to have been of central importance.

To examine the empirical association between the extent of suffrage (a proxy for the degree of inequality in political power) and the investment in schooling institutions more directly, let us look at the ratio of students in primary and secondary schools to the population between ages five to nineteen and at the fraction of the total population who cast votes in a wide range of countries in the Americas and Europe (see table 9). Several features are immediately evident. First, the United States and Canada stood out early as having the highest proportions of school-age children attending school in the world—62 and 60 percent, respectively, in 1895. The only other nations that come close are the only three of the countries in

36. See Cubberley, *History of Education*, pp. 641–44.

TABLE 9

Ratio of Students in School to Population Ages 5–19 and Proportion of the Population Voting for Selected Countries, 1895–1945

	CA. 1895		CA. 1920		CA. 1945	
	Schooling Ratio [a]	Suffrage [b] (in percent)	Schooling Ratio [a]	Suffrage [b] (in percent)	Schooling Ratio [a]	Suffrage [b] (in percent)
Argentina	0.21	1.8%	0.41	10.9%	0.44	15.0%
Bolivia	0.07	—	—	—	0.18	—
Brazil	0.08	2.2	0.10	4.0	0.22	5.7
Chile	0.16	4.2	0.37	4.4	0.40	9.4
Colombia	—	—	0.20	6.9	0.21	11.1
Costa Rica	0.22	—	0.22	10.6	0.29	17.6
Cuba	—	—	0.31	—	0.37	—
Mexico	0.13	5.4	0.22	8.6	0.28	11.8
Peru	—	—	—	—	0.31	—
Uruguay	0.13	—	0.36	13.8	—	—
Canada	0.60	17.9	0.65	20.5	0.64	41.1
United States	0.62	18.4	0.68	25.1	0.76	37.8
Austria	0.45	7.9	0.52	46.1	0.58	46.9
Belgium	0.42	20.1	0.46	26.3	0.53	28.9
Denmark	0.49	9.9	0.49	30.3	0.50	50.8
Finland	0.12	4.6	0.29	27.3	0.53	44.3
France	0.56	19.4	0.43	21.0	0.60	49.3
Germany	0.54	14.6	0.53	45.6	0.55	48.8
Ireland	0.32	—	0.54	21.9	0.53	41.1
Italy	0.27	4.1	0.36	16.2	0.47	52.5
Netherlands	0.44	5.1	0.45	20.5	0.56	49.5
Norway	0.48	7.9	0.50	32.1	0.52	47.5
Portugal	0.14	—	0.17	—	0.26	—
Spain	—	—	0.27	—	0.34	—
Sweden	0.50	2.8	0.42	11.2	0.45	46.4
Switzerland	0.53	11.8	0.54	19.2	0.49	20.5
United Kingdom	0.45	9.8	0.51	30.4	0.66	49.9

SOURCES: For the schooling data: B. R. Mitchell, *International Historical Statistics: The Americas 1750–1988* (New York: Stockton Press, 1993), and *International Historical Statistics: Europe 1750–1988* (Basingstoke, Hants, Eng.: Macmillan; New York: Stockton Press, 1992). For the data on suffrage: Peter Flora et al., *State, Economy and Society in Western Europe: 1815–1975*, vol. 1 (Frankfurt am Main: Campus Verlag; Chicago: St. James Press, 1983); Dieter Nohlan, ed., *Enciclopedia Electoral Latinamericana y del Caribe* (San José, Costa Rica: Instituto Inter-americano de Derechos Humanos, 1993).

[a] Schooling ratios were calculated by dividing the total number of students (regardless of age) by the population between the ages of 5 and 19. When groups of population were different from this range, we assumed the same number of people in each age group and weighted the population figures so as to make them comparable. An example of this was Bolivia.

[b] Suffrage is used here to represent the proportion of the population that votes in each country.

Europe that attained universal equal male suffrage in the nineteenth century: France (56), Germany (54), and Switzerland (53); notably, Britain fell behind its neighbors by this measure of investment in education, despite dominating them in per capita income. The United States and Canada were also distinguished in 1895 as having, with the exception of Belgium, the highest fractions of their populations voting as well. The Latin American countries generally lag both their North American neighbors and the European countries in both schooling ratios and the extension of the franchise. In South and Central America, Argentina had the highest schooling ratio in 1895, but it was barely a third of the levels prevailing in the United States and Canada. This may partially reflect the preferences of the substantial flows of immigrants from Europe, who were much more literate than those born in Argentina. Given the particularly small proportion of the population voting in 1895, 1.8 percent, it is difficult to explain the country's relatively high schooling ratio as arising from a broad demand for schooling registered through the ability to vote. It was, however, the only Latin American nation to have done away with both wealth and literacy restrictions at this point, and although even qualified immigrants were reluctant (mysteriously so to the many scholars who have studied the phenomenon) to change their citizenship to obtain the right to vote, their children would be doing so within a generation. By 1920, both Argentina and Uruguay had introduced the secret ballot and made other reforms (Uruguay doing away with wealth and literacy restrictions), and both the schooling ratios and the proportions voting soared. Thus Argentina and Uruguay had the highest proportions voting as well as the highest schooling ratios (with the exception of Chile nosing out Uruguay for second place) in Latin America.

From 1895 to 1945, generally, nearly all the European countries, as well as the United States and Canada, implemented further extensions of the franchise, through both broadening male suffrage and giving women the right to vote. Those such as the United

States, Canada, France, Germany, Switzerland, and Belgium, which had already achieved high schooling ratios and relatively high voting percentages by 1895, experienced only modest increases in schooling ratios through 1945. Those that began in 1895 with rather low schooling ratios and proportions voting, such as Finland, Ireland, Italy, and the Netherlands, experienced both a great expansion of suffrage and substantial advances in the fraction of the school-age population in school. Those that remained monarchies (Portugal and Spain) had no significant elections and maintained the lowest schooling ratios in Europe throughout the entire period. Only three of the Scandinavian countries—Sweden, Norway, and Denmark (the Netherlands is perhaps a marginal case)—deviate significantly from the general pattern. Despite restrictions on the franchise and low proportions of the population voting, those countries already had high schooling ratios in 1895; these remained roughly stable through 1945 while the proportions voting jumped.

In Latin America, both the schooling ratios and the proportions voting rose over time for all of the countries on which we were able to obtain information. They remained consistently low by general international standards, however, with the exception of Argentina, Uruguay, and Chile, who approached the schooling ratios in the European democracies near the bottom of their distribution by 1945 (Italy, Sweden, and Switzerland), and the European monarchies (Portugal and Spain), who fall comfortably within the Latin American distribution in schooling ratios. In cross section, the empirical association between the extent of the franchise and the extent of schooling is strong and obvious from a broad international perspective, but it holds as well, though in a weaker form, within Latin America alone.

These comparative statistics are informative, but a multivariate analysis with controls for variation across countries and over time in per capita income would improve our understanding of the systematic patterns in the data. In table 10 we present a set of six

TABLE 10
Pooled Cross-Country Regressions with the Schooling Ratio
as the Dependent Variable, 1895–1945

Independent Variable	DEPENDENT VARIABLE					
	School-ing Ratio	School-ing Ratio	School-ing Ratio	Log (School-ing)	Log (School-ing)	Log (School-ing)
	(1)	(2)	(3)	(4)	(5)	(6)
Constant	−0.616	−0.578	0.424	−4.809	−5.33	−0.415
	(−2.09)	(−1.95)	(15.00)	(−4.54)	(−5.05)	(−1.85)
D 1920	−0.012	0.009	0.039	−0.126	0.018	0.038
	(−0.37)	(0.32)	(1.25)	(−1.04)	(0.19)	(0.29)
D 1945	−0.04	0.004	0.072	−0.321	−0.101	0.079
	(−0.78)	(0.09)	(1.69)	(−1.80)	(−0.71)	(0.49)
D Latin America	−0.118	−0.153	−0.226	−0.176	−0.376	−0.563
	(−2.48)	(−3.80)	(−6.23)	(−1.02)	(−2.62)	(−3.93)
D U.S.-Canada	0.116	0.116	0.155	0.084	0.102	0.239
	(3.29)	(3.25)	(4.23)	(0.68)	(0.81)	(1.79)
D Low PCY Europe	−0.032	−0.035	−0.089	−0.019	−0.307	−0.248
	(−1.04)	(−1.13)	(−3.06)	(−0.18)	(−0.33)	(−2.33)
Log(PCY)	0.136	0.134		0.561	0.58	
	(3.55)	(3.47)	—	(4.18)	(4.22)	—
Voting	0.157		0.156			
	(1.35)	—	(1.24)	—	—	—
Log(Voting)				0.162		0.206
	—	—	—	(1.97)	—	(2.30)
Number of Observations	58	58	61	58	58	61
Adjusted R-squared	0.78	0.77	0.73	0.73	0.72	0.65

NOTES: t-stats in parentheses. Third and sixth equations have three additional Latin American observations: Costa Rica (1920 and 1945) and Uruguay (1920). The variable "voting" represents the proportion of the population that voted in each country (it is equivalent to the variable "suffrage" in table 9).

pooled cross-section regressions with the ratio of students in school to the school-age population as the dependent variable; the first three employ the ratio and the second three use the ratio in logarithmic form. The independent variables include year dummies (for 1920 and 1945), regional dummies (for the United States and Canada, Latin America, and those European nations with per capita incomes below the European average in 1920), the log of per capita income, and the proportion of the population voting (in logarithmic form in the last three regressions).

Although one cannot feasibly distinguish between alternative paths of causation from these regressions alone, the results indicate that inequality in political power, as reflected in the proportion of the population who voted, was significantly related to the fraction of the population provided with schooling. To begin with, the coefficients on the variables representing the proportion of the population voting are consistently positive and large. They are, moreover, of an analytically important magnitude as well as statistically significant in the latter three regressions, where the equations were estimated in logarithmic form. They are only marginally significant in the specifications without logarithms, however. Part of the problem may be that per capita income and the proportion voting are highly correlated (r is about 0.7), reflecting a multicollinearity problem that tends to increase standard errors and diminish statistical significance. Overall, it is impressive that the proportion of the population voting is significantly related to schooling ratios, even after controlling for time, region, and per capita income. Moreover, in equation 4, where both per capita income and the proportion of the population voting were included as independent variables, the regional dummy variables are insignificant. The implication is that the regional differences in schooling can be fully accounted for by differences in per capita income and our measure of inequality in political influence.

IV

Many scholars have long been concerned as to why the United States and Canada have been more successful than other New World economies since the era of European colonization. As we and others have noted, all the societies of the Americas enjoyed high levels of product per capita early in their histories. The divergence in paths can be traced back to the late eighteenth and early nineteenth centuries, when the United States and Canada began to achieve sustained economic growth. Others did not manage to attain this goal until the late nineteenth or twentieth centuries, if ever. In previous work we highlighted the potential relevance of substantial differences across societies in the degree of inequality in wealth, human capital, and political power and argued that the roots of these disparities lay in differences in the initial factor endowments of the respective colonies. In our hypothesis, the extent of inequality exerted significant influence on the way in which strategic economic institutions evolved over time. Where inequality was relatively low, institutions tended to develop so as to make opportunities more accessible to the general population; this served, in our view, to promote growth by stimulating productivity and a broad participation in commercial activities, as well as to preserve relative equality in the society at large. Where inequality was relatively high, institutions tended to evolve so as to restrict access to opportunities, favoring elite groups and preserving relative inequality but reducing the prospects for sustained economic growth. In addition, the close associations between standing (whether economic or political) and race may also have contributed to the persistence of substantial inequality, either through natural, unconscious processes or by increasing direct action by elites to retain their privileged positions and holdings. The record of both growth and inequality over time, as well as the general outlines of institutional development across the economies of the Americas, seemed to correspond with our framework.

Here we have tried to subject our hypothesis to another test of consistency with the evidence by examining the record over time of the development of education institutions in the Americas. Indeed, we have found significant support for our theory. Not only were the United States and Canada well ahead of their neighbors in establishing institutions of primary education open to virtually all segments of the population, but even among the other countries in the New World, those societies that had relatively more equality or population homogeneity organized public schools earlier and attained higher levels of literacy. The strong cross-sectional patterns are not the only features of the record that are consistent with the theory. Particularly relevant for identifying a causal mechanism is the observation that in both the United States and Canada (and in Britain as well), political decisions to expand public schools with open access followed shortly after the extension of suffrage to broad segments of the population. Moreover, the indications that in many Latin American societies the goal of increasing schooling rates was frequently frustrated by collective action problems at the local or state/provincial levels, especially where there was great inequality and populations were heterogeneous, and that progress typically required the intervention of national governments, also lend support to our view.

Although our account focuses on the importance of the extent of inequality for how education institutions like universal primary education and literacy evolved in specific countries of the Americas, other factors, both systematic and idiosyncratic, also played significant roles. Perhaps foremost among them is immigration. As illustrated by the experiences in Argentina and Chile, both the desire to attract immigrants and the success at doing so tended to encourage public schooling and increase literacy rates. Immigrants to Latin America were generally more literate, and placed a higher value on education, than the native born. Another factor of importance in Latin America was the relationship between the national government and local and state authorities. National governments were almost always the central force behind an extensive system of public schools, as they were well positioned to appreciate the economic returns of raising educational levels and to overcome the collective action problems that made it difficult for local and even provincial governments to raise sufficient revenue. Even when the national governments decided to provide resources to promote the expansion of schooling, however, they had to resolve difficulties in the demarcation of legal authority, principal-agent issues, and general political economy considerations. Both the form and the severity of these problems varied across countries and influenced the timing and effectiveness of national government intervention in educational policy. Finally, another factor of importance in accounting for the variation across economies is what might be called the *British colony effect*. Although it seems unlikely that the early investments in public schooling by the United States and Canada can be attributed to their British heritage, the rapid increase in schooling throughout the British colonies in the Caribbean basin in the late nineteenth century may well have been related to the activities of the British Colonial Office during that period.

Despite these influences, we regard the evidence as in general consistent with the hypothesis that the extent of inequality and heterogeneity had a major impact on the evolution of educational institutions in the New World and that the relative equality characteristic of the United States and Canada from the beginning was a major reason why these economies were committed early and strongly to the establishment of universal primary schools and successful at attaining high rates of literacy. The relative inequality characteristic of the rest of the hemisphere, however, helps account for why universal schooling and high literacy came much later elsewhere in the New World and may also help us understand why extreme inequality has persisted to the present day in these latter areas. Our hypothesis remains speculative and requires further study, but we hope that this attempt to examine how the paths of various New World economies diverged will stimulate more work on the interplay between factor endowments, inequality, institutions, and economic growth—in this context and in general.

References

Acemoglu, Daron, and James A. Robinson. "Why Did the West Extend the Franchise?" University of Southern California; Massachusetts Institute of Technology, 1998. Manuscript.

Alboites, Luis. *Breve Historia de Chihuahua.* Mexico: Colegio de Mexico, 1994.

Albright, Spencer Delancey. *The American Ballot.* Washington, D.C.: American Council on Public Affairs, 1942.

Annino, Antonio. "The Ballot, Land and Sovereignty: Cadiz and the Origins of Mexican Local Government, 1812–1820." In Eduardo Posada-Carbó, ed., *Elections before Democracy: The History of Elections in Europe and Latin America.* New York: St. Martin's Press, 1996.

Arce Gurza, Francisco. "En Busca de una Educación Revolucionaria: 1924–1934." In Josefina Zoraida Vazquez et al., eds., *Ensayos sobre historia de la educación en México.* Mexico, D.F.: Colegio de Mexico, 1981.

Bazant, Milada. "La República Restaurada y el Profiriato." In Francisco Arce Gurza et al., eds., *Historia de las Profesiones en México.* Mexico, D.F.: Colegio de Mexico, 1982.

Bethell, Leslie, ed. *The Cambridge History of Latin America.* 5 vols. Cambridge, Eng.: Cambridge University Press, 1984.

Britton, John A., ed. *Molding the Hearts and Minds: Education, Communications, and Social Change in Latin America.* Wilmington, Del.: Scholarly Resources, 1994.

Bulmer-Thomas, Victor. *The Economic History of Latin America since Independence.* Cambridge, Eng.: Cambridge University Press, 1994.

Censo de Educación. Vols. 1–3. Buenos Aires: República Argentina, 1909.

Cubberley, Ellwood P. *The History of Education.* Boston: Houghton Mifflin, 1920.

Dominion Bureau of Statistics. *Illiteracy and School Attendance in Canada.* Ottawa: F. A. Acland, 1926.

Egnal, Marc. *Divergent Paths: How Culture and Institutions Have Shaped North American Growth.* New York: Oxford University Press, 1996.

Engerman, Stanley L., and Kenneth L. Sokoloff. "Factor Endowments, Institutions, and Differential Paths of Growth among New World Economies: A View from Economic Historians of the United States." In Stephen Haber, ed., *How Latin America Fell Behind.* Stanford: Stanford University Press, 1997, pp. 260–304.

Fernández Rojas, José. *El Proceso de la Educación Pública en México.* Saltillo, Mexico: Impresora de Coahuila, 1933.

Fischel, Astrid. *Concenso y Represión: una interpretación socio-política de la educación costarricense.* San José, Costa Rica: Editorial Costa Rica, 1987.

———. "Politics and Education in Costa Rica." Ph.D. dissertation, University of Southampton, 1991.

———. *El uso ingenioso de la ideología en Costa Rica.* San José, Costa Rica: Universidad Estatal a Distancia, 1992.

Flora, Peter, et al. *State, Economy and Society in Western Europe: 1815–1975.* Vol. 1. Frankfurt am Main: Campus Verlag; Chicago: St. James Press, 1983.

Goldin, Claudia, and Lawrence F. Katz. "Human and Social Capital: The Rise of Secondary Schooling in America, 1910 to 1940." Harvard University, 1997. Manuscript.

Helg, Aline. *La Educación en Colombia, 1918–1957: Una historia social, económica y política.* Bogotá, Colombia: Fondo Editorial, CEREC, 1987.

Higgs, Robert. *Competition and Coercion: Blacks in the American Economy, 1865–1914.* Cambridge, Eng.: Cambridge University Press, 1977.

Instituto Nacional de Estadística Geografía e Informática (INEGI). *Estadísticas Históricas de México.* Vols. 1 and 2. Aguascalientes, México, 1994.

Martínez Jiménez, Alejandro. "La Educación Elemental en el Porfiriato." *Historia Mexicana* 22, no. 4 (1973): 514–52.

Mitchell, B. R. *International Historical Statistics: Europe 1750–1988.* Basingstoke, Hants, Eng.: Macmillan; New York: Stockton Press, 1992.

———. *International Historical Statistics: The Americas 1750–1988.* New York: Stockton Press, 1993.

Mulhall, M. G., and E. T. Mulhall. *Handbooks of the River Plate.* London: Trubner, 1885.

Newland, Carlos. "La Educación Elemental en Hispanoamérica: Desde la

Independencia hasta la Centralización de los Sistemas Educativos Nacionales." *Hispanic American Historical Review* 71, no. 2 (May 1991).

———. "The Estado Docente and Its Expansion: Spanish America Elementary Education, 1900–1950." *Journal of Latin American Studies* 26, no. 2 (May 1994).

Nohlan, Dieter, ed. *Enciclopedia Electoral Latinoamericana y del Caribe*. San José, Costa Rica: Instituto Interamericano de Derechos Humanos, 1993.

North, Douglass. *Structure and Change in Economic History*. New York: Norton, 1981.

Oficina Nacional de Estadística. *Resúmenes Estadísticos: Años 1883–1910*. San José, Costa Rica: Imprenta Nacional, 1912.

Phillips, Charles E. *The Development of Education in Canada*. Toronto: W. J. Gage, 1957.

Recchini de Lattes, Zulma L., and Alfredo E. Lattes. *Migraciones en la Argentina*. Buenos Aires: Centro de Investigaciones Sociales; Instituto Torcuato di Tella, 1969.

Resúmen de la República. Buenos Aires: República Argentina.

Roberts, George W. *The Population of Jamaica*. Cambridge, Eng.: Cambridge University Press for the Conservation Foundation, 1957.

Schultz, Theodore W. *The Economic Value of Education*. New York: Columbia University Press, 1963.

Sibaja, Luis Fernando. "Ayuntamientos y Estado en los Primeros Años de Vida Independiente de Costa Rica (1821–1835)." In *Actas del III Congreso de Academias Iberoamericanas de la Historia: El Municipio en Iberoamérica (Cabildos e Instituciones Locales)*. Montevideo, Uruguay: Instituto Histórico Geográfico, 1995.

Solana, Fernando, Raúl Cardiel Reyes, and Raúl Bolaños Martínez, coordinators. *Historia de la educación pública en México*. Mexico: Fondo de Cultura Economica, 1981.

Soltow, Lee, and Edward Stevens. *The Rise of Literacy and the Common School in the United States*. Chicago: University of Chicago Press, 1981.

Staples, Anne. "Panorama Educativo al Comienzo de la Vida Independiente." In Josefina Zoraida Vazquez et al., eds., *Ensayos sobre historia de la educación en México*. Mexico, D.F.: Colegio de Mexico, 1981.

Tanck de Estrada, Dorothy. "Las Cortes de Cádiz y el desarrollo de la educación en México." *Historia Mexicana* 29, no. 1 (1979): 3–34.

U.S. Bureau of Census. *Seventh Census of the United States: 1850*. Washington, D.C.: Government Printing Office, 1853.

————. *Education of the American Population*, by John K. Folger, and Charles B. Nam (a 1960 census monograph). Washington, D.C.: Government Printing Office, 1967.

U.S. Department of the Interior. *Annual Reports of the Department of the Interior. Report of the Commissioner of Education*. Washington, D.C.: Government Printing Office, 1898.

Valenzuela, J. Samuel. "Building Aspects of Democracy before Democracy: Electoral Practices in Nineteenth Century Chile." In Eduardo Posada-Carbó, ed., *Elections before Democracy: The History of Elections in Europe and Latin America*. New York: St. Martin's Press, 1996.

Vaughan, Mary Kay. *The State, Education, and Social Class in Mexico, 1880–1928*. DeKalb: Northern Illinois University Press, 1982.

————. "Primary Education and Literacy in Nineteenth-Century Mexico: Research Trends, 1968–1988." *Latin American Historical Research Review* 25, no. 1 (1990).

Vedoya, Juan Carlos. *Cómo fue la enseñanza popular en la Argentina*. Buenos Aires: Plus Ultra, 1973.

West Indian Census. *General Report on the Census of Population 9th April, 1946*. Kingston: Government Printing Office, 1950.

Wilcox, Martin, and George Edwin Rines. *Encyclopaedia of Latin America*. New York: Encyclopedia Americana, 1917.

Wilson, J. Donald, Robert M. Stamp, and Louis-Philippe Audet. *Canadian Education: A History*. Scarborough, Ont.: Prentice-Hall of Canada, 1970.

Privately and Publicly Induced Institutional Change: Observations from Cuban Cane Contracting, 1880–1936

Scholars of Latin America often point to inappropriate institutions as the main obstacles to long-term economic growth. Without caution, however, new institutional analyses often slip into tautology and imputed functionalism,[1] for if the "appropriateness" of institutions is identified by the performance outcome of the economy, then the proposition that economic growth depends on the appropriate institutional change is irrefutable.

To avoid tautology, one needs to seek another means of identifying the appropriate institutions. A positive approach to the study of the effects of institutional change on growth may begin simply by identifying different kinds of institutional change that are not

Paper presented at the Conference on Institutional Change and Latin American Economic Growth: Empirical Studies in the New Institutional Economics at the Hoover Institution, Stanford University, February 6, 1998. Contact Alan Dye, Department of Economics, Barnard College, 3009 Broadway, New York, NY 10027, *ad245@columbia.edu.* I am indebted to Steve Haber, Douglass North, Richard Sicotte, Alan Taylor, and Barry Weingast for their suggestions on an earlier version of this essay.

1. Robert Bates, "Social Dilemmas and Rational Individuals: An Assessment of the New Institutionalism," in John Harriss, Janet Hunter, and Colin M. Lewis, eds., *The New Institutional Economics and Third World Development* (London: Routledge, 1995), p. 44; John Toye, "The New Institutional Economics and Its Implications for Development," in Harriss, Hunter, and Lewis, eds., *The New Institutional Economics and Third World Development*, pp. 57, 65.

dependent on growth. One can then seek to determine whether a particular kind of change is correlated with a high rate of long-run growth. In the study of the less-developed world, however, it is difficult to separate out the influences of all the factors that might have impeded growth. Still, this seems the best path to follow. This chapter takes the first step in this path of investigation by focusing on a specific case of institutional change in the Cuban sugar industry. The practice of outside contracting for cane, along with supporting institutions, emerged in the 1880s and developed through the 1930s. In this specific case, existing information permits one to identify different kinds of institutional change independently from the effects they may have had on the growth performance of the industry.

Privately and Publicly Induced Institutional Change

The notion of institution in the new institutional economics covers such a broad range of phenomena that it is difficult to identify the key differences between institutions of various kinds without devolving into an unbearable typology. One key division that stands out in the literature is that some institutional changes are the outcome of the accumulation of private decisions, whereas others are enacted by the state. It remains vague as to how the precise distinction should be made between these two kinds of institutional change, but it is compelling that a fundamental distinction exist. For example, if one considers the neoclassical view that self-interest working through free markets will generate an efficient set of institutions—a statement with Panglossian implications about institutions—it is clear that the implicit mechanism of institutional change is a multitude of decentralized individual decisions. In a less idealized version of the influence of private decisions on institutions, the decentralized character of the force of change is still key. The best theoretical analogue appears to be technical change, which is now viewed as driven by cumulative processes of discovery, learning by doing, and diffusion.[2] Alternatively, when one ponders the state's role in the formation of institutions, as a general characterization the force of change is centralized. It involves a political process in which many voices are heard but in which the decisions reached are handed down as fiat.[3] In short, the processes of change in privately and publicly induced institutional change typically are very different. The mode of change itself may help determine the efficacy of the institutional change for growth.

Having made this distinction between decentralized privately induced institutional change and centralized authoritative institutional change, two propositions stand out. First, centralized change may suffer from less or inadequate information as it designs or modifies institutions. Because it is costly, the state is forced to economize on the collection of information, which limits its ability to optimize institutional design. Second, one cannot assume that the state would choose to optimize institutional design for the public good. There are two reasons: (1) the ruling authority has its own goals, such as tax collection; (2) it must answer to its constituency to remain in power.[4] Therefore, the probability of failure of an institution enacted by fiat is relatively high. By contrast, the cumulative outcome of decentralized decision making economizes on the col-

2. Nathan Rosenberg, *Inside the Black Box: Technology and Economics* (Cambridge University Press, 1982); Brian Arthur, "Competing Technologies, Increasing Returns, and Lock-in by Historical Events," *Economic Journal* 99 (1989): 116–31.

3. R. C. O. Matthews, "The Economics of Institutions and the Sources of Growth," *Economic Journal* 96 (1986): 903–18. This is not true in every case. As an example, the influence of common law decisions on institutions may be seen as decentralized. Therefore, judge-made laws or rulings may need to be treated separately from statutes and decrees pronounced by the government. Richard A. Posner, *Economic Analysis of Law,* 2d ed. (Boston: Little, Brown, 1977).

4. Douglass North, *Structure and Change in Economic History* (New York: W. W. Norton, 1981); Douglass North and Barry Weingast, "Constitutions and Commitment: The Evolution of Institutions Governing Public Choices in Seventeenth Century England," *Journal of Economic History* 49 (1990): 803–31.

lection of information. All things equal, each individual decision is likely to be more faulty than the state's decision might have been. A single decision, however, has a negligible effect on existing institutions, and its failure will not result in institutional failure. Meanwhile, the external effects of learning by doing result in a process that selects good decisions, diffuses them, and embeds them slowly into the institutional framework. If the objectives of private decision makers, or parties to transactions, are commensurate with economic growth, then institutional change induced in this way is likely to promote growth.

A final point is that these two modes of generating institutional change interact with one another. Any self-interested decision maker or group of decision makers has two avenues with which to pursue economic goals—the market and politics. Which, or how much of each, is chosen will depend on the perceived relative net benefits. If the perceived net benefits were to change for any group, then one should expect a shift in activity between the market and politics within that group.

The emergence and development of cane contracting arrangements in Cuba is an opportune case for looking into this set of issues. This is an instance in which a market, or more precisely, a practice of outside contracting for cane, went from being insignificant to being the principal means by which the production of cane was organized in Cuba over a period of no more than thirty years. The available data make it possible to identify the influence of private individual decisions on institutional change and contrast them with institutional changes established by the state through legislation. Information about private decisions or agreements to transact cane are reflected in samples of contracts I have collected from the 1890s and the 1920s. Information about actions of the state is also available concerning the kinds of laws passed, the problems they intended to address, and unintended consequences.

Institutions are the formal and informal rules—including conventions and norms of behavior—that govern exchange.[5] The contracts or private agreements that I examine below are not institutions because they represent the outcomes of negotiations between parties.[6] Institutions are rules that constrain those outcomes. Nevertheless, some features of a contract will reflect the underlying institutions that govern the negotiation. Furthermore, when institutional change is induced by the accumulation of decentralized private decisions, the contract is one place where the individual influence is felt and where the cumulative outcome is revealed.

Examination of how cane contracts changed between the 1890s and the 1920s in Cuba reveals a process of selection of contractual features that reduced the costs (moral hazard and holdup) of the cane transaction. Selected contractual features converged into a standard (or relatively standard) set of provisions. Formally, except where legal limitations prohibited it, these provisions were negotiable. But to reduce the scope and costs of negotiation, some standard features reflected norms of cooperative behavior that evolved into standard practice and thus became expected by incipient parties to a contract. As machinery may embody technology, contracts may embody institutions. Learning by using contracts to organize the cane transaction diffused and slowly embedded some norms of behavior into the institutional framework, and these had positive effects on the productivity and growth of the sugar industry.

State-enacted institutional change specifically designed to alter the cane transaction in Cuba came later than privately induced change. Until the 1920s, state interventions in the sugar industry remained limited and generally sought to accommodate the direction of private agreements. The late 1920s and 1930s inaugurated a

---

5. Douglass North, *Institutions, Institutional Change, and Economic Performance* (Cambridge, Eng.: Cambridge University Press, 1990), pp. 36–40.
6. John Wallis, "Towards a Positive Economic Theory of Institutional Change," *Journal of Institutional and Theoretical Economics* 145 (1989): 98–112.

spate of interventionist policies that radically changed the specification of rights in the cane transaction. Consistent with the proposition that the state may have been less well informed about appropriate modifications to the rules governing the transaction or less motivated by productivity concerns, these changes undid some of the positive contractual features that had evolved through private arrangements.

Emergence of Cane Contracting

The practice of contracting for cane was first adopted widely in Cuba in the late 1880s and 1890s when innovating producers in Cuba adopted new large-scale technology in sugar milling. The abandonment of the traditional plantation organization was not a trivial development. In Cuba, as well as other sugar-exporting countries or colonies, sugar cane had traditionally been grown on the same plantations where it was milled into sugar. The reason was not only slave labor, which was better suited to large-scale operations, but organizational separation of cane growing and sugar milling could lead to high production costs, either as transformation costs or as transaction costs. The harvesting of cane had to be closely coordinated with the grinding and the boiling and crystallization of its juices because sugar cane, once cut, deteriorated rapidly; efficient grinding required that cane be ground within a day or two after it was cut. Historically, those problems of coordination were solved by keeping the cutting and grinding of cane in close spatial proximity and within the same organization.[7]

7. Dye 1998a, chap. 3. The first attempts in Cuba to separate cane growing and milling came about gradually in the 1860s and 1870s in response to labor shortages. The slave population in Cuba was declining with the ending of the slave trade, and some producers were experimenting with new means of attracting white and free black laborers to cane fieldwork. These first attempts at outside contracting for cane affected only a small amount of the cane grown in Cuba, and they represented only

The movement to promote cane contracting that emerged in the 1880s was an organizational innovation to encourage the adoption of new milling technology, rationalized by contemporaries as an application of the concept of the division of labor.[8] Innovative mill owners attempted to adapt new continuous-process machinery from the European beet sugar industry. The minimum efficient scale of the new milling equipment was much larger than that of the traditional plantation, so the innovating planter entrepreneurs suddenly needed to expand their sources of cane supplies. To do this, the first entrepreneurs arranged with neighboring (traditional) plantation owners to supply cane under contract for a period of several years. Similar offers of cane contracts were made to other neighboring landowners, either smaller landholders or sometimes ranchers.[9]

In Cuba, those producers who had access to capital were able to finance the purchase of the new machinery and hire the services of skilled personnel who understood the industrial technology. As those entrepreneurs focused on adapting their operations to the demands of the new milling technologies, it must have seemed natural to contract out with owners of existing plantations for the additional cane needed to operate at the larger scale. Existing plantation owners had the experience and skills for growing cane. Meanwhile, a lower reigning price of sugar no longer covered the costs of growing and milling using the outmoded technology.[10]

---

marginal changes to the organization of the plantation. (Rebecca Scott, "The Transformation of Sugar Production in Cuba after Emancipation," in Bill Albert and Adrian Graves, *Crisis and Change in the International Sugar Economy 1860–1914* [Norwich, Eng.: ISC Press, 1984]).

8. *Revista de Agricultura* 1881–90, passim.

9. Ramiro Guerra y Sánchez, *Azúcar y población en las Antillas*, 3d ed. (Habana: Cultural, 1944); Laird Bergad, *Cuban Rural Society in the Nineteenth Century: The Social and Economic History of Monoculture in Matanzas* (Princeton, N.J.: Princeton University Press, 1990).

10. Edwin Atkins, *Sixty Years in Cuba* (Cambridge, Mass.: Riverside Press, 1926);

These contractual arrangements were not primarily for labor services, as were the earlier attempts at settlement contracting in Cuba in the 1870s or as Shlomowitz found for Australia.[11] Outside cane growers, known as *colonos*, were managers of cane plantations that granted exclusive rights to their cane to a mill, known as a "central mill," for the expected life of the cane planting. Their responsibilities included hiring labor for planting, cultivating, cutting, and hauling cane. The harvest and grinding season lasted between five and six months of each year, between December and May. A single planting of cane produced annual crops for between six and fifteen years. Contracts were written typically for the duration of the expected life of a cane planting (six to fifteen years). It quickly became common for the price of cane to be fixed in terms of sugar; that is, the grower would contract to receive x arrobas of cane per 100 arrobas of sugar (1 arroba = 25 lbs.) for the duration of the contract. Many *colonos* were landowners, others were tenants. If the *colono* was a tenant, the contract would combine the grinding agreement with a lease and sometimes a credit agreement.[12]

Hernán Venegas Delgado, "Acerca del proceso de concentración y centralización de la industria azucarera en la región remediana a fines del siglo XIX," *Islas* 86 (1987): 63–121.

11. Scott, "Transformation of Sugar Production"; Ralph Shlomowitz, "Plantations and Smallholdings: Comparative Perspectives from the World Cotton and Sugar Cane Economies, 1865–1939," *Agricultural History* 58 (1984): 1–16.

12. It is worth noting that *colonos* were not a class of peasants; they were business people from many walks of life. As opportunities for *colono* contracts grew over the years, new *colonos* came from a wide variety of former occupations both rural and urban. Some of the fieldwork was performed by independents who contracted out to *colonos*, and upwardly mobile independent contractors sometimes became *colonos*. Urban middle-class professionals had considerable interest in getting into the cane business, that is, obtaining a *colono* contract. Because some *colonos* were former planters and others were smallhold owners or tenants, the size distribution of *colonias* varied widely. For instance, at harvest, some would hire a few fieldworkers to cut their cane; others employed up to 300 or so fieldworkers during the harvest season and half that many permanently. U.S. National Archives, Spanish Treaty

TABLE 1
Sugar Production in Cuba, 1877–1929

Year	Number of Active Mills	Sugar Produced (in thousands of metric tons)	Sugar per Mill (in thousands of metric tons)	Ratio of Sugar to Cane (in percent)	Cane Produced by Colonos (in percent)
1877	1,190	526.8	0.4	6.1	—
1894	450	1110.9	2.5	—	30.0
1905	174	1078.7	6.2	9.9	—
1913	172	2515.1	14.6	10.9	69.7
1916	189	3104	16.5	11.5	—
1929	163	5352.6	32.8	12.4	81.7
1933	125	2073.1	16.6	11.7	74.3
1937	157	3094.1	19.7	12.4	—
1941	158	2506.2	15.9	12.6	—

SOURCES: Dye 1998a, tables 1.1 and 6.2; Cuban Economic Research Project, Grupo Cubano de Investigaciones Económica, *Un estudio sobre Cuba* (Coral Gables, Fla.: University of Miami Press, 1963), p. 935; Manuel Moreno Fraginals, *El Ingenio: El Complejo Económico Social Cubano del Azúcar*, vol. 3 (Habana: Editorial de Ciencias Sociales, 1978), pp. 243–48; Commission on Cuban Affairs, *Problems of the New Cuba* (New York: Foreign Policy Association, J. J. Little and Ives Co., 1935); Ramiro Guerra y Sánchez, *Azúcar y población en las Antillas*, 3d ed. (Habana: Cultural, 1944).

Technical and organizational change had a profound effect on the Cuban sugar industry in these years (see table 1). Mill performance, measured as the sugar-to-cane yield, increased on average from around 6.1 to 12.4 arrobas of sugar per 100 arrobas of cane from 1877 to 1929. This had a significant effect on Cuba's relative competitiveness in the world market. Sugar production (almost all for export) increased more than tenfold between 1877 and 1929 (see table 1). This growth represented a mild increase in Cuba's share of the world sugar market (cane and beet combined) at a time other sugar colonies were suffering serious declines in their market shares against innovative latecomers from Europe (beet) as well as the

Claims Commission (USNA—STCC); *Revista de Agricultura*, 1889; Robert P. Porter, *Industrial Cuba* (New York: G.P. Putnam's Sons, 1899).

Pacific (cane), namely, Java, Australia, and Hawaii. By the 1920s, Cuba, along with Java, was producing sugar more cheaply than anywhere else in the world.[13] Also characteristic of the technical change was an enormous and continual increase in the scale of production. Average production per mill increased from 443 to 32,838 metric tons between 1877 and 1929 (see table 1).

The Cane Transaction

Defining characteristics of Cuban cane contracts in both their origins and their history were exclusive grinding rights, payments in sugar, and long-term duration. Early cane contracts were very different from later contracts, as the parties learned by using the contracts and made modifications over time. A model postulating that boundedly rational sugar producers through experience updated their subjective perception of the optimal contract fits the evidence well.[14] Evidence suggests that, in the early contracts, producers did not fully understand how to use the contractual mechanism to mitigate the high transaction costs of coordinating the deliveries and grinding of cane with outside contractors. As they became cognizant of and responsive to these problems, they gradually improved the specific areas of weakness in the design of cane contracts.

Two kinds of transaction costs dominated. First, the high costs of coordination failure dictated a need to synchronize grinding at the mill with the harvest of the various *colonos*, who could number between a half dozen and fifty. Because the sucrose content deteriorated rapidly, it was not efficient to permit cane to accumulate at the mill waiting to be ground; also, because of the capital intensity

13. Francis Maxwell, *Economic Aspects of Cane Cultivation* (London: Norman Rodger, 1927), pp. 91–101; Dye 1998a, table 2.1, pp. 27, 245.
14. North, *Institutions*, pp. 16, 95.

and high fixed costs of the milling operation, it was not cost-efficient to leave the mill idle at any time. The length of the grinding
season was fixed by seasonal factors; therefore, idle time meant
underutilized capacity and an increase in the unit fixed costs of
production. Second, investments in site-specific assets—cane fields
and railroads—were required to complete the transaction, which
created a need for contractual means to mitigate potential holdup
problems. As described above, a cane field, with its six- to fifteen-
year life, represented a site-specific asset; the cane could be sold
only locally because of deterioration during transport. Furthermore,
central mills used private railroads (also site-specific assets) to haul
the cane from the *colonia* to the mill. Without contractual protection,
if the ex ante expectation or agreement about the price of cane was
adequate to evoke a party to invest in the site-specific asset, once
the investment was made, the other party could hold up completion
of the transaction and force a renegotiation of the price. Both coordination and holdup costs had important effects on the design of
cane contracts.

Holdup costs were reduced by exclusive grinding agreements,
in which a fixed rate of payment (in sugar) for cane was made for
the duration of the contract, which corresponded with the expected
life of a cane field. Because the life of the railroad was considerably
longer, mills remained subject to holdup problems, especially at the
termination of the contract. A grower could effectively hold up a
mill, however, only if he was the owner of the cane property and if
another mill was close enough to provide an alternative outlet for
his cane.[15] Therefore, the holdup costs mills might have incurred
depended on the local distribution of land and access to railroads.
To reduce the threat of holdup, mills gradually acquired a larger

15. If the land had any alternative use with comparable profitability, such as the
provision of food to Havana, if Havana were near enough, the *colono's* threat could
be effective.

proportion of their own cane lands and leased them to growers. Hence, the percentage of cane produced by owner-operators gradually fell. This had important political and economic consequences, discussed below.[16]

Costs of coordination failure were reduced by contracts that included additional clauses to establish rules of governance for deliveries and grinding. Identifying, negotiating, and enforcing such clauses was costly; therefore, many contingencies that might have affected coordination were left unspecified, and contracts were incomplete. From this we may derive some predictions about the effects of learning. The higher the transaction costs of identifying, negotiating, and enforcing additional clauses, the more incomplete the contracts would be. If the boundedly rational parties did not fully understand how best to design their cane contracts, then the initial transaction costs were high. Learning by using the contracts would lower the costs of identifying which kinds of clauses were most effective. Experience would result in a lowering of negotiation costs, as both parties became more familiar with the expected outcomes of different clauses. Experience would also likely lead to more effective enforcement, as parties encountered problems in the original agreements and sought remedies. Learning and experience would also exhibit external economies as parties to contracts could learn from others' experience. These predictions about effects of experience and learning by using are compared below with observations about how contracts were modified between the 1890s and 1920s.

16. Alan Dye, "Avoiding Holdup: Asset Specificity and Technical Change in the Cuban Sugar Industry, 1899–1929," *Journal of Economic History* 54 (1994a): 628–53; Benjamin Klein, Robert G. Crawford, and Armen A. Alchian, "Vertical Integration, Appropriable Rents, and the Competitive Contracting Process," *Journal of Law and Economics* 21 (1978): 297–326; O. E. Williamson, *The Economic Institutions of Capitalism* (New York: Free Press, Macmillan, 1985).

Early Conventions

At first producers did not know what they were doing when they wrote a cane contract. Contemporary testimony describes how experience and wider use of the contract led to the establishment of rules or conventions for conducting the cane transaction. The following is a candid description of the early contracts by one of the contributors to the *Revista de Agricultura.*

> Each person established colonias on his plantation [*ingenio*] adjusting [the agreements] at his convenience, without much attention to details, as something new and as an experiment that he was conducting. Experience instructed these mill owners, and the contracts, made only as God willed or in good faith, came to be modified. They began to weigh the cane which before was calculated "by the trained eye," as is commonly said. They standardized the computation on 100 arrobas of cane, or one cartload. They sought a price for this quantity that seemed equitable for both parties. They determined with more or less precision the amount of sugar obtained from that cane, which many did not know. In conclusion, owners and colonos showed their intelligence by their successive careful observations.[17]

Note the observer's remarks about the imprecision of the first contracts and their inattention to details. Experience led, first, to some very basic conventions that soon came to be taken for granted, such as the custom to quote the price of cane in units of 100 arrobas of delivered cane, the average cartload at the time (1 arroba = 25 lbs.). To give better information about performance and the distribution of gains, producers began weighing the cane and calculating the sugar-to-cane ratio. Beforehand, in the vertically integrated plantations, planters had disregarded weighing the cane and used the

17. *Revista de Agricultura* 9, no. 36 (8 September 1889): 423.

ratio of sugar to land planted in cane as the standard measure of performance.[18]

Another example of some early conventions and operating procedures is that of liquidating the value of sugar paid to *colonos*. Although the price of cane was specified in sugar, mills were often in a better position to warehouse and market it, so contracts often provided for the mill to sell the *colono*'s sugar. When that was the case, it became customary to make payments (liquidate the grower's sugar) using average monthly or semimonthly sugar prices, yet early contracts often did not specify how that average price was to be determined. Sometimes contracts stated that the average price would be determined by the prices quoted in the newspapers in one of the port cities; even in those cases, however, negotiations were problematic because parties complained about the variation and inaccuracy of the daily newspapers. Growers accused mill managers of pricing opportunistically.[19] Eventually, the Colegio de Corredores (Brokers' board) began publishing monthly and semimonthly average prices of sugar for each province, and it became common for cane contracts to specify that payment using those quotes.[20]

Early Contracting and Subsequent Modifications

Even after these first conventions were established, early contracts remained rudimentary and incomplete. The characteristics of early contracts can be observed in a sample of thirty-five contracts I

18. One observes the practice of measuring performance by sugar/land planted in the nineteenth-century agricultural censuses. Presumably, planters did not weigh the cane to save on measurement costs, but as transactions of cane with other parties were introduced, the absence of an objective measure of the quantity of cane exchanged would have suffered repeated negotiations over how much had been exchanged.

19. *Revista de Agricultura*, 1881–90, passim.

20. USNA—STCC; the Braga Brothers Collection (BB) RG 2, series 10a, 10c.

collected from the late 1880s and 1890s. Modifications made in contracts later on can be observed by comparing them with contracts written in the 1920s.[21] In this comparison, a number of observations suggest that parties learned by using the contracts and modified them to solve transaction-cost problems.

1. In the 1890s, contracts were usually less complete than their 1920s counterparts. One presumes that the selection of clauses in the 1920s contracts reveals the discovery of more successful clauses.

2. In the 1890s, the clauses of contracts varied considerably, but by the 1920s clauses had converged and were similar between mills. This suggests that the early contracts were characterized by experimentation with different clauses and that over time the best clauses were discovered and diffused among users so that by the 1920s many features of cane contracts had become standardized within the industry.

3. The clauses that had been standardized by the 1920s, in most cases, were drawn from the pool of clauses that had been in use by some mill in the 1890s. This observation suggests that the best clauses diffused from mill to mill.

4. One feature of the standard 1920s contract not present in my sample 1890s contracts was that broad powers of in-contract enforcement of the agreement were given to mill

---

21. Contracts of the 1920s were obtained from BB and, in the Cuban National Archives (ANC), Havana, from the Fondos of the Protocolos Notariales and the Secretaría de la Presidencia; Guerra y Sánchez, *Azúcar y población en las Antillas;* and U.S. Department of Commerce, Bureau of Foreign and Domestic Commerce, *The Cane Sugar Industry: Agricultural, Manufacturing, and Marketing Costs in Hawaii, Puerto Rico, and Louisiana, and Cuba* (Washington, D.C.: Government Printing Office, 1917). Contracts from the 1890s were obtained from the USNA—STCC.

managers. Provisions for enforcement in the 1890s contracts were infrequent and not typically broad in their application.

5. Finally, reinforcing point 4, the clauses adopted between the 1890s and the 1920s tended to reduce the autonomy of the grower by transferring specific rights of control, especially over daily operations, to the mill. This general tendency became a source of contention between growers and mills in the 1920s.

A closer examination of the changes made in particular clauses demonstrates that many were made in response to transaction costs associated with coordination problems inherent in early contracts. To show this, I looked at the clauses in the contracts that dealt with the delivery and grinding of cane—the point in the production process where coordination costs were the greatest. It was also the portion of contracts in which the clauses had become most uniform by the 1920s. A summary of the provisions of the delivery and grinding agreements is found in the appendix.

The propositions about the effects of experience and learning, expressed above, closely fit the patterns of change observed between the 1890s and 1920s contracts. The relative incompleteness of the sets of clauses that governed grinding and deliveries was reduced and standardized over these decades. Clause by clause, one can observe a pattern of change that corroborates the proposed changes in the costs of identification, negotiation, and enforcement.

The most common provision for governing deliveries in 1890s contracts stipulated that the cane had to be delivered "in good condition, fresh, ripe, and free of straw, roots, shoots and earth" (see appendix, issues 3 and 4). This clause sought to deter delays in deliveries after the cane was cut and ensure that it was delivered in good condition to reduce the deterioration in sucrose content. Mill managers' testimonies indicate that delays in cane were a continual problem in the 1890s and were never completely eradicated.[22] About 80 percent of the contracts in my 1890s sample included a clause of this nature. By the 1920s, this provision had become a standard in all cane contracts but was supplemented by a provision explicitly granting the mill the right either to reject or discount cane that did not meet the required conditions, which made the provision more enforceable.

Other provisions that seem to be straightforward components in the 1920s agreements were often not included in the 1890s contracts. For example, in the 1920s, mills as a rule were granted rights to determine when the grinding season would begin and what the daily quota of each grower would be (see appendix, issues 1 and 2). In the 1890s sample, 63 percent of the contracts had no explicit provision to determine the beginning of the grinding season and 14 percent made no provision to determine how much would be delivered each day. In those contracts in which provisions for beginning the grinding season were made, most granted the mill the right to decide; of those that made some provision for daily quotas, 23 percent required the mill and grower to reach an agreement each season, and 20 percent fixed the quota in the contract.[23] Granting the right to decide to the mill reduced the costs of conducting periodic negotiations at critical times in the production process and enhanced the mill management's ability to act as the central coordinator of the deliveries of multiple growers.[24] Fixing the quota in the

---

22. ANC—ICEA, BB, Dye 1998a, chap. 4.

23. Implicit in this discussion is the distinction between specific and residual rights of control. The specific rights are those assigned specifically by the contract. The residual rights are those left unspecified, which by default typically reside with the owner of the assets involved. See Oliver Hart, "Incomplete Contracts and the Theory of the Firm," *Journal of Law, Economics and Organization* 4, no. 1 (1988): 119–39; "An Economist's Perspective on the Theory of the Firm," *Columbia Law Review* 89 (1989): 1757–74.

24. Just before the commencement of grinding, mill management was typically very occupied as it attempted to ready the mill for the season's grinding campaign;

contract, however, was too rigid. It did not provide for changes in the expected crop from season to season or that the volume of cane tended to diminish somewhat with each successive crop obtained from one planting. The uncertain effects of weather and other factors made it difficult to predict the size of each annual crop as the contract was written. Consequently, giving the mill control over the decision eventually won out.

In each of the above examples, the provision ultimately selected, as revealed by the 1920s contracts, represented a transfer of specific rights of control from the grower to the mill. Presumably, the cost of identifying these clauses was small. Still, a successful negotiation of such transfer of rights would have involved estimating benefits and costs, including the costs of negotiating and enforcing the agreement and determining how they would be allocated.[25] Including the relevant clause contributed to the accumulation of information that over time reduced the costs of estimating benefits and costs. Mills and growers would enjoy external economies as they learned from the experience of others. In the earlier contracts, there was considerable variety in the clauses that were included or omitted. The outcomes of each of these trials contributed information that ultimately would be diffused throughout the industry, either directly or indirectly.

One major difference between the 1890s and 1920s contracts was that the later contracts included general provisions to permit mills to supervise and enforce the agreements, whereas the earlier contracts usually did not. The 1920s contracts granted mills the right

---

therefore, it faced a high opportunity cost in the time and effort spent dealing with an additional problem and more so if one negotiator attempted to hold out for a better deal. The concept of the mill as central coordinator is motivated by Alchian and Demsetz 1972: 777–95.

25. Lack of experience with such provisions could be accompanied by exaggerated suspicions about the costs of giving up rights of control one is accustomed to holding.

to enter and supervise the *colonias* whereas none of the contracts in my 1890s sample included such explicit provisions. The 1920s contracts also provided that, if plantings, cutting, or deliveries were not given proper attention, the mill could take charge of the *colonia's* operations at the expense of the *colono*. None of the 1890s contracts granted such a right.[26]

The provisions for supervision and enforcement in the 1920s contracts reduced the costs of enforcement for mills. It is noteworthy that similar provisions were not included to reduce growers' costs of enforcement. Enforcement provisions, then, represented a further transfer of rights of control from growers to mills. The historiography of Cuba has typically interpreted this shift of control as contributing to the coercive power of mills.[27] Without denying that the market power of mills tended to increase during these decades, the next section discusses how this pattern of transferring rights of control using specific provisions in the contracts was motivated by transaction costs and resulted in improved efficiency.

Besides reflecting outcomes of negotiations between individuals, the provisions of contracts reflect the influence of cumulative effects of individual decisions that, through their influence on mass behavior, create behavioral norms that govern transactions. For example, the presence of a provision that the grower's sugar would be liquidated according to the price quotes of the Colegio de Corredores reflected more than an individual decision; it was a customary and expected practice, reputably objective, that aided in reducing costs of negotiation and enforcement. More to the point, the standardization of provisions and practices by the 1920s suggests that some of these features were accepted as norms of the transaction rather than as negotiable outcomes. As a feature became expected practice, departures from it were not impossible; however, the cost

26. BB Record Group IV, series 10c.
27. Guerra y Sánchez, *Azúcar y población en las Antillas*.

of negotiating an unfamiliar practice would be greater than the cost of negotiating the familiar or expected one.[28] The more incipient contracting parties expected a specific provision, the higher the opportunity costs of departing from it. If the costs of negotiating a departure were high enough, one might say the practice had become institutionalized.

The Transfer of Rights of Control

The broad transfer of property rights from the grower to the mill reflected in the appendix seems one-sided, and one wonders how, absent coercion, it was ever accepted by growers. A careful look at the method of payment for cane suggests that the broad transfer of rights of control enhanced productivity, and the decentralization of decisions suggests the mechanism by which it was accepted by growers.

To frame the issue, the method of payment was key to the effectiveness of the contract to coordinate the harvest and grinding. The usual method of paying x arrobas of sugar per 100 arrobas of cane delivered actually introduced an incentive adverse to the maximization of sucrose content, for the weight of the cane and its sucrose content were not perfectly correlated. Using the weight of the cane as the basis of payment weakened the built-in incentive for the grower to cooperate with the mill to maximize the sucrose content.[29] Even though the total amount of sugar to be divided up depended on the sucrose content, for a given weight of cane the payment to the grower was not reduced by losses of sucrose. Pro-

28. Robert Cooter and Thomas Ulen, *Law and Economics*, 2d ed. (Reading, Mass.: Addison-Wesley, 1997), p. 252.

29. In the growing cycle, the ripeness (measured in sucrose content) and the weight of the crop peaked at different times. In fact, it created an incentive for growers to plant, cut, and deliver cane so as to maximize the cane's weight, not its sucrose content.

ducers in the 1890s, who were well aware of this problem,[30] proposed a solution, which was never adopted, of a payment based on
the sucrose content rather than the weight of the cane. In another
work, I adapted a model of residual rights of control from Hart
(1988) to demonstrate that this imperfect payment method was evidently preserved because it provided protection to the grower that
no other plausible payment method offered.[31] Space permits only a
sketch of the analysis.

Consider the following the division of the production function:

$$A(m, g) = r(m)\, s(m, g)\, c(g)$$

where A is sugar produced, c is the weight of cane delivered, s is the
sucrose content of the cane, r is the rate of extraction of the available
sucrose, and m and g represent the efforts of the mill and the
grower. The expression illustrates that the grower was responsible
for growing the cane and the mill was responsible for processing it
but that they shared the responsibility of maintaining the sucrose
content from the time at which the cane was cut to the time it was
ground. Losses of sucrose could be caused by factors under the
control of either the grower or the mill.

The responsibility was shared because each party managed one
segment of the delivery from fields to mill and the sucrose content
was not measured until the end of the shipment. Growers hauled
the cane by oxcart to the railroad loading station, and then mill
management continued delivery by railroad to the mill. Furthermore, the entire interval of time in which the cane was cut, loaded,
and hauled away was under the direction of the grower. Delays in
any of these activities meant a loss of sucrose. Meanwhile, coordinating the deliveries of multiple growers was under the direction of

30. *Revista de Agricultura* 10, no. 15 (13 April 1890): 172.
31. Dye 1998b.

the mill management. Large queues at the mill or breakdowns of milling equipment meant sucrose losses. Because growers' incomes were insensitive to losses of sucrose, on the one hand, they were more likely to engage in opportunism that lowered sucrose content; however, on the other hand, they were also protected from opportunistic behavior by the mill that might lower sucrose content. Suppose, contrary to the actual contracts, growers' incomes had been sensitive to losses of sucrose. Under that circumstance, if mills underinvested in railroad rolling stock, mill maintenance, or skilled personnel, the opportunity costs would have been shared by growers. Mills would thus have an incentive to act opportunistically because they would incur all the benefits but only a portion of the costs of the underinvestment. Therefore, the method of payment that made growers' receipts insensitive to sucrose content protected the grower from any opportunistic lowering of sucrose content caused by the mill's actions. But the same provison, absent other contractual provisions, made the mill more open to opportunism by growers.[32]

Contracts may have been designed to base payment on sucrose content, including specific provisions to protect the grower against opportunism from the mill—just as the actual contracts included specific provisions to protect the mill. Any such provision, however, required monitoring and enforcement, and mills were in a better position to monitor and enforce the behavior of growers than vice versa. First, mill managers understood the technology of cane growing but growers did not have intimate knowledge of the new milling

32. This problem might have been resolved if the costs of measuring sucrose content were not high. Sucrose content was estimated using scientifically based instruments that required laboratory conditions and formal training to use. In the 1890s, mills were just beginning to use laboratories and employ trained chemists for factory control. Formally trained chemists were scarce in Cuba, however, and even though their employment in mills became common by the 1920s, such skills were scarce and probably prohibitively costly for the budgets of cane growers.

technology or railroad operations. Second, mill managers probably had better access to the courts to enforce stipulations or obtain judgments in their favor. Growers with less understanding of the legal system or access to the courts were better off with a price mechanism that provided them a built-in protection. Third, in the configuration of the sugar enterprise, the mill could most effectively occupy the role as central coordinator to direct the team-production aspects of milling the cane of multiple growers.[33]

Elsewhere, I have argued that the protection that growers received and retained through the method of payment on the basis of cane weight was sustainable only because rights of control were transferred to mills to offset the incentives for coordination failure. A comparison of the 1920s contracts with the 1890s contracts shows that significant changes in the clauses governing deliveries and grinding increased mills' specific or residual rights of control over the relevant activities, including delivery, grinding, prevention of cane fires, and receipt of burnt cane (see appendix). The transfer of rights of control was unidirectional, but the way the transfer was realized depended on the issue. For example, regarding issues of timing and cane quality—the rights to decide when to begin grinding, what the grower's quota would be, and in what condition the cane had to be delivered—the contracts specified (formerly residual) rights that, by the 1920s, had been transferred to the mill. However, regarding mill responsibilities—for providing steady grinding services and supplying rail cars for loading—mills' discretion in making those decisions increased. In 1920s contracts, for example, mills were given the right to suspend grinding under "any motive or cause" without prior notification or compensation, whereas in the 1890s, when such provisions were included, the contracts required notification and/or compensation and limited the right to suspend

33. Alchian and Demsetz, "Production, Information Costs, and Economic Organizations."

grinding only to cleanings, machinery breakdowns, and unforeseen events. Each such provision either restrained the ability of the grower to neglect sucrose maintenance or increased the mill's powers to coordinate the deliveries of multiple growers more effectively. Regarding the activities of delivering and grinding cane, the mills' increased powers did not encourage them to behave opportunistically toward growers because the mills bore the full cost of not maintaining sucrose content. This was the effect of the payment for cane by its weight rather than by its productive (sucrose) value.

In exchange for the transfer of rights of control, growers did receive higher rates of payment, in terms of sugar. The average rates of payment that went to growers increased from 4.3 arrobas to 6.11 arrobas per 100 arrobas cane between the 1890s and 1917 (see table 2). The average rate probably remained the same or rose slightly from 1917 to 1925. This can be explained as an outcome of the increased milling productivity, which resulted in an increase in the mill's sugar-to-cane yield. For best-practice mills, the share of sugar that went to growers stayed roughly the same between the 1890s and the 1920s, with a perhaps slight increase between the 1890s and 1917 (see table 2), which suggests that growers were compensated for the loss of control over their operations by receiving roughly half of the gains from the higher sugar-to-cane ratio. The increase in the growers' share is downwardly biased because only best-practice mills, with higher yields, contracted with outside growers to any significant extent in the 1890s, whereas all mills, except one, contracted with outside growers by 1917. The rates of payment to growers did not vary systematically between best-practice and other mills, at least by 1917. Comparison of the growers' share at best-practice mills in the 1890s with the growers' share at the average mill in later years likely offers a more accurate comparison. If so, growers received more than half of the increase in the sugar-to-cane yield. Although one cannot say with certainty that the increased rates of payment fully compensated growers for their

TABLE 2
Growers' Shares of Sugar Output

Period		Payment to Grower (lbs. sugar/ 100 lbs. cane)	Yields (sugar-cane ratios; lbs. sugar/ 100 lbs. cane)		Growers' Share (in percent)	
			best practice	average	best practice	average
1890s	Mean	4.28	9.39		45.6	
	(Standard deviation)	(0.78)	(1.10)			
	N	37	10			
1917	Mean	6.11	12.24 [a]	10.40	49.9	58.8
	(Standard deviation)	(0.95)	(0.28)	(1.26)		
	N	23	10	199		
1925	Mean	6.11 [b]	12.59	11.16	48.5	54.7
	(Standard deviation)		(0.43)	(0.82)		
	N		10	183		

SOURCES: Author's calculations using data collected from U.S. National Archives, Spanish Treaty Claims Commission, Record Group 76; Braga Brothers Collection, Ser. 127, University Archives, University of Florida at Gainesville; Fe Iglesias García, *De El ingenio al Central* (Havana: Editorial de Ciencias Sociales, 1996), pp. 88–94; Cuba, Secretaría de Hacienda, *Industria azucarera y sus derivados* 1917, 1925; U.S. Department of Commerce, Bureau of Foreign and Domestic Commerce, *The Cane Sugar Industry: Agricultural, Manufacturing, and Marketing Costs in Hawaii, Puerto Rico, and Louisiana, and Cuba* (Washington, D.C.: Government Printing Office, 1917).

[a] The best-practice yield in 1917 is estimated by the average yield of the top 10 mills. This approach introduces a slight downward bias in the difference between the 1917 and 1890s growers' shares since the 1890s sample includes ten high-productivity mills but not necessarily the top ten.

[b] Scattered evidence suggests that average rates of payment rose slightly in the 1920s. Assuming the same rate in 1917 and 1925 will be a lower-bound estimate of the growers' share in 1925.

lost autonomy, growers unambiguously shared, in an equitable way, in the productivity gains of the combined technical and organizational innovations.

Cuban historiography has generally attributed growers' lost autonomy, reflected in the terms of the contracts, to the imbalance of power between North American capitalists and nationals.[34] North American investors began after 1903 to acquire sugar properties. During and after the First World War, North American acquisitions of land accelerated so that by 1925 only six of the top twenty sugar companies (by volume production) were exclusively Cuban or Spanish owned.[35]

Despite North American control of the prime Cuban sugar property, the pattern of change in the contracts is not explained solely by their power. Why not? That cane contracts converged to an optimal design is a predicted outcome of the transaction-cost explanation but not of the power explanation. In the transaction-cost explanation, the optimal design of the contract was effectively determined by the technology of using cane as a raw material in sugar production, which was the same for all mills. So if contract modifications were made in pursuit of the optimal design, mills would have adopted similar contract designs in the long run because they used the same technology. By contrast, in the asymmetric power explanation, one would expect contracts to differ depending on the relative bargaining power of the grower to the mill.[36] The features discussed above were standard features of all contracts by the 1920s.

This is not to say that the bargaining power of mills did not

34. Guerra y Sánchez, *Azúcar y población en las Antillas*; Manuel Moreno Fraginals, "Plantaciones en el Caribe: el caso de Cuba - Puerto Rico - Santo Domingo (1860–1940)," in Manuel Moreno Fraginals, *La historia como arma: y otros estudios sobre esclavos, ingenios y plantaciones* (Barcelona: Editorial Crítica, Grupo Editorial Grijalbo, 1983); Oscar Pino Santos, *El asalto a Cuba por la oligarquía financiera yanqui* (Havana: Casa de las Américas, 1973).

35. Antonio Santamaría García, "La industria azucarera y la economía cubana durante los años veinte y treinta: La crisis del sector exportador, comercial y azucarero y su incidencia en la sociedad y en la economía insular" (Doctoral thesis, Universidad Complutense de Madrid and Instituto Ortega y Gasset, 1995), p. 310.

36. Dye 1997 gives additional evidence that the bargaining power reflected in the distribution of contracts does not corroborate the asymmetric-power explanation.

their abilities to bargain effectively at contract renewal either to threaten holdup or to resist terms in the contract that would result in a loss of autonomy.

As a means of reducing holdup costs, the measures that increased mills' bargaining power increased the efficiency of the sugar enterprise as a whole because it ensured effective use of sunk investments. If, before acquisition, a grower could pose an effective holdup threat (prior to land concentration), he possessed market power to obtain a noncompetitive rate of payment and to extract rents from the mill to be used for replacement of fixed capital. It follows that the elimination of that threat through land acquisition permitted the mill to charge prices that reflected the resource's marginal costs and encouraged its efficient use.

Did the increased market power of mills reduce the growth potential of the sugar industry? If one considers only the economic effects, independent of the political instability that eventually emerged, evidence suggests that growth potential was enhanced. In an econometric study of the rate of adoption of new technology (Dye, 1994b), I found that mills least subject to holdup were better able both to keep up with best-practice technology and to grow faster. Mills that obtained a higher proportion of their cane from landowning growers grew more slowly, used more outmoded technology, and were more likely to shut down as the profitability of sugar fell in the late 1920s. But as discussed below, the broad transfer of rights of control contributed to a growing political instability as Cuban nationals became less willing to accept the contractual terms and business prospects offered them in the market when economic control became more heavily concentrated in the hands of North American financial interests.

Legal Changes

Over the course of development of the cane contract from its origins into the 1920s, in certain instances private agreements were accommodated by new legislation or alterations in the courts' application of existing laws. Changes described in this section suggest a continuation of the private decentralized mode of institutional change described above into more direct and formal rulings.

As noted, the Colegio de Corredores became an important third-party organization when its sugar price quotes became the basis for the liquidation of growers' sugar in private agreements. An early important legislative act was an executive decree in 1915 that regulated how the quotations of the Colegio de Corredores were to be determined. In 1921 a decree mandated the existing practice of pricing growers' sugar according to the quotes of the Colegio and in effect guaranteed growers that price as a minimum.[39]

Legal scholars in the 1890s noted that customary application or interpretation of the civil code was not always suited to the needs of the cane transaction. Problems arose, for example, over whether the courts interpreted the payment to the grower in sugar as a share payment for the use of land, which would place it under the code for *aparcería* (share tenancy), or not, which would place it under the code for *arrendamiento* (lease). In Spanish legal code, *aparcería* introduced ambiguity about the residual rights of property owners because it was sometimes viewed as a *sociedad* (partnership) rather than as an arm's-length lease agreement. Another problem was the application of the code for *compra-venta* (purchase-sales) to the grinding agreement. In exchanges that involved goods that were counted, weighed, or measured, the civil code provided that the risk was not borne by the buyer until the goods were counted, weighed,

39. Cuban Economic Research Project, Grupo Cubano de Investigaciones Económica (CERP) 1963, pp. 450–51.

or measured. Although legal scholars noted that cane burned in fire could be ground profitably, the high incidence of cane fires in Cuba did not offer appropriate protection to the grower.[40] Some contracts guaranteed the grower that burnt cane would be ground, but the hazard existed that the courts would determine the private provision inconsistent with the law. Courts eventually adjusted their interpretations to account for these inconsistencies, and clauses considered problematic for legal reasons became standard later on.[41] Not all such inconsistencies were solved so automatically, however; interested parties argued that a special law was needed for cane contracts.

Another important issue involved the property rights in cane. It had become customary in the contracts to assign the property rights of the cane and its roots, the *cepa*, to the grower. In its general disposition regarding property in land, the civil code considered all fruits of the land as the property of the landowner. Private agreements that assigned the property rights of the cane and the *cepa* to the grower were inconsistent with this provision. The Law of Agrarian Contracts of 1922, which defined the *contrato de colonato*, accommodated this practice by explicitly stating that the *colono* was the legal owner of the cane and the *cepa*. Further, the new law corrected a ruling in the general code on *arrendamiento* (lease) whereby the lease was extinguished if the lessee failed to pay the rent or fulfill the conditions of the lease. The Law of Agrarian Contracts of 1922 ensured that the grower's property rights to the *cepa* did not require removing it from the land but rather it blocked the landowner's right to access the property during the contracted period or until the matter was resolved.[42]

40. *Revista de Agricultura*, 4 May 1890, p. 210.
41. Angel Usátegui y Lezama, *El colono cubano* (La Habana: Jesus Montero, 1938), p. 44.
42. CERP, *Un estudio sobre Cuba* (Coral Gables, Fla.: University of Miami Press, 1963), pp. 451–53.

Another important article in the Law of Agrarian Contracts of 1922 gave growers the right to use the pending fruits of the land as security for credit independent of the land itself. Before this ruling, a lien could not be placed on pending fruits separately from the land that produced them. (Growers and creditors found ways to reach credit agreements using their cane as security, but the new law removed uncertainties about creditors' legal rights to cane given in security.)[43] This ruling helped enforce credit agreements between growers and third parties and enhanced the mobilization of capital.

These rulings reduced costs of negotiation and enforcement by clarifying the assignment of property rights and encouraged the capitalization of the future value of cane and *cepa*. In character, they tended to accommodate or complement the direction and spirit of change in the standard contractual practice as it had evolved in private agreements.

State-Enacted Crop Restriction

The foregoing analysis demonstrated that private decentralized institutional change successfully reduced the costs of transacting cane by contract, although the gains did not come without distributional costs since the innovations in cane contracts generally transferred greater rights of control to mills. Through 1922, state interventions in the sugar industry, which were generally conservative, incremental attempts to correct perceived problems in the contractual relationship, generally sought to accommodate the in-

---

43. CERP, *Un estudio sobre Cuba*, pp. 451–52; Angel Usátegui y Lezama, *El colono cubano* (La Habana: Jesus Montero, 1938). Although the absence of this law does not seem to have hurt growers' access to credit during the sugar boom of World War I, it might have been a brake on the withdrawal of credit to growers as prices fell afterward. Enrique Collazo Pérez, *Una pelea cubana contra los monopolios (Un estudio sobre el crac bancario de 1920)* (Vicerrectorado de Relaciones Internacionales, Universidad de Oviedo, 1994).

tentions of private agreements. As described in the last section, they appear to have been informed by the accumulation of years of experience in private dealings. This conservative approach to state interventions in the sugar industry was abandoned after 1925. The populist government of Gerardo Machado (1925–33) and the anti-imperialist government of Ramón Grau San Martín (1933–34) sought to rectify perceived injustices. The new orientation was not aimed solely at the sugar industry, but the sugar industry was a principal target.

As regarded the sugar industry, a reopening of political bargaining over who should gain from Cuba's natural resources in sugar emerged as the distribution of gains and losses became skewed against nationally owned mills. Distributional reform focused on the plight of national mills during the crisis of the late 1920s and 1930s, not on the cane transaction per se. A more thorough analysis of the politics of reform is warranted, but it would take us beyond the scope of the present essay. I hope to demonstrate in this section that the political outcome resulted in state-enacted institutional change that sought a redistribution of losses as the crisis in the sugar industry deepened. Unintentionally, however, it also undermined efficiency gains attributable to private cane contracting agreements that had enjoyed the benefits of accumulated experience in addressing the transaction-cost problems inherent in contracting out for cane.

The first important economic act of the Machado regime was the passage of the Verdeja Act of 1926, which implemented crop restrictions to buoy up the price of sugar on the world market. With only 20 percent of the world market, however, Cuba's unilateral attempt to stabilize the world sugar price could not possibly succeed. But besides the stabilization policy, the act had been intended as a mechanism to preserve threatened Cuban-owned sugar mills. The state, by appropriating the right to set quotas for all sugar mills and cane growers, was able to redress the growing distributional imbalance between national and foreign-owned mills. The state had the power to assign quotas during the years 1927, 1928, and then from 1931 until the Second World War.[44] The crisis of the 1930s evoked further defensive distributional actions by the state. By 1933, revolutionary politics had taken over in Cuba, and legislation was passed to redistribute property rights and further alter the balance of power in the sugar industry. This section first outlines the most relevant legislation and then discusses the economic interests that the redistributive measures were intended to address and some of its consequences for the efficient operation of the cane transaction.

The Verdeja Act ordered the reduction of the 1927 Cuban sugar crop by 10 percent (to 4.5 million tons) and authorized the president to establish production quotas at all levels of the sugar enterprise. As the policy was implemented, production quotas were set for each mill. Then to prevent mills from giving preference to their own cane, they were restricted to grinding their internal "administration cane" and each *colono*'s cane in proportion to its availability. The crop restrictions were renewed for the 1928 crop, but the unilateral price stabilization measures on Cuba's part were failing. Cuba's efforts at orchestrating an international price support agreement fell through, so the crop restriction policy was abandoned for the 1929 crop.

In 1930, the effects in Cuba of the world crisis were compounded by the passage of the Hawley-Smoot Tariff Act in the United States, which raised the tariff on Cuban sugar to an unprecedented level. The result was a decline in sugar production in Cuba from 5.3 million metric tons in 1929 to 2.1 in 1933, a loss of annual export earnings of more than 75 percent.[45] Despite the earlier fail-

44. CERP, *Un estudio sobre Cuba*, pp. 453–54; Santamaría García, "La industria azucarera."

45. Oscar Zanetti Lecuona, *Cautivos de la reciprocidad* (Havana: Editorial ENPES, 1989); Ballinger 1971.

ure, a new and more comprehensive unilateral sugar stabilization program was instituted in 1930 that included aggressive redistributional measures. It reinstituted the system of production quotas at all levels of sugar production, but it also explicitly sought to avert a decline in the regions most severely hurt by the crisis. This meant providing disproportionate protection to the smaller, less cost-efficient mills. Production quotas were assigned on a progressive rather than a pro rata basis—smaller mills were assigned proportionately larger quotas relative to their capacities. Similarly, in the assignment of grinding quotas to cane growers, smaller growers were assigned proportionately larger quotas, relative to their available cane.[46] Legislation in 1932, 1933, 1934, and 1937 gave further protection to smaller mills and their *colonos*. Quota rights were not transferable, except that after 1933 mills whose production did not exceed 60,000 bags (9630 metric tons) were granted the right to sell cane (and quota assignments) to other mills.

Other legislation regulated and redistributed property rights between growers and mills. These had the effect, of course, of nullifying parts of the private agreements that were in force. Laws passed in 1934 and 1935 established a minimum rate of payment to growers of 5.5 arrobas of sugar per 100 arrobas of cane for tenant *colonos* and 6 arrobas for landowning *colonos*. A 1935 law guaranteed that growers receive 48 percent of the overall yield of sugar (the sugarcane ratio) when the yield did not exceed 12 arrobas of sugar per 100 arrobas of cane ground. Landowning *colonos* also received an additional 5 percent of the sugar produced from cane grown on their land. The Law of Sugar Coordination of 1937 further reassigned property rights by granting the "right of permanence" by

46. Oscar Zanetti Lecuona, *Dinámica de estancamiento. El cambia tecnológico en la industria azucarera cubana entre 1926 y 1958* (working paper series, Avances de Investigación 1/, Havana: Instituto de Historia de Cuba, 1996), p. 21.

which tenant growers were granted broad rights to continual use of the land they occupied.[47]

State-enacted institutional change originated in individual decisions to pursue political measures to reverse the direction of private competition that increasingly threatened many Cuban-owned sugar mills. Central to individual decisions to pursue political reform was the growing industrial concentration of the sugar industry and a polarization after 1923 in the distribution of gains and prospects of sugar mills as the crisis in the sugar industry worsened. Thus owners of technically outmoded mills had an incentive to abandon competitive "business as usual" and to seek protection from the state. Because most technically outmoded mills were nationally owned, the costs of organization were reduced.

Three factors interacted to forge the polarization of mill-owner interests. Technical progress of milling in Cuba exhibited vintage-capital effects: outmoded mills delayed updating plant and equipment until the relative productivity of outmoded plant and equipment had depleted sufficiently to warrant the investment in new fixed capital.[48] Construction of new mills was stimulated by the interruption of European sugar production during the First World War. After the war, there was a leveling off of demands for Cuban sugar, and credit either for updating outmoded mills or for construction of new mills became more restricted. Despite the slowed growth in demand for Cuban sugar, the average milling capacities in the newly constructed mills continued to grow. The inverse trends in overall demands and average milling capacities implied that in the long run the number of mills in the industry would decline. Creditors had to infer that not all active mills in Cuba could survive, and, consequently, investment in sugar mills involved pick-

47. CERP, *Un estudio sobre Cuba*, pp. 642–53.
48. Dye 1998a, chap. 4.

ing the winners. Under the new circumstances, credit was rationed to those most likely to survive.

One can see how foreign and national interests became polarized under these circumstances. First, after World War I, despite falling prices and reports of growing unsold stocks of sugar on the market, production capacity continued to grow. The reason was that mills founded during the war were initially built at small scales because of high adjustment-cost barriers.[49] Achievement of state-of-the-art productivity required subsequent construction—additions to mill capacity—for several years. Therefore, new mills founded to accommodate the high sugar demands during the war continued to adjust their capacities toward the large optimal scale of production after the war despite the leveling off of demand for Cuban sugar exports.

Second, as credit became more restricted the mill owners most adversely affected were those who had rationally delayed updating their outmoded mills because of vintage-capital effects.[50] Especially after the Cuban banking crisis of 1920–21, adopting new milling technology depended almost exclusively on North American sources of credit. But the provision of this credit was necessarily rationed because of the inverse movements of the optimal milling capacity and the secular trend in the market for sugar. By 1925, export sales of Cuban sugar had peaked, and there were reports of gluts on the market. Prospects for growth overall in the sugar industry for the next few years were dim.

Meanwhile, state-of-the-art mills founded during the war were in the midst of expanding, which because of adjustment costs took several years to complete. The new mills had a competitive advantage in raising the capital needed for expansion because they could reduce unit costs of production by continuing their existing devel-

49. For explanation, see ibid.
50. Dye 1998a, ch. 4.

opment programs into which they had already sunk some of the necessary physical investments. It was more costly to update the older, technically outmoded mills that had not yet begun improvement programs. In short, the number of mills in the industry would have to decline, which produced a negative-sum game over market share in the Cuban sugar industry in the late 1920s. Investors were now more cautious about which mills they invested in, knowing that, under current market conditions, some mills would not survive. Therefore, credit was offered only to those mills declared most likely to succeed. The mills that survived tended to be newer or sounder mills that North American investors would identify as the likely winners in the negative-sum game for the declining market.

Third, access to credit was further affected by information asymmetries. After 1920, the industry had undergone a process of consolidation of mills into larger sugar corporations controlled by either North American interests or jointly between North American and national interests.[51] Between 1921 and 1925, New York banks had positions in all the major consolidations. The banking houses involved included National City, Chase National, J. P. Morgan, J. & W. Seligman, Hayden & Stone, and Sullivan and Cromwell; also important were the Royal Bank of Canada, the Bank of Nova Scotia,

51. The first truly significant such action was the consolidation of seventeen existing sugar mills in 1915–1919 into the Cuba Cane Sugar Corporation, a joint project of the Manuel Rionda family, J. P. Morgan, J. & W. Seligman, and National City Bank. Other key figures in the American sugar industry were Horace Havemeyer, Claus Spreckels, and James Jarvie; important Cuban industrial figures and congressmen were Orestes Ferrara, J. A. Sánchez de Bustamante, and Regino Truffin. Louis A. Pérez, *Cuba under the Platt Amendment, 1902–1934* (Pittsburgh, Pa.: University of Pittsburgh Press, 1986), p. 229; Pino Santos, *El asalto a Cuba*, p. 102. Other important acquisitions happened during the banking crisis of 1920–21, in which many sugar properties came into the hands of New York banks. For example, National City Bank consolidated ten mills into a subsidiary, the General Sugar Company; the American Sugar Refining Company purchased and consolidated six; and so forth.

and a group of Boston banks.[52] Given satisfactory technology and performance, the mills of those companies were likely to receive credit because they were the mills over which bankers and other financiers had more information and control.

Finally, the problems of holdup, discussed above, continued to plague those mills that were less successful in land acquisition or otherwise limiting the options of growers. Creditors were also sensitive to this issue. They perceived mills with holdup problems as unable to control cane costs; consequently, they were discouraged from committing financial resources to those operations.[53]

In sum, mill owners' ability to update their mills' technology depended on their access to credit and abilities to address holdup problems; such a situation favored both newer mills and those in North American hands. Given these conditions, milling interests in Cuba became polarized between those with good prospects of survival and those without. The groups most clearly at risk were outmoded Cuban-owned mills with few or no connections with North American creditors. As this polarization occurred, owners of nationally owned mills merged into a homogeneous group at risk of extinction which perceived the state's rights to assign quotas in the crop restriction legislation of 1926 and 1930 as advantageous to their interests.

Both crop restriction programs, especially that of the 1930s, protected mills at risk by adopting a principle that all active mills were to be preserved. Effectively, it prevented the closure of less-efficient mills and protected growers under contract with those mills.

Regarding growers, the state-determined cane-grinding quotas protected them from suffering a greater-than-proportionate share of the required crop reductions. From the viewpoint of the crop restriction program, control over cane quotas seemed necessary to

---

52. Pino Santos, *El asalto a Cuba*, pp. 101–29; Quigley 1989.
53. Ayala 1995; Dye 1994a.

prevent mills from shifting too great a portion of the costs of the program onto growers. From the viewpoint of the internal organization of production, however, taking control of cane quota assignments out of the hands of mill owners removed one of the key mechanisms to ensure contract enforcement—that is, to ensure that growers performed their duties of sucrose maintenance satisfactorily. Quotas interfered with mills' abilities both to select the best cane for grinding and to discourage poorly tended cane. Both weather and growers' efforts affected the cane's condition. The mills' rights, according to the private agreements, to determine the quotas of growers was in part to permit flexibility for the optimal selection and timing for grinding the available cane. They were also intended to ensure that growers attended their cane, delivered it promptly, and acted to prevent cane fires. Quotas impeded the abilities of mills to take action against *colonos* who did not perform these duties according to the contract. The "right of permanence," granted by the Law of Sugar Coordination of 1937, further weakened mills' abilities to remove growers who did not fulfill their contractual obligations.

Regardless of their immediate benefits to growers' interests, these measures were harmful to the prospective productivity of mills because they interfered with the organizational design that had evolved to reduce transaction costs. The evidence suggests that the state's assigning quotas limited the potential aggregate earnings of mills, growers, and all others whose incomes were linked to Cuba's dominant industry. Such a statement is consistent with the observed trend in sugar-to-cane yield, which was a standard measure of a mill's effectiveness at gathering and extracting sucrose (see table 1). The average sugar-to-cane yield steadily rose from 6.1 to 12.4 arrobas of sugar per 100 arrobas cane ground between 1877 and 1929, but it leveled off and stayed at its 1929 level throughout the 1930s. Without the policy of preserving the inefficient mills, one would have expected the trend to continue to rise. But even with the policy of preserving inefficent mills, absent offsetting factors, one would have expected some increase in productivity from the effect of selectively choosing the best among heterogeneous cane fields when the preexisting availability of cane remained the same but the amount to be ground was reduced.[54] The offsetting factors appear to have been ineffective contracts and poor coordination between mills and growers.

Conclusion

The contrast between institutional change when the primary moving force was decentralized private decision making and when it was collective action through legislation is striking, and its implications deserve more systematic investigation. The accumulation of multiple private contracting decisions led, through learning by using, to a standard contractual form. As provisions effective at reducing transaction costs were identified, selected, and diffused, cane contracts approached this form. Key to the transaction-cost reducing properties of private decisions is decentralized information and the economization of information transmission between actors. The effectiveness of the selection mechanism to reduce transaction costs depended not on a conscious decision or on a political bargain but on the spontaneous incorporation of the information content of many trials and errors.

Contrast this mode of change with the grand acts of the Cuban state in enacting crop restrictions. It is a puzzle of Cuban history why policymakers attempted unilaterally to stabilize the price of sugar after 1926 because, with a 20 percent share of the world market, Cuba was sure to lose market share. At least some producers were well aware of that likelihood.[55] Regardless of the reasons of

54. This follows from the effects of Ricardian differential rents.
55. BB RG series 10c.

each constituent group involved in supporting that policy, Cuban mill owners at risk of extinction in the technically competitive but capital constrained world of the late 1920s and 1930s had more to gain by supporting crop restriction than by opposing it. The state-controlled quota system, a by-product of the implementation of the crop restriction program, permitted inefficient mills to survive by guaranteeing them a share of the market. Changing the rules from the top appeared to be the only plausible tactic. Therefore, they considered a state-controlled system of quotas to be in their best interest even though it meant an overall reduction in the market for Cuban sugar and higher production costs in the sugar mill (since contractual relations with growers would be less flexible and less enforceable).

The effectiveness of the policy decision mechanism to reduce the costs of producing sugar or transacting cane depended on information transmitted from specialists. That is, if the crop restriction policy was to function well, information transmitted by sugar producers had to be filtered and assessed through the political process. Cuban producers at risk of extinction had an incentive to transmit information consistent with their own self-interest. If we assume legislators were unambiguously in pursuit of a policy that would have preserved the efficiency properties of the sugar enterprise and the cane transaction, the information they received from constituent producers was nonetheless imperfect and not necessarily suited to the task. Unlike the decentralized case, the transmission of information to the state legislative body was consciously filtered through the self-interested behavior of constituent parties. The expression of nationalist interests would have received greater representation in the current legislative climate, with the growing anti-imperialist sentiment, than that of foreign interests. Although we have not explicitly analyzed the process of collective bargaining, the analysis of state interventions in the Cuban sugar industry suggests that the information that reached that sphere of decision making was incomplete in its representation of the predictable effects of crop restriction policies.

In the final analysis, one is left acutely aware of the complex interactions of economic and political incentives. The information content of private decentralized versus state-enacted institutional change suggests the superiority of the private mode of institutional change. One cannot ignore, however, the distributional consequences, in this case, of private competitive forces versus state actions to alter the rules and norms of exchange in the sugar enterprise. As is often the case, the standard cane contract solved transaction-cost problems by concentrating control through the unilateral transfer of rights of control and property in land from growers to mill owners. This also meant a concentration of market power in the hands of mills. Evidence suggests that, for the sugar industry, it had positive consequences both for efficiency and for growth in the sugar industry, but the effects of concentrated market power on the rest of the economy are unclear. Furthermore, the progression of historical events suggests that the concentration of market power in the hands of the foreign-owned mills was politically destabilizing. Whatever the efficiency gains from transaction-cost reducing private contracting arrangements, given a stable set of institutions, the endogeneity of distributional effects and the incentives of parties to alter the existing rules of the game through political bargaining cannot be ignored.[56] Furthermore, the distributional effects of private bargaining over rights of control, which may not have been Pareto improving, cannot be ignored. If the prospects of market competition seemed dim, self-interested actors could choose to change the rules of the game through political channels. It is difficult to say that the institutions were appropriate, regardless of their efficiency properties, if the distribution of gains could not

---

56. Jack Knight, *Institutions and Social Conflict* (New York: Cambridge University Press, 1992), pp. 112–13.

sustain a stable institutional equilibrium. The interaction of economic and political activities must be better understood before we have a conclusive understanding of the differences between privately and publicly induced institutional change.

Appendix: Summary of the Grinding Agreement Provisions of the Sample of 35 Contracts from the 1890s

HOW TO READ THE TABLE: Issues 1–20 give groupings of provisions used in at least one contract in the 1890s or in the standard set of provisions of the 1920s contracts. A *provision* is the manner in which an issue is treated in a particular contract, identified in the table by (a), (b), et cetera. One might think of each issue as a random variable and each provision as a realization in a contract of an issue. The Frequency column gives the number of observations in the sample of thirty-five contracts that fit each provision. The corresponding relative frequency is given in the last column. The provisions that were part of the standard 1920s contract are identified in **bold** print. In some cases, more than one provision is bolded. In those cases, one or the other of the provisions was standard in 1920s contracts.

Unless noted with an *, the provisions are mutually exclusive categories. In some cases, the frequencies and relative frequencies are for appropriate conditionals rather than for the sample as a whole. Either in this case or in the case of nonmutually exclusive categories, the frequencies of all provisions for the issue will not sum to thirty-five.

Issue	Provision	Frequency	Relative Frequency
	GRINDING AND DELIVERIES		
1	Beginning of grinding and deliveries		
	Right to determine the beginning of each year's grinding season given to		
	(a) **mill (with no limits specified)**	5	14.3
	(b) **mill (within limits)**	7	20.0
	(c) mill & grower	1	2.9
	(d) not specified	22	62.9
2	Daily quota of cane		
	Right to determine the daily quota of cane to be delivered by the grower given to		

Issue	Provision	Frequency	Relative Frequency
	(a) **mill (with no limits specified)**	15	42.9
	(b) mill (within limits set by contract)	2	5.7
	(c) mill and grower	7	20.0
	(d) quota fixed in contract	6	17.1
	(e) not specified	5	14.3
3	Requirements on the condition of delivered cane		
	(a) **standard clause only** [a]	25	71.4
	(b) **standard clause + some additional conditions** [b]	3	8.6
	(c) not specified	10	28.6

[a] The standard condition stated that the cane must be delivered "in good condition, fresh, ripe, and free of straw, roots, shoots and earth."
[b] Additional conditions included specifying a maximum specific density of the cane juice extracted, or specifying a time limit on the interval of time between cutting and delivery.

Issue	Provision	Frequency	Relative Frequency
4	Right to refuse or discount cane that does not meet the above conditions		
	(a) **stated explicitly**	0	0.0
	(b) not stated	35	100.0
5	Where to be delivered? (at mill or specified loading station)		
	(a) **stated explicitly**	22	62.9
	(b) not stated explicitly	13	37.1
6	If contract includes provision that mill will supply rail cars, how was the number of cars determined?		
	(a) **stated as those needed**	13	
	(b) fixed number by contract	1	
	(c) **left unspecified**	6	
	Contract includes provision that mill will supply rail cars	20	20
7	Conditions under which mill may suspend grinding and/or require grower to suspend deliveries:		
	(a) **Any motive or cause**	3	8.6
	(b) Only for cleanings, breakdowns, or unforeseen events	7	20.0
	(c) not specified	25	71.4

Issue	Provision	Frequency	Relative Frequency
8	Requirements of mill in case of suspension:		
	(a) Mill must notify grower of suspension and must accept deliveries of cane cut before notification*	7	20.0
	(b) Provision for cane to be sold elsewhere, if delay > x*	6	17.1
	(c) Provision for mill to compensate grower for losses	5	14.3
	(d) **None specified**	15	42.9
	not mutually exclusive		
9	Weight of cane for payment to be taken at		
	(a) **mill**	16	45.7
	(b) **loading station**	5	14.3
	(c) not specified	14	40.0

CANE FIRES

Issue	Provision	Frequency	Relative Frequency
10	If fire occurs in a field of the mill or one of its growers, the grower is obligated to		
	(a) **suspend deliveries**	16	45.7
	(b) **suspend deliveries and provide aid**	8	22.9
	(c) no explicit requirement	11	31.4
11	Grower is required to maintain firebreaks and firelanes as mill directs:		
	(a) **Stated explicitly**	5	14.3
	(b) Not stated	30	85.7
12	Grower may not set fire to grasses, weeds, etc., without		
	(a) **authorization from mill**	3	8.6
	(b) notification to mill	1	2.9
	(c) Not stated	31	88.6
13	Grower is liable for damages caused to mill or another by fire set on his *colonia*:		
	(a) **Stated explicitly**	3	8.6
	(b) Not stated	32	91.4

RECEIPT OF BURNT CANE

Issue	Provision	Frequency	Relative Frequency
14	(a) Mill promises to receive burnt cane	18	51.4
	(b) **Mill will receive burnt cane, only if it meets certain conditions:**	5	14.3
	*only if it is in good condition**	2	5.7
	*only for the first [3] days after the fire**	1	2.9

Issue	Provision	Frequency	*Relative Frequency*
	*only if it has not rained**	0	0.0
	*only if accidental**	2	5.7
	(c) No provisions	12	34.3
	not mutually exclusive		
15	Mill promises to assist in grinding the grower's burnt cane before it deteriorates:		
	(a) Mill requires suspension of other growers' deliveries to give preference to the burnt cane*	22	62.9
	(b) Mill promises to provide additional rail cars as needed to burn all the cane as quickly as possible*	14	40.0
	(c) Mill requires its other growers to assist in putting out the fire, and cutting and hauling the burnt cane*	4	11.4
	(d) **Not stated or mill retains discretion**	7	20.0
	not mutually exclusive		
16	Discounts on the price of burnt cane		
	(a) **may be applied at discretion of mill***	1	2.9
	(b) **may be applied only after the first ___ days of fire†***	17	48.6
	(c) may be applied if it has rained*	4	11.4
	(d) no provisions for discounting	16	45.7
	not mutually exclusive		
	†*Number of days in 1890s specified usually as three or five. Number of days specified in 1920s usually three.*		
17	Discounted price to be determined by		
	(a) agreement between mill and grower	4	21.1
	(b) an objective third party	3	15.8
	(c) **If discounting provided, how to determine if not specified**	12	63.2
PAYMENT FOR CANE			
18	The price of cane is expressed as		
	(a) **x lbs. sugar/100 lbs. cane delivered**	31	88.6
	(b) a scaled monetary price equivalent to (a)	1	2.9
	(c) a scaled monetary price not equivalent to (a)	3	8.6
	(d) not specified	0	0.0
19	Liquidation of grower's sugar If the price is expressed as (a), payment is made physically in terms of		

Issue	Provision	Frequency	Relative Frequency
	(a) sugar at grower's free disposal	18	51.4
	(b) **the value of the sugar due the grower**	13	37.1
	(c) not specified	4	11.4
20	The basis price of sugar		
	If payment is expressed as (a) and payment is made as the value of the sugar due, the basis price of sugar is determined by		
	(a) **the monthly average of the Colegio de Corredores at the nearest port**	7	20.0
	(b) the monthly average at the local market	3	8.6
	(c) two commercial notaries, one chosen by each party	1	2.9
	(d) **the average price received by the mill for its sugar‡**	0	0.0
	(e) not specified	24	68.6
	‡by law, after 1921, the grower may demand the monthly average of the Colegio de Corredores as a minimum regardless of the private contractual agreement		

INSPECTION AND SUPERVISION

21	The mill has the right to inspect the *colonia*:		
	(a) **Stated explicitly**	0	0.0
	(b) Not stated	35	100.0
22	The grower is obligated to follow the instructions of the mill in planting and cultivation:		
	(a) **Stated explicitly**	0	0.0
	(b) Not stated	35	100.0

ENFORCEMENT

23	If plantings and cultivation are not performed as the mill instructs, or cutting and deliveries do not proceed according to the contract, the mill has the right to take charge of the *colonia* at the grower's expense:		
	(a) **Stated explicitly**	0	0.0
	(b) Not stated	35	100.0

SOURCE: U.S. National Archives, Spanish Treaty Claims Commission.

NOTE: Inspection, supervision, and enforcement excluded

References

Primary Sources

Archivo Nacional de Cuba (ANC). Havana, Cuba. Fondos consulted were the Instituto Cubano del Estabilización de Azúcar (ICEA), Protocolos Notariales (PN), and Secretaría de la Presidencia (SP).

Braga Brothers Collection (BB). University Archives, University of Florida at Gainesville.

Cuba, República de, Secretaría de Agricultura, Comercio y Trabajo. 1916/17–1930. *Industrial azucarera, Memoria de la zafra.* Havana.

Cuba, República de, Secretaría de Agricultura, Comercio y Trabajo. 1914. *Portfolio azucarero.* Havana.

Cuba, República de, Secretaría de Hacienda. 1903/4–1930. *Industria azucarera y sus derivados.* Annual series. Havana.

U.S. National Archives (USNA). Washington, D.C. Record Group 76. Spanish Treaty Claims Commission (STCC).

Published Sources

Alchian, Armen, and Harold Demsetz. "Production, Information Costs, and Economic Organization." *American Economic Review* 62 (1972): 777–95.

Arthur, Brian. "Competing Technologies, Increasing Returns, and Lock-in by Historical Events." *Economic Journal* 99 (1989): 116–31.

Atkins, Edwin. *Sixty Years in Cuba.* Cambridge, Mass.: Riverside Press, 1926.

Bates, Robert. "Social Dilemmas and Rational Individuals: An Assessment of the New Institutionalism." In John Harriss, Janet Hunter, and Colin M. Lewis, eds., *The New Institutional Economics and Third World Development.* London: Routledge, 1995, pp. 27–48.

Bergad, Laird. *Cuban Rural Society in the Nineteenth Century: The Social and Economic History of Monoculture in Matanzas.* Princeton, N.J.: Princeton University Press, 1990.

CERP (Cuban Economic Research Project, Grupo Cubano de Investigaciones Económica). *Un estudio sobre Cuba.* Coral Gables, Fla.: University of Miami Press, 1963.

Collazo Pérez, Enrique. *Una pelea cubana contra los monopolios (Un estudio sobre el crac bancario de 1920).* Gijón, Spain: Vicerrectorado de Relaciones Internacionales, Universidad de Oviedo, 1994.

Commission on Cuban Affairs. *Problems of the New Cuba.* New York: Foreign Policy Association, J. J. Little and Ives, 1935.

Cooter, Robert, and Thomas Ulen. *Law and Economics.* 2d ed. Reading, Mass.: Addison-Wesley, 1997.

De Abad, L. V. *Azúcar y caña de azúcar.* Havana: Editora Mercantil Cubana, S.A., 1945.

Dye, Alan. "Avoiding Holdup: Asset Specificity and Technical Change in the Cuban Sugar Industry, 1899–1929." *Journal of Economic History* 54 (1994a): 628–53.

———. "Cane Contracting and Renegotiation: A Fixed Effects Analysis of the Adoption of New Technologies in the Cuban Sugar Industry, 1899–1929." *Explorations in Economic History* 31 (1994b): 141–75.

———. "Organizational Innovation and the Latifundium: The Purpose of the Colono Contract in Cuban Sugar, 1880–1929." Working Paper series #98–xx, Barnard College, Department of Economics, September 1997.

———. *Cuban Sugar in the Age of Mass Production: Technology and the Economics of the Sugar Central, 1899–1929.* Stanford: Stanford University Press, 1998a.

———. "Why Did Cuban Cane Growers Lose Autonomy?" In John Coatsworth and Alan Taylor, eds., *Latin America and the World Economy since 1800.* Cambridge, Mass.: Harvard University Press, 1998b.

Eggertsson, Thráinn. "Mental Models and Social Values: North's Institutions and Credible Commitment." *Journal of Institutional and Theoretical Economics* 149 (1993): 24–28.

Guerra y Sánchez, Ramiro. *Azúcar y población en las Antillas.* 3d ed. Habana: Cultural, 1944.

Hart, Oliver. "Incomplete Contracts and the Theory of the Firm." *Journal of Law, Economics and Organization* 4, no. 1 (1988): 119–39.

———. "An Economist's Perspective on the Theory of the Firm." *Columbia Law Review* 89 (1989): 1757–74.

Hoernel, Robert. "Sugar and Social Change in Oriente, Cuba, 1898–1946." *Journal of Latin American Studies* 8 (1976): 215–49.

Iglesias García, Fe. "The Development of Capitalism in Cuban Sugar Production, 1860–1900." In Manuel Moreno Fraginals, Frank Moya Pons, and Stanley Engerman, eds., *Between Slavery and Free Labor: The Spanish-Speaking Caribbean in the Nineteenth Century.* Baltimore: Johns Hopkins University Press, 1985, pp. 54–76.

———. *De El ingenio al central.* Havana: Editorial de Ciencias Sociales, 1996.

Johnson, Ronald, and Gary Libecap. "Contracting Problems and Regulation: The Case of the Fishery." *American Economic Review* 72 (1982): 1005–22.

Khan, Mushtaq. "State Failure in Weak States: A Critique of New Institutionalist Explanations." In John Harriss, Janet Hunter, and Colin M. Lewis, eds., *The New Institutional Economics and Third World Development.* London: Routledge, 1995, pp. 71–86.

Klein, Benjamin, Robert G. Crawford, and Armen A. Alchian. "Vertical Integration, Appropriable Rents, and the Competitive Contracting Process." *Journal of Law and Economics* 21 (1978): 297–326.

Knight, Jack. *Institutions and Social Conflict.* New York: Cambridge University Press, 1992.

Libecap, Gary. "Distributional Issues in Contracting for Property Rights." *Journal of Institutional and Theoretical Economics* 145 (1989): 6–24.

Martinez-Alier, Juan. "The Cuban Sugar Cane Planters, 1934–1960." *Oxford Agrarian Studies* 2, no. 1 (1974).

Matthews, R. C. O. "The Economics of Institutions and the Sources of Growth." *Economic Journal* 96 (1986): 903–18.

Maxwell, Francis. *Economic Aspects of Cane Cultivation.* London: Norman Rodger, 1927.

Mokyr, Joel. *The Lever of Riches: Technological Creativity and Economic Progress.* New York: Oxford University Press, 1990.

Moreno Fraginals, Manuel. *El Ingenio: El Complejo Económico Social Cubano del Azúcar.* 3 vols. Habana: Editorial de Ciencias Sociales, 1978.

———. "Plantaciones en el Caribe: el caso de Cuba - Puerto Rico - Santo Domingo (1860–1940)." In Fraginals, *La historia como arma: y otros estudios sobre esclavos, ingenios y plantaciones.* Barcelona: Editorial Crítica, Grupo Editorial Grijalbo, 1983.

Nelson, Lowry. *Rural Cuba.* Minneapolis: University of Minnesota Press, 1950.

North, Douglass. *Structure and Change in Economic History.* New York: W. W. Norton, 1981.

———. *Institutions, Institutional Change, and Economic Performance.* Cambridge, Eng.: Cambridge University Press, 1990.

North, Douglass, and Barry Weingast. "Constitutions and Commitment:

The Evolution of Institutions Governing Public Choices in Seventeenth Century England." *Journal of Economic History* 49 (1990): 803–31.

Pérez, Louis A. *Cuba under the Platt Amendment, 1902–1934.* Pittsburgh, Pa.: University of Pittsburgh Press, 1986.

Pino Santos, Oscar. *El asalto a Cuba por la oligarquía financiera yanqui.* Havana: Casa de las Américas, 1973.

Porter, Robert P. *Industrial Cuba.* New York: G.P. Putnam's Sons, 1899.

Posner, Richard A. *Economic Analysis of Law.* 2d ed. Boston: Little, Brown, 1977.

Rosenberg, Nathan. *Inside the Black Box: Technology and Economics.* Cambridge, Eng.: Cambridge University Press, 1982.

Santamaría García, Antonio. "La industria azucarera y la economía cubana durante los años veinte y treinta: La crisis del sector exportador, comercial y azucarero y su incidencia en la sociedad y en la economía insular." Doctoral thesis, Universidad Complutense de Madrid and Instituto Ortega y Gasset, 1995.

Scott, Rebecca. "The Transformation of Sugar Production in Cuba after Emancipation." In Bill Albert and Adrian Graves, eds., *Crisis and Change in the International Sugar Economy 1860–1914.* Norwich, Eng.: ISC Press, 1984.

Shlomowitz, Ralph. "Plantations and Smallholdings: Comparative Perspectives from the World Cotton and Sugar Cane Economies, 1865–1939." *Agricultural History* 58 (1984): 1–16.

Toye, John. "The New Institutional Economics and Its Implications for Development." In John Harriss, Janet Hunter, and Colin M. Lewis, eds., *The New Institutional Economics and Third World Development.* London: Routledge, 1995.

U.S. Department of Commerce, Bureau of Foreign and Domestic Commerce. *The Cane Sugar Industry: Agricultural, Manufacturing, and Marketing Costs in Hawaii, Puerto Rico, and Louisiana, and Cuba.* Washington, D.C.: Government Printing Office, 1917.

Usátegui y Lezama, Angel. *El colono cubano.* La Habana: Jesus Montero, 1938.

Venegas Delgado, Hernán. "Acerca del proceso de concentración y centralización de la industria azucarera en la región remediana a fines del siglo XIX." *Islas* 86 (1987): 63–121.

Wallis, John. "Towards a Positive Economic Theory of Institutional Change." *Journal of Institutional and Theoretical Economics* 145 (1989): 98–112.

Williamson, O. E. *The Economic Institutions of Capitalism.* New York: Free Press, Macmillan, 1985.

Zanetti Lecuona, Oscar. *Cautivos de la reciprocidad.* Havana: Editorial ENPES, 1989.

———. *Dinámica de estancamiento. El cambia tecnológico en la industria azucarera cubana entre 1926 y 1958.* Working Paper series, Avances de Investigación 1/. Havana, Instituto de Historia de Cuba, 1996.

Zanetti Lecuona, Oscar, and Alejandro García Alvarez. *Caminos para el azúcar.* Havana: Editorial de Ciencias Sociales, 1987.

Concluding Remarks:
The Emerging New Economic
History of Latin America

This volume represents the application of three separate and exciting trends in social science to Latin American development: the new economic history, the new institutional economics, and the new political economy. The papers in this volume bring together these literatures in different ways but all focus on aspects of the question "Why did Latin America fall behind?"[1] The result is a series of new insights into the history of this important region, as well as insights into the causes of economic growth and stagnation.

The application of the analytic tools and quantitative techniques of these three fields of social science to the question of the causes of Latin American underdevelopment is, in our view, an exciting development. First, it makes a break with a long tradition in Latin America area studies that focused on dependency explanations of the region's lagged growth.[2] Second, it integrates history, economics, and politics in a way that has not been part of either the literature on Latin American development or development economics.

The authors wish to thank Stephen Haber for helpful conversations.

1. Stephen Haber, ed., *How Latin America Fell Behind: Essays on the Economic Histories of Brazil and Mexico, 1800–1914* (Stanford: Stanford University Press, 1997).

2. Peter Evans, *Dependent Development* (Princeton: Princeton University Press, 1979), represents one of the principal works in dependency theory. For critical reviews, see Haber, *How Latin America Fell Behind,* and Robert Packenham, *The Dependency Movement* (Cambridge, Mass.: Harvard University Press, 1992).

Third, because it integrates techniques from the new economic history—with its emphasis on the testing of clearly specified hypotheses—it holds the promise of revising the theoretical insights that have come out of the new institutionalism and the new political economy.

The new economic history of Latin America brings the theoretical and empirical tools of modern economics to bear on the question of Latin America's economic performance. As many of the papers in this volume attest, the initial results are impressive and suggest the power of this approach.

With respect to the new institutional economics, we now have overwhelming evidence that institutions matter,[3] but we know less about *how* they matter. Moreover, if the new institutional economics is to take its proper place as an essential part of the social sciences in general—and in economics in particular—we must not only demonstrate how institutions matter, but also integrate institutional analysis with other social sciences and particularly with price theory of neoclassical economics. This integration will provide us with a powerful framework with which to better understand how an economy works and why some economies consistently outperform others.

The advantage of the new institutional economics is that it brings time into the picture, which is essential if we are to understand economic development. Institutions connect the past with the present and the future. Put simply, history matters. The major contribution of the new institutional analysis is that it affords a means of understanding the complex interplay among institutions, eco-

---

3. See, for example, Douglass C. North, *Institutions, Institutional Change, and Economic Performance* (New York: Cambridge University Press, 1990), and Oliver E. Williamson, *The Mechanisms of Governance* (New York: Oxford University Press, 1996).

nomic performance, and the path-dependent pattern of development.

The new political economy focuses on how and why the political system designs the economy in particular ways.[4] Economists have long emphasized that the character of an economic system depends on its system of property rights, the degree to which contracts are enforced, and the stability of the macroeconomy. Politics determines the pattern of policy decisions in each of these domains and thus determines long-term economic performance. Indeed, any government strong enough to protect property rights, enforce contracts, and provide a stable macroeconomy is also strong enough to confiscate the wealth of its citizens. The principal question of the political economy of growth is why some countries tend toward enforcing rights and others toward predation. In short, the new political economy seeks to understand how politics interacts with the economy over time to produce particular patterns of growth.

In the comments that follow, we explore the interplay of these three bodies of knowledge in each of the volume's papers. First, we suggest how each of the papers contributes to the principal question of why Latin America fell behind. Second, we discuss the degree to which each paper draws on the three strands of the new economic history of Latin America, the new institutional economics, and the new political economy. Finally, we discuss a range of questions for further research that each of the papers raise. Indeed, as is always the case with a newly emerging literature, these papers raise many issues that are, as yet, unanswered.

We begin with the essay by Mariscal and Sokoloff. These scholars have made a promising start by providing us with detailed data

---

4. North, *Institutions,* and Barry R. Weingast, "The Economic Role of Political Institutions: Market-Preserving Federalism and Economic Development," *Journal of Law, Economics, and Organization* 11 (April 1995): 1–31.

and evidence both on the nature of income and wealth inequality and its relationship to inequality in educational opportunity, schooling, and literacy rates. As a quintessential application of the new economic history, Mariscal and Sokoloff have brought new data to bear on an important historical question. The differences in educational investment between Canada and the United States versus Latin America are striking and require explanation. The empirical evidence provided by Mariscal and Sokoloff presents an extremely detailed and nuanced portrait of this phenomenon. Among other things, Mariscal and Sokoloff emphasize the sources of income and wealth inequality as the source for inequality in schooling. Without doubt the underlying economic inequality is a critical factor in inequality in education. Because of its new evidence and bold thesis, this paper is likely to create a lively debate.

The focus on data and evidence means, to a degree, that the paper underdevelops the role of the other two modes of analysis, the role of institutions and political economy. Pursuing these two themes would complement Mariscal and Sokoloff's analysis and also deepen it. Although they are correct to point to inequalities of income and wealth as an important factor in determining policy choices, including that toward education, these factors alone do not provide an adequate model of political choice or economic development. Further, delving back into the sources of the inequality in wealth and income would provide a richer picture of the Latin American heritage and its effect on policy choice and economic development. This heritage carried many institutions over from Spain and Portugal, providing both political and economic rules of the game that set in motion substantial inequality. The plantation economy and its economies of scale—and, indeed, slavery—undoubtedly contributed to Latin America's having the most unequal distribution of income in the world.[5] But in our view, this alone does

5. Stanley L. Engerman and Kenneth L. Sokoloff, "Factor Endowments, Insti-

not fully explain either the underlying unequal income distribution or the inequalities of education.[6] In addition, the set of rules in both the political and the economic realms amplified and elaborated that initial differential opportunity. This includes critical elements inherited from Spain and Portugal, such as the distribution of land, a hierarchical political organization, and the rules governing markets.

Mariscal and Sokoloff provide fascinating data that offer us important new clues to the way in which the educational system in particular and the economy in general evolved in Latin America. What is particularly striking is the persistence of inequality, which has its roots in the institutional heritage carried over from the founding of Spain and Portugal's new world colonies.

Summerhill's contribution is exciting because it provides important new insights into how specific political rules produce particular economic results. It epitomizes a mature combination of all three modes of analysis—the new economic history's emphasis on using the tools and techniques of modern economics, including the appeal to evidence as a way of adjudicating among competing explanations; the new institutionalism's emphasis on the effects of institutions on the economy; and the new political economy, which helps explain why the political system biases economic decisions in a particular direction.

Summerhill focuses on the problem of the economic development of Brazil, investigating how railroads evolved during the nineteenth century. Without railroads, much of Brazil's interior would not have developed. Summerhill argues that a range of problems

---

tutions, and Differential Paths of Growth Among New World Economies: A View from Economic Historians of the United States," in Haber, *How Latin America Fell Behind.*

6. Douglass C. North, William Summerhill, and Barry R. Weingast, "Order, Disorder, and Economic Change: Latin America vs. North America," in Bruce Bueno de Mesquita and Hilton Root, eds., *Governing for Prosperity* (New Haven: Yale University Press, 1999).

hindered the purely private development of railroads, including a major difference between the social and private rates of return and—a topic we will return to in Haber's paper—the lack of modern capital markets. As a consequence, the Brazilian government became heavily involved in financing railroads.

Using modern political economy methods to study the pattern of political decision making, Summerhill derives several hypotheses about the political biases toward Brazilian railroad development, notably, that public subsidies will be too large and that they will be inefficient. His empirical investigations find support for these and other propositions. Had the subsidies been switched from the poor to good performers, Brazil's gross domestic product would have been several percentage points larger and the social savings from railroads 36 percent higher.

Summerhill's approach holds the promise of a revolutionary reinterpretation of Brazilian economic history. Drawing on the new economic history, he provides new characterizations of the economic effects of railroads, evidence that differs greatly from the prevailing wisdom of foreign investment.[7] Drawing on the new institutional economics, he demonstrates how particular institutions affected the evolution and development of the Brazilian economy. Finally, relying on the new political economy, he shows the political forces underlying the political decisions funding the railroads. Using these tools, Summerhill demonstrates why the development of railroads in Brazil deviated from the optimal pattern of investment.

This approach promises new insights across a range of questions in Latin American history. We look forward to his extending the analysis beyond the application to one policy area during the latter half of nineteenth century Brazil, connecting it backward in

7. See William Summerhill, "Order against Progress: Government, Foreign Investment, and Railroads in Brazil, 1852–1913," unpublished manuscript, University of California, Los Angeles, 1999, for an elaboration.

time to the long-run Brazilian heritage from Portuguese domination and forward in time into the twentieth century.

Dye's essay draws on the new institutional economics to produce a new economic history of how the Cuban sugar cane market evolved from the late 1880s through the early twentieth century. Dye compares the way in which economic rules evolved under two sets of circumstances: markets relatively unfettered by political intervention and, subsequently, markets under substantial political control. Dye shows that, in the first case, unfettered markets fostered a process of learning by doing which gradually made for greater efficiency. He then argues that, beginning in the 1920s, the Cuban government became more interventionist, pursuing nationalist and anti-imperialist goals. A range of new policies had adverse effects on efficiency, quite the contrary of the results when market decisions were made.

We hope Dye's future work will expand these themes, in part because we see the issues as more complex. The new institutional economics and the political economy approaches suggest that markets produce more efficient means of organizing production only when politics structures them in a way that encourages the players to compete via price and quality instead of via other dimensions, such as preferential political rules or even killing one another. As Haber's paper makes clear for the case of Brazil, the absence of appropriate political foundations for particular markets often inhibits the formation of markets altogether. The Cuban case makes clear that, before the 1920s, the market was structured in a way that led to greater efficiency. The story becomes more complex when the polity gets involved. What accounts for the new pattern of interventionist policies? We agree with Dye's finding that market decision making, made by entrepreneurs attempting to maximize their wealth or income, produced increased efficiency. But this outcome must be seen in the context of institutions protecting property rights and, to a degree, enforcing contracts.

Political intervention began to occur in this market when a larger set of constituencies became involved, which typically occurs whenever the political process allows access for diverse groups. The result is that political innovations are constrained by the demands of conflicting constituencies, including those adversely affected by the ruling. By its nature, political decision making is a more diverse and difficult issue to analyze but points up the crucial importance of political institutional decision making for understanding the process of economic change.

Taylor begins his paper by focusing on the way in which growth theory provides insights into the process of economic change and into the nature of successful economic development. An exemplary application of the new economic history, Taylor provides new insights into the question of how Latin America fell behind. His paper focuses on policies that distorted capital flows and investment, with significant long-term consequences for economic growth. Taylor thus provides new and important insights into the question of how political decisions and policy making steered Latin America off the path of economic development.

Taylor's paper suggests two questions for further research. The first concerns the new institutionalism. Growth theory tells us that economic growth depends on capital investment (including that in human capital), technological change, economies of scale, and so on. Missing from this approach is an analysis of the incentive structures that lead economic players to engage in the types of activities necessary for growth, such as investment. Taylor's focus on distortions in the capital market represents one element of the larger story of Latin America's failure to develop incentives fostering the kinds of activities that lead to growth. As Taylor emphasizes, history matters. In Taylor's case, history matters from the beginnings of Latin American and Argentine development because of the initial institutional framework and the way it evolved, shaped, and constrained the players with respect to producing incentives for increasing productivity. Argentina's pattern of development, like that of Latin America more broadly, reflects a complex interaction of this institutional framework, the political and economic choices made under it, and the opportunities arising from comparative economic advantage.

This brings us to our second question for further research, the interplay of politics and economic performance. If government policies distorted capital and investment, why did these polities choose them? Taylor did not address this question directly, and his cross-sectional evidence does not provide an unambiguous answer. A different perspective is to look longitudinally over time. The economy constantly alters existing interests and creates new ones. These changes, in turn, have implications for political decision making, as the new configuration of interests attempt to acquire access to politics. A greater understanding of this process will give us deeper insights into the interplay between democracy and economic performance than we get simply by the cross-sectional framework. Importantly, this will give us a deeper understanding into why Latin American polities have often chosen policies that hindered economic development.

Finally we come to Haber's fine analysis. Haber's work represents a marvelous integration of institutional analysis with the new economic history, giving us deep insights into the process of performance of an economy over time. Haber studies how the Brazilian textile industry was fundamentally influenced by changes in the rules of the game that made it possible to improve economic performance. He shows how different configurations of institutions underpinning markets have different long-term implications for growth.

Haber picks up the story in late-nineteenth-century Brazil, where the political foundations of capital markets were completely inadequate. The absence of limited liability companies, for example, inhibited the formation of banks. The absence of banks, in turn, placed striking impediments on the mobilization of capital and hence on the ability to make productive investments. Rapid economic growth took place when, after major political changes in the late nineteenth century, Brazil improved the political foundations of capital markets. Haber demonstrates that these changes help explain the fast-paced growth of the textile industry from 1885 through the mid-1920s.

We hope that Haber's future work will expand these themes in two ways. First, if combined with the type of political analysis employed by Summerhill, Haber's approach holds the promise for deep insights into the political impediments preventing Brazil from creating efficient capital markets during the nineteenth century. In particular, what were the forces after the 1889 revolt that led Brazil to alter the political rules to improve the efficiency of capital markets? In this sense, our question for Haber is similar to that for Taylor, though the political decisions each studies had opposite economic outcomes.

Second, embedding this story in a historical background will not only help explain the beginnings of the textile industry but also show how the initial pattern of institutions provided the basic background for the story that he tells so effectively in his paper.

All in all, this wonderful group of papers demonstrates the power and significance of the three new approaches: the new economic history, the new institutional economics, and the new political economy. The combination of these approaches holds the promise of a deeper understanding of why Latin America fell behind. One theme running through all the papers concerns the political choice of rules governing markets. Economists have a well-developed theory about the form of these rules to produce economic development. What is striking about Latin America, as these papers reveal, is how political decisions in Latin America so frequently bias the rules away from those that produce efficient markets. Explaining this political bias, in our view, will dominate the literature in the years to come.

References

Engerman, Stanley L., and Kenneth L. Sokoloff. "Factor Endowments, Institutions, and Differential Paths of Growth among New World Economies: A View from Economic Historians of the United States." In Stephen Haber, ed., *How Latin America Fell Behind: Essays on the Economic Histories of Brazil and Mexico, 1800–1914.* Stanford: Stanford University Press, 1997.

Evans, Peter. *Dependent Development.* Princeton: Princeton University Press, 1979.

Haber, Stephen, ed. *How Latin America Fell Behind: Essays on the Economic Histories of Brazil and Mexico, 1800–1914.* Stanford: Stanford University Press, 1997.

North, Douglass C. *Institutions, Institutional Change, and Economic Performance.* New York: Cambridge University Press, 1990.

North, Douglass C., William Summerhill, and Barry R. Weingast. "Order, Disorder, and Economic Change: Latin America vs. North America." In Bruce Bueno de Mesquita and Hilton Root, eds., *Governing for Prosperity.* New Haven: Yale University Press, 1999.

Packenham, Robert A. *The Dependency Movement.* Cambridge: Harvard University Press, 1992.

Summerhill, William. "Order against Progress: Government, Foreign Investment, and Railroads in Brazil, 1852–1913." Unpublished manuscript, University of California, Los Angeles, 1999.

Weingast, Barry R. "The Economic Role of Political Institutions: Market-Preserving Federalism and Economic Development." *Journal of Law, Economics, and Organization* 11 (April 1995).

Williamson, Oliver E. *The Mechanisms of Governance.* New York: Oxford University Press, 1996.

Index